Understanding the
Enterprise Culture

Understanding the Enterprise Culture

Themes in the Work of Mary Douglas

edited by
SHAUN HARGREAVES HEAP
and
ANGUS ROSS

EDINBURGH UNIVERSITY PRESS

© Edinburgh University Press, 1992

Edinburgh University Press
22 George Square, Edinburgh

Typeset in Lasercomp Palatino
by MS Filmsetting, Frome, and
printed in Great Britain by
Robert Hartnoll Ltd, Bodmin

British Library Cataloguing
    in Publication Data
    Understanding the enterprise
    culture: Themes in the work
    of Mary Douglas.
    I. Hargreaves Heap, Shaun
    II. Ross, Angus
    306.3

ISBN 0 7486 0323 9

Contents

Foreword

This book originated in a conference around the work of Mary Douglas at the Centre for Public Choice Studies at the University of East Anglia.

Of the contributions by Mary Douglas, Chapter 2 first appeared in *The Listener* of 8 September 1977, Chapter 3 was prepared for a meeting of the Tocqueville Society in October 1982, and an earlier version of Chapter 4 was given at a conference on the enterprise culture at Lancaster University in 1989.

We would like to thank the Centre for Public Choice Studies for their support on this project.

1

Introduction: Mary Douglas and the enterprise culture

SHAUN HARGREAVES HEAP AND ANGUS ROSS

AN OVERVIEW

The government of Margaret Thatcher engaged in a long crusade to change not simply economic conditions but values and attitudes. By removing constraining regulations, and kicking away the crutches of public subsidy and over-generous welfare benefits, her government sought to foster a new spirit of enterprise in the UK. The 'dependency culture' which the nanny state had fostered under previous governments was to be replaced by an enterprise culture. This ambition has occasioned much debate, both in political and in academic circles; and these debates have assumed a fresh urgency with the governments of the USSR and Eastern Europe apparently embarking on a similar path. Is it really possible for a government to achieve such wholesale change in the values of a culture?[1] Will the encouragement of individual initiative and the free play of market forces succeed without an accompanying change in the culture? And if the attempt were to succeed, what would be the costs? Can the public virtues of citizenship, and what is now to be thought of as the private virtue of caring for those unable to care for themselves, survive in this new order? The questions quickly multiply. There have been many voices in this debate, but one that has a special claim to be heard is that of the distinguished anthropologist Mary Douglas.

From her earliest writings on the Lele of the Kasai (1963), Mary Douglas has pursued the Durkheimian project of tracing the hidden social influences on thought, though unlike Durkheim she has insisted on including our own modern, industrialised society within the scope of her enquiry. Her central proposition is that the way we think, from our ideas about justice to our beliefs about the cosmos, is a function of our social experience. In classifying kinds of social experience for this purpose, Douglas rejects any simple contrast between 'modern' and 'primitive' societies. The individualism of modern capitalism is a special case of a more widespread form of social organisation in which the barriers preventing individuals from transacting with each other are at a minimum, and much can be learned about the implications of individualism and deregulation by looking at other examples of this social type. There is much more to it than the readiness to take risks and accept responsibility for failure that are urged upon us by advocates of the enterprise culture. For example, the value placed on the individual as consumer and as entrepreneur goes along with an unfortunate short-term perspective on the future and a tendency to neglect the environment. Douglas's anthropological approach provides a convincing and also rather alarming picture of something very familiar suddenly seen from an unfamiliar perspective.

In drawing out the connection between modes of thought and forms of social organisation, Douglas also helps us to approach the question of whether it is possible for a government to change the values of a culture. The connection she proposes is non-reductive, in that both culture and social organisation retain a degree of autonomy. Each form of social organisation both generates and is sustained by certain beliefs and values which provide it with the political legitimation it needs. She tells us, in fact, that

> the political rhetoric reveals a minimal three types of legitimation each so distinctive that no speaker in one such type can appeal to the justifying principles which uphold another type without being landed in contradiction ... Each kind of society is stabilized in a uniquely specialised normative order. Its principles cannot be borrowed by either of the others without grave inconsistency. This is the central argument of cultural theory.[2]

If Douglas is right, we must expect culture to possess a considerable degree of resistance to change, with a consequent inertia in forms of social organisation. The autonomy which culture enjoys acts as a brake favouring the practices of the status quo. On the other hand, since there are other pressures on forms of social organisation (economic pressures, for example), a flip from one type of society to another cannot be ruled out. If such a flip were to occur, the implication is that it would not be easy to reverse. Thus, should a government succeed in generating an enterprise culture, we could well be stuck with it.

THE RATIONAL CONSUMER

There are three interlocking elements in Mary Douglas's work on culture: a picture of individual motivation, a theory of the relationship between culture and forms of social organisation, and a taxonomy of the possible combinations of culture and social organisation. We shall consider each of these elements in turn.

Individuals for Douglas are never just the instrumentally rational agents we find in neoclassical economic theory. Naturally, individuals have objectives and they wish to see these objectives satisfied, but it is wrong to see all action as reflecting a choice of the most efficient means to serve a given end. As rational beings, we also need to make sense of the world and our place in it, and this 'making sense' is not just a matter of grasping a pattern that is already there. It involves imposing an intelligible pattern on the world, and since sanity requires that our world be one we share with others, the project of creating and sustaining an intelligible world involves communicating the sense *we* see in the world to others and getting their agreement. The intelligibility of the social world is a human construct, and one that is in constant need of reaffirmation and reinterpretation. In the first of her contributions to the present volume, Douglas spells out the implications for our picture of consumer motivation.

> Man is a social being, and he needs goods for communicating with others, and for making sense of what is going on around him ...
> Yes, they serve phsyical needs, but at the same time goods are used as the visible part of a general social effort to get on with other people and to make sense of life ... the individual uses consumption to say something about himself, and about his family and his locality, but he is saying it to other people, and he is listening to other people's remarks of the same kind about themselves ... this is what I think is the main point about consumption: the effort to get some agreement from your fellow consumers to define some events in some kind of agreed way ... the main basis

of making sense is getting other people's agreement that what we think is there is really there.[3]

In *The World of Goods* (1978), written with Baron Isherwood, Douglas applies this picture of consumer motivation to the problem of explaining changes in patterns of consumption and in the ratio of consumption to savings. Another theme taken up in that work, and which is also broached in Chapter 2 below, is that any attempt to moralise about 'materialism' or the 'affluent society' will miss the point if it seeks to convict the consumer of irrationality, or of being moved by trivial or essentially unworthy motives like envy or vanity, or of being the victim of a 'false consciousness' generated by the economic system. It is not that Douglas wishes to defend the consumer society against all criticism. Rather, she wants to focus the moral debate on the way in which wealth, and the consumption patterns it makes possible, are used to secure access to, and exclude others from, the real, informational sources of power and control in society:[4] 'the ultimate object of consumption activity is to enter a social universe ... Relative deprivation is like relative deafness: someone who is outside one conversation misses the clues and can't adapt quick enough to get into the next conversation, so the chance of making sense, and the chance of playing a respected role diminish.'[5]

Thus for Douglas, individuals do often act rationally in the sense of the economic textbooks, but they also act expressively. An individual sees certain food or clothes as right or appropriate for a certain occasion, not because they are a means of attaining some further end, but because they are an apt expression of that individual's view of the importance of the occasion, of his/her own standing in the community, etc. Taken together, such choices made over a period of time express his/her view of the kind of universe she/he takes himself or herself to be in and the relative importance of everthing in it, and these choices are made *because* they are expressive of his/her view on these matters. The result is that each individual is in a continuing dialogue with others over the way the world is to be understood and over what is of value or importance in it.

Culture comes into the picture here in a number of ways. Without agreement on the most general features of their shared universe, without a web of shared categories and shared beliefs and values, there could be no agreement between individuals on the meaning of particular actions or consumption choices, and thus no possibility of using such choices as a means of communication. Without a shared culture, actions would not have this all-important symbolic dimension. On the other hand, each choice an individual makes helps to determine the culture: 'Goods are endowed with value by the judgement of fellow consumers.'[6] 'Consumption is a very active process in which all the social categories are being continually surveyed and redefined by everybody engaged in it.'[7] Thus while it is culture that serves to determine the meaning of any given choice, the whole assemblage of choices being made within a community at a given time helps to define the culture in existence at that time.

It is also culture, in the shape of a shared cosmology, that supplies the terms in which individuals make sense of their own experience. Indeed, this need to see our experience as fitting into some intelligible pattern must be part of the reason culture arises in the first place. Our need for intelligibility is such that where no explanation is available we are prepared to invent one. In our determination to make sense of our world, we require our cosmology to explain everything. We seem unwilling to admit ignorance or chance. Confronted with what are, from a coldly objective point of view, purely random events, we weave stories around them to provide an air of intelligibility, however spurious. Sometimes this takes the form of invoking the will of an inscrutable deity, but there are quite mundane examples too. We invoke the idea of winning and losing streaks in sport to describe the phenomenon of how one success or failure builds on another in a sequence of victories or losses, despite that fact that there are very few examples of runs which do not conform with the predictions of statistical theory when teams have a constant probability of winning. In fact the popularity of the idea of 'luck' in our culture is itself testimony to our need to offer something, however, tenuous, by way of explanation for good and ill fortune.

CULTURE AND SOCIAL ORGANISATION

On its own, of course, the individual's need to see an intelligible pattern in his/her experience yields at most an individual cosmology, or rather as many individual cosmologies as there are individuals. To understand the emergence of a shared cosmology, we need to take account of the social need for agreement. A shared culture is a condition of the possibility of mutual understanding, and mutual understanding is most urgent, Douglas points out, where there are disputes to be settled. If society is to be possible at all, there must be agreement on the terms in which claims are legitimated, actions justified and honour defended, though to say we *need* culture is not in itself to explain how it arises or why it persists, or what form it will take in a given society.

Douglas specifically warns us against seeing culture as something imposed on individuals from outside. The beliefs and values that are accepted in a given society at a given time represent the outcome of countless individual disputes and agreements, and thus reflect countless judgements on the part of individuals. Nonetheless, it might be thought that we should see a society's culture as reflecting, or deriving from, something beyond itself, something more fundamental, either in nature or in society. The simplest thought is that the beliefs and values on which agreement is reached will reflect truths about the world, but Douglas rejects any appeal to objective values that are somehow part of the fabric of the universe. To understand why certain values are agreed on, we need to examine the role those values play in ordering social relations, though note that it does not follow that the values will be 'pro-social' in any simple sense. Not all cultures expect the individual to be committed to the general good. An enterprise culture, notoriously, expects the reverse to be true, and accepts this as wholly legitimate. More controversially, Douglas sees the same point as applying to a community's beliefs about the world, natural and social. We must, of course, assume some tendency for individuals to agree on beliefs that are true, or for which there is evidence, but that cannot be the whole story. There are other motives for agreement in belief, for the importance of shared belief lies in its role in the legitimation of disputed claims, where questions of fact and value are inextricably linked. A community's shared beliefs, like its values, will be in part at least a function of its form of social organisation.

However, in proposing that a community's culture reflects its form of social organisation, Douglas is at pains to reject any simple determinism. Thus she rejects the familiar Marxist thesis that culture (or 'ideology') reflects the operation of a deeper set of economic forces. That thesis holds that we have the beliefs and values we do because those are the beliefs and values that enable the economy to perform in the most efficient manner. Thus a capitalist economy will give rise to a capitalist ideology and a socialist economy to a socialist ideology. Culture is here seen as the outcome of a deeper teleological process which selects economic systems according to their efficiency. As before, culture is seen as reflecting something more fundamental, and the eye is naturally drawn away from culture to that more fundamental thing. But for Douglas, the relationship between culture and other aspects of society or nature is more intricate and defies the reduction of one to the other.

It is in *How Institutions Think* (1986) that Douglas offers her most explicit account of the relationship between culture and other objective features of society. She focuses there on the need for conventions that enable individuals to co-ordinate their activity to mutual benefit. Consider the problem of two drivers approaching an intersection on different roads. It is in the interests of both that there be a convention which assigns priority to one road or driver over the other, because without such a convention either both must slow down or you get the occasional crash. Or consider the economic advantages which flow from a division of labour. These advantages only obtain when there is a mechanism for co-ordinating individual decisions, because all would lose if all were to decide to become bakers: they would have done better to remain self-sufficient rather than specialise. Once again, something that is needed does not emerge simply because it is needed. There is always more than one convention that would perform the task of co-ordination, and the fact that *some* convention is needed does not guarantee that there will be agreement on *which* convention is to be observed. At the crossroads, we could have the convention that one gives way to the right or to the left, or to the older driver, or to the wealthier driver. To be sure, some conventions are demonstrably more efficient than others from the point of view of effective co-ordination. A crossroads convention based on age or wealth would be very inconvenient. But such considerations only narrow the field. They are unlikely to single out one convention on which all must agree.

We are happy enough to say that who gets priority at the crossroads is *simply* a matter of convention, and it does not matter *very* much what convention we use as long as it keeps the traffic moving. But in that respect it is an untypical example of social co-ordination. Where there are conflicting claims to priority, we are usually unhappy to accept just any convention that serves the purpose of co-ordination. The question of the justice or appropriateness of the convention arises. For Douglas, our insistence on raising such questions is another example of the need to see an intelligible order in things, and it is of course the culture, rather than considerations of economic efficiency, that leads us to see one convention rather than another as uniquely fitting or appropriate. In a word, it is culture that provides us with reasons for preferring one convention to another, and in this way' culture makes its own contribution to shaping social institutions.

Douglas sees culture as meshing with the social practices of a society to form a unity, where each supports the other but neither can be seen as determined by, or reducible to, the other. A community's shared beliefs and values help to determine which co-ordinating conventions will strike individuals as legitimate, but equally, it is the usefulness of those beliefs and values in defending claims to priority when disputes arise in operating those conventions that ensures that those beliefs and values remain a part of the shared culture. This general approach enables Douglas to avoid the suggestion that there is just one optimal culture. Every culture, in her view, has both strengths and weaknesses. Considered solely from the point of view of economic efficiency, we can say that in so far as a culture helps us to establish co-ordinating conventions by providing reasons for following one convention rather than another, that is a strength. But in claiming that a certain convention is the *only* acceptable convention to follow, a culture may make claims which are not justified by its co-ordinating capacities alone and blind us to the merits of economically more efficient conventions. The extra baggage which our demanding cosmology brings may blind us to dangers which threaten the co-ordination game itself. For example, it is a weakness of the individualism characterisitic of an enterprise culture that it focuses attention on the short term, to the neglect of longer-term dangers.

Another kind of worry is that different conventions may distribute the rewards arising from co-ordination very differently across the population. Thus a certain culture may be seen as serving the interests of one particular group, and we may want to criticise it from the point of view of justice. However, in seeking to criticise a culture on moral grounds, we are likely to be criticising it on the basis of the value commitments of a *different* culture, and it is less clear what objective basis there can be for such criticism. The claim that every culture has its strengths and weaknesses is not intended by Douglas as an invitation to a general relativism on questions of value, though that is clearly a possibility that has worried some of her readers. To appreciate what she means by this claim, and to appreciate her special contribution to our understanding of culture, we need to turn to the specifics of her attempt to correlate different kinds of social organisation with different kinds of culture.

GRID AND GROUP: A TAXONOMY OF CULTURES

To understand the way in which our social experience affects how we think, we need to recognise two distinct ways in which society may exert pressure on an individual, two distinct ways in which society may restrict his/her options. Douglas uses the term 'grid' to refer to restrictions that arise from the system of social classficiation, for example, the distinction between lord and commoner or between man and woman. Grid in this sense is the set of rules which govern individuals in their personal interactions. Strong or 'high' grid means strongly defined roles which provide a script for individual interaction. Towards the weak end of this axis, the public signals of rank and status fade and ambiguity enters relationships. Individuals no longer have the guidance of a script, but are valued as individuals and relate to each other as such. The constraints become correspondingly weaker, until they take only the generalised form of respect for each person as a unique individual.

Douglas uses the term 'group' to refer to the extent to which an individual's interactions are confined within a specific group of people who form a sub-group within the larger community. Where group is strong, there is a clear boundary between members and non-members, and though it may be possible for an individual to leave the group, that will have high costs in that membership of the group confers many benefits. As a result, members of the group are able to exert considerable pressure on the individual to conform to its requirements. By contrast, where group is weak, the individual is free to form relationships or negotiate exchanges with anyone, and the resulting network of interactions constitutes a myriad of overlapping groups, with no sub-group of individuals who interact only with themselves.

A market-oriented, individualist society will come out as 'low grid-low group' on this classification because in such a society an individual's interactions are relatively unconstrained in each of these dimensions. By contrast, a society characterised by hierarchies will come out as 'high grid-high group', since its members are likely to be constrained in both dimensions. But to appreciate the significance of this scheme of classification, we need to see that there are two other possibilities, for grid and group can vary independently of each other. Mary Douglas has fractured the familiar markets versus hierarchies (or individualist versus bureaucratic) opposition across two dimensions, rather than one, to produce four distinct types of social organisation:

high grid:	anarchic/isolates	hierarchies
low grid:	individualist	sect/enclave

| | low group | high group |

High group-low grid is a very recognisable social type, the best example being the commune with its strong commitment to equality combined with an equally strong sense of group identity. High grid-low group is perhaps less recognisable. It is the situation of those excluded from all groups but who are nonetheless highly restricted in their possibilities of interaction by their status in the classification system. In some societies widows, or the old generally, may be in this position. However, it is plain that Douglas sees the locus of power in most societies as lying somewhere along the diagonal linking individualist and hierarchical forms of organisation. The other two types are usually found at the margins of power within a society, though that does not exclude the possibility that a large bulk of the population is sometimes located in those positions.

The importance of distinguishing these two dimensions of social control, grid and group, lies in the insight they provide into the relationship between social organisation and systems of belief and value. What follows is a brief summary of the mode of thought that Douglas associates with the three ideal types which have received most attention: Hierarchies, Individualism and Sects, based on her discussion in 'Cultural bias'.[8] We begin in each case with a description of the ideal type and then turn to the beliefs characteristic of each arrangement. It is convenient to distinguish these beliefs broadly according to the central organising ideas about nature and about the relation between nature and society. This is a familiar method of classifying beliefs used by anthropologists. To illustrate how these broad differences translate into some more mundane ones, we have noted some specific ideas on time, education, punishment and justice. In part Douglas treats these associations as empirical descriptions, though her claim is that they exhibit a certain internal coherence and can be understood as a response to the particular form of social experience in question.

Hierarchy: high group-high grid

Groups exist with a strong, constraining boundary between insiders and outsiders. Individuals have well-defined rights and obligations in relation to other individuals and to their group. Roles are highly differentiated allowing for much specialisation, and the group has many ways of overcoming internal conflicts and ensuring its own persistence.

Nature is locally stable and benign, but if it is disturbed too much it will become unstable.

Society and nature: strong parallels are drawn between the natural order and the social order; nature is good and provides moral justification for the social order.

Time and death are part of the closed cycle of life which the group encompasses and transcends by its own persistence. Time is regulated by the routines of the group, just as it is ordered by the laws of nature. History is an important record and monument to the group. Traditions are almost a part of nature, and just as nature will continue, so will social institutions. There is no reason to fear tomorrow; tomorrow will come as it has done since time immemorial.

Education is important because children require direction. There may be a natural order here as there is a social order, but just as species are accommodated within that order painfully, so the same applies to children and the social order.

Punishment is often exemplary and appeals to the need for

12 Shaun Hargreaves Heap and Angus Ross

deterrence. The only unforgivable deviation is disloyalty which is revealed in the failure to observe the internal rules.

Justice: inequality is seen as posing no problem because it is found in nature.

Individualism: low group-low grid

Individuals are free-wheeling. All classifications are provisional and negotiable. Obligations are ambiguous and at best implicit. It is a competitive environment where rank and group count for nothing. Instead, there is value in popularity, in being able to persuade others to join you, and in stealing a march on others by innovating.

Nature is regarded as benign and stable over all disturbances.

Society, by contrast, is experienced as anonymous, merciless, an unremitting source of worry. Nature is thus idealised as good and simple, but a wistful sense of alienation never wins against the excitement and rewards of competition. Society is therefore separate from nature, with its own rules and its own resources. It has culture with a capital C.

Time is used flexibly; there are no set routines and this makes the future always uncertain. To focus on tomorrow and the short term is about all that you can do in the cut-throat competitive world where individuals make their own rules and they get remade overnight. History provides a stockpile for culture with a capital C.

Education appeals to the natural sense of goodness supplied by nature, and thus there are voluntaristic conceptions of education as a form of self-realisation and self-expression, coupled with a belief that individuals should be allowed to move at their own pace.

Punishment is based on desert. There is no need for exemplary displays. The great fear is that people who lose out under the competitive market will seek succour in hierarchies.

Justice: the low-grid ethic of individual equality is daily affronted by the gross inequality generated by market competition. This can be satisfactorily explained only by reference to innate differences in ability.

Sects/enclaves: high group-low grid

The group is as crucial to sects as it is to hierarchies, only here there is no internal differentiation. Low grid leads to a strong commitment to internal equality between group members. This creates leadership problems and a tendency to fracture.

Nature is regarded as unstable. It contains both wolves and lambs and one can easily unbalance the other.

Society is like nature, and the task of the group is to 'fight the good fight' and unmask all the wolves who wander in sheep's clothing. The boundary between insiders and outsiders is an attempt to hold the line.

Time is more pressing for sects than hierarchies because history, like nature, is full of convulsions. Sects are concerned with the long run, but that cannot look after itself. The future must be fought for.

Education and punishment follow closely that of hierarchies, except that disloyalty is not revealed in the failure to observe internal rules. Rather, disloyalty expresses itself in contamination from relations with those outside the group.

Justice: there is strong commitment to mechanisms which guarantee equality within the group.

To illustrate the insight that this two-dimensional classification of social types can yield, we refer to an essay written jointly with James Douglas comparing British and Swedish trades unions.[9] In terms of a simple contrast between markets and hierarchies, there is no obvious reason for distinguishing British from Swedish trades unions: both look like bureaucratic organisations. However, the Douglases suggest that while both score highly along the group dimension, they differ in respect of position on the grid dimension. Swedish trades unions are high-grid, and so come out as genuine hierarchies, whereas their British counterparts are low-grid, having more of the characteristics of the sect or commune. This difference helps to explain why Swedish trades unions have successfully participated in corporatist decision-making while British trades unions have not. In Douglas's terms, hierarchical organisations can do deals with other hierarchical organisations, whereas sects are handicapped both by their low-grid suspicion of contamination from compromising contact with outsiders, and by the way in which their commitment to equality makes strong leadership difficult.

FRAMING THE DISCUSSION OF THE ENTERPRISE CULTURE

The enterprise society and its culture corresponds very closely to the ideal type 'low grid-low group' in Douglas's taxonomy. Indeed, she refers to the basic guiding principle of this ideal type as 'frontier individualism' which is invoked 'at the frontiers of knowledge and experiment, as well as at territorial and political frontiers' (1978, p. 9). Douglas's particular contribution is to help us to see how this social type tends to generate a number of distinctive beliefs and attitudes which yield their own particular problems. Taken together with her insights into the motives that underlie consumption, her taxonomy of social types puts us in a position to make a more objective and better informed assessment of the contemporary call to enterprise. One weakness of the Individualist ideal type to which Douglas draws attention is particularly noteworthy. If she is right, the often-criticised preoccupation with the short term which seems to run through much British and North American economic decision-making is an inevitable feature of an enterprise culture. The frequently remarked long-termism of Japan is exactly what we should expect from a society in which the group is all-important. It is unlikely to be nurtured by a society that insists on placing ultimate value on the freedom of the individual entrepreneur.

Another major weakness of the Individualist social type is discussed by Douglas for the first time in Chapter 4 below, 'The person in an enterprise culture'. There is, she suggests, a strange silence about the nature of the person or 'self' that is celebrated by an individualist culture. This can be understood if we see the thesis of the ineffability of the self as a way of guarding against the political coercion that can arise when a particular view of personhood is asserted, as when the Nazis declared there to be two kinds of person, Aryans and others. However, Douglas argues that what is designed as a defence is actually a source of weakness, for to fend off the threat posed by those who press partisan views of personhood, the liberal needs to assert a positive view of his or her own. The best vehicle for developing such a view is anthropology, Douglas argues, because by helping us to be clear about the way in which our idea of the self serves social purposes it brings the discussion of the self within the ambit of politics.

In Chapter 3 below, 'An institutional ecology of values', Douglas addresses the question of the way in which social institutions structure our perceptions of risk and danger, looking specifically at the risks arising from modern technology.[10] The chapter provides a useful statement of the general thesis of the institutional influences on thought, as well as reminding us of some of the specific problems facing societies committed to market individualism. Such societies tend to be short-term in outlook, over-optimistic about the environment, and reluctant to entertain collective solutions that would threaten to move society in the direction of hierarchy (or 'corporatism'). This issue is taken up in O'Riordan's chapter which reviews the contemporary debate over environmental risk. He is more sanguine than Douglas, recommending a mixture of self-regulation, independent regulatory bodies and government-imposed standards, though he acknowledges that there may be difficulties in achieving the first within a pure enterprise culture.

The difficulty relates in part to a third weakness which Douglas sees as afflicting the Individualist social type. The provision of public goods, and the associated free-rider and prisoner's-dilemma problems, is a major theme of Douglas's *How Institutions Think* (1986). In societies where group affiliations are strong, the group can impose effective sanctions against free riders. In societies which endorse the free-wheeling individualism of the enterprise culture, the group lacks this authority and the problem of public goods surfaces in an acute form. It is an issue that exercises a number of the contributors to this volume. It surfaces in Hargreaves-Heap's discussion of entrepreneurship, where he suggests that Douglas's cultural analysis can help economics to understand the crucial activity which propels the economy away from one equilibrium towards another, and thus help with the problem of explaining equilibrium selection. As an illustration, he considers possible solutions to the prisoner's-dilemma-type problems created by the move to 'flexible specialisation'. He concludes that the form of organisation characteristic of Japanese companies, where elements of low grid combine with high group, will be more able to rise to these challenges than the typical North American company.

A similar conclusion is drawn by Weale in a different context. In his contribution to this volume he argues that private charitable organisations should not be regarded as a substitute for state provision. Instead, building on the arguments of James Douglas,[11] he suggests that private charities are a valuable complement to state provision, for by combining elements of high group and low grid, charities are able to do things, particularly experimental things, which public bodies cannot do. Thompson, in his contribution, takes the idea of complementarity between different social types and their cultures a stage further. He argues that Douglas's four social types form a symbiotic whole: each type requires the presence of the other, so there can be no society that is purely individualist in type, or purely hierarchical. This is a significant amendment to Douglas's cultural analysis, and carries with it the implication that the attempt to build a pure enterprise culture could not succeed.

Perhaps more worryingly, Thompson argues that it is an inevitable feature of an individualist market economy that it should give rise to an underclass of rejects who are excluded from effective participation, ending up either as isolates (high grid-low group) or as members of (possibly revolutionary) sects (low grid-high group). He is, of course, reminding us of a further weakness of the enterprise culture: its attitude to the inequalities that arise from the operations of the market. How are those who lose out to be persuaded not to throw their allegiance behind other more 'caring' forms of social organisation? What conception of justice can reconcile the losers to their predicament?

Attempts to answer this question by some of the great proponents of market individualism—Hume, Adam Smith and Hayek—are the focus of Sugden's contribution to this volume. He finds that they confirm Douglas's prediction that attempts to legitimate social institutions will appeal to analogies with nature. As Sugden demonstrates, these attempts to represent the operations of the market as uniquely 'natural' are highly questionable, but he doubts that any other option is open to the proponents of the market because no theory of justice can stand independently of culture. In this respect, he appears to accept the relativity of values.

Hollis addresses a closely related worry in his discussion of citizenship in the enterprise culture. How can a society that celebrates the energetically self-seeking individual generate sufficient commitment to the public virtues of citizenship to make civilised life possible? Given the terms of Douglas's discussion, in particular the assumption of individual rationality, this is in part a question about whether values other than self-interest have a rational, and thus an objective, claim on our attention, which once more raises the issue of relativism. Hollis argues that the perception of strengths and weaknesses in different cultures, on which Douglas lays such stress, itself presupposes values that are not merely relative, and the same goes for any solution to the public goods problem. O'Neill, too, is worried by a suggestion of relativism in Douglas's discussion of justice, but she argues that it is possible to accept the thesis of the 'artificiality' of justice without a collapse into relativism. The key is to rely less on the arguments of Hume and more on those of Kant.

Douglas's most important contribution to our understanding of inequality in an enterprise culture is to be found in her work on consumption. Street's essay takes up that discussion of consumer motivation, with its implicit defence of the consumer against charges of false consciousness, and finds parallels with recent attempts on the part of the British left to come to terms with consumerism. Finally, Ross seeks to place Douglas's claim that we are social beings in a wider perspective. Reflection on the evolutionary history of our species suggests that we are indeed social by nature, and that it is therefore a mistake to represent liberty (and by implication the market) as a 'natural' state. But the thought that we are biologically adapted for a social way of life also, Ross argues, provides independent support for the assumptions underlying Douglas's distinctive picture of consumer motivation.

Taken together, the contributions to this volume offer both some penetrating reflections on the implications of the contemporary call to enterprise and an assessment of an important aspect of the work of one of our most distinguished anthropologists.

NOTES

1 For evidence that it has not in fact achieved total success, see R. Jowell, S. Witherspoon and L. Brooks (eds) *British Social Attitudes*, *7th report*, (Aldershot, Gower, 1990).

2 Mary Douglas, 'Culture and Collective Action', in M. Feilich (ed.), *The Relevance of Culture*, (New York, Burgin and Garvey, 1989).

3 'Why do people want goods?', Chapter 2 below. This piece was

originally broadcast as two talks on Radio 3 and published in *The Listener*, 8 and 15 September 1977.

4 On this theme, see also Mary Douglas, *In the Active Voice*, (London, Routledge, 1982) Chaper 2.

5 Mary Douglas, *In the Active Voice*, pp. 25 and 31.

6 Mary Douglas, *The World of Goods*, (London, Allen Lane, 1979), p. 75.

7 'Why do people want goods?', Chapter 2 below.

8 Mary Douglas, *In the Active Voice*, Chapter 9.

9 Mary Douglas and James Douglas, 'Institutions of third kind: British and Swedish labour markets compared', (mimeo, 1987).

10 This problem is discussed further in Douglas and Wildavsky, *Risk and Culture: An Essay on the Selection of Technological and Environmental Dangers*, (Berkeley, University of California Press, 1982), and in Mary Douglas, *Risk Acceptability According to the Social Sciences*, (London, Routledge, 1986).

11 James Douglas, *Why Charity? The Case for a Third Sector*, (Beverley Hills, California, Sage, 1983).

2

Why do people want goods?

MARY DOUGLAS

Why do people want goods? This is an absolutely basic question. It is crucial to incomes policy, and it is the background to all the theorising about how to deal with inflation today. Demand theory is at the centre, even the origin, of economic theory. And it is amazing to discover, when one goes into it, that no-one knows why people want goods at all. Economists meticulously avoid the question. They even count it a virtue, a sign of methodological purity, not to offer suggestions on the whys and why-nots of consumer behaviour. Their expertise is in the analysis of choice; they have deliberately made a self-denying ordinance which stops them from making judgements, as they say, outside their field of competence, about the value of the things that people choose. In consequence, we have got a vacuum here, and, like all vacuums, it tends to get filled by very dubious, difficult and rather insulting assumptions about the rationality of the consumer.

I find it very worrying when I hear some economists warning us that we should not give way to our destructive greed, that our greed for goods is destroying our environment, that it would be very much better to return to a simple life. I have the sense that they do not understand at all our motives when we buy things. They allocate to us, the consumers, in their theories, something that they call sovereign choice, and yet that does not in the least describe what it feels like to be buying anything. There is something obligatory in that experience which the theory does not explain at all.

We know that we are not just mindless automatons or helpless victims of advertisers' sales talk; we do, to some extent, support the economists' view of ourselves. We are very rational; we agree that, once we have decided to get something, we do choose between brands, and we know that, when we make the decision, our income level does have a part to play. But in the economists' analysis, there is so much left unexplained. We do not always feel that we are choosing at all. The thing, whatever it is—a better lawnmower, or a bigger freezer or colour television—has somehow become a necessity, and endowed with its own imperative demand to be acquired, as if, without it, the whole household threatens to return to time-consuming complications of a much more primitive era, in which we just will not be able to manage. Really, instead of being a sovereign consumer exerting his free choice as the books describe us, the wretched consumer often feels like the passive holder of a wallet whose contents are being sucked out by impersonal forces. And, in this predicament, moral reproaches seem quite impertinent. Somewhere, there will have to be less empty theorising about consumers' wants.

Let me start with the whole idea of choice. Choice assumes that the individual is a rational being. We are supposed to respond to a fall in prices by being ready to buy a larger quantity, and to a rise in prices by buying less. Also, as we get more of a particular good, our wish to have more of it weakens. This is the minimal rationality that economic theory requires us to assume about the consumer. But the thing that is missing in that minimal rationality is that the individual who is making these choices is completely isolated, impossibly isolated, and as a result of being cut off in the theory from all other consumers, his fellow human beings, the theory makes his concerns absurdly trivial. The normal social dimension of his wants is missing, and that is what has got to be put back.

Consumption decisions are a vital source of the culture of the time. People reared in a particular culture see it change in their lifetime. They are playing some part in the change. And consumption is that very sphere in which culture is generated. Let me supply an example. The shopper comes home with a selection on purchases. There are some things in it that will be kept for the household, some allocated to particular members of the family or, put aside for the children. Other things have been bought for the special pleasure of future guests. Decisions are also made about what parts of the house people are to be invited into, and what parts of them are available to one degree of outsiders, what parts are available to a more intimate group of people who might be expected to come in further into the home. Decisions are made about how often to throw open the house to other people, as well as how much of it, and what should be offered to them—if it is music, or if it is food and drink, or if it is just drink and conversation.

These sort of choices are the mainspring of culture. They are not trivial choices at all, they are absolutely fundamental for the whole life of a people. In the end, the consumer's choices should be seen as moral judgements about everything: about what a man is, about what a woman is, how a man ought to treat his aged parents, how much of a start in life he ought to give his children, how he expects himself to grow old—should he put aside something for his old age, or should he hope that something else will be done for him by other people? Has he got the kind of family obligations that stop him from migrating? How many other people would agree with him that he ought to stay behind if he is offered a highly paid job somewhere else? Should he insure for his own funeral? All these are consumption choices, and I have picked them to indicate that they are not all trivial, and that, if everybody is making them in the same direction, and it is a new direction, then the culture is changing, because these choices involve heavy costs.

So, instead of supposing that goods are primarily needed for subsistence, plus something rather pejoratively called display, we should assume that they are needed for making visible and stable the categories of culture. It is said by some linguists, and others, that the essential nature of language is not for giving instructions about how to do practical things, but in its creative capacity—for poetry, for example. And I think it would be in the spirit of anthropology to make a similar assumption about the nature of consumption—that its essential capacity is to make sense of things, creatively.

So let us forget the idea of consumer irrationality and let us keep in our minds the idea that the consumer is a rational being. Let us forget that commodities are good for eating and clothing and shelter (though, of course, that is the origin of their importance), and try instead the idea that commodities are good for thinking. They can be treated as a non-verbal communication medium for the human creative faculty. That would be a new approach to consumption, and certainly the time is right for such an approach. An anthropologist might pose the question of why any tribesman uses goods to serve his physical needs. Yes, they serve his physical needs, but, at the same time, the goods are being used as the visible part of a general social effort to get on with other people, and to make sense of life. Given some time and some space, people use consumption to say something about themselves, and about their families and their localities, but they are saying it to other people, and they are listening to other people's remarks of the same kinds about themselves.

The kinds of statements the individual is making about the kind of universe s/he is in may be affirming it or trying to change it; they may be defiant; they are not necessarily competitive—though they could be. An individual can proceed, through consumption activities, to get some agreement from his fellow men and women, and this is what I think is the main point about consumption: the effort to get some agreement from your fellow consumers to define some events in some kind of agreed way. S/he may be wanting them to redefine events, to change the decisions that we have been given from our past. And the same thing really holds good for the decoration of the home, and even for the constitution of a meal—an ordinary meal or a special meal. So consumption is a very active process, in the course of which all the social categories are being continually surveyed and redefined by everybody engaged in it.

Goods are for making sense. Goods are for rational beings to make sense of their universe. Consuming is finding consistent meanings. You cannot make sense of an individual item of information. You cannot make music out of one note, make poetry out of one word. Sense lies in the whole discourse, in the whole poem, the whole tune, and the problem for the anthropologist looking at the uses of goods is to scan his/her material for the whole structure of meanings.

Let us take, for example, the meaning of their cattle to the pastoral peoples of the Sudan, the Nuer. They use cattle, they eat cattle, they drink their milk and drink their blood. They use the cattle dung for fire. They use the horns and skins for containers. There is not any part of the cattle for which they do not have a practical use. But also, they marry with cattle, they pay debts with cattle, they pay for homicide with cattle, they affirm all their relationships with cattle. By insisting that the proper livestock owed to you be paid over, you are showing that you are willing to accept the obligations of that relationship, and to pay up when it is your turn. Above all, they use the cattle for sacrifice to God. It is not possible to list the uses of their cattle without running through every item, every aspect of their culture, and you could use the movements of the cattle as a kind of shadow map for all social relationships. The hoofmarks from camp to camp show all the changes in marriage relationships, and some of the hoofmarks of cattle being returned show a wrong being repaired, so that you have a kind of shadow description of the society in the transfers of goods. Meaning is made visible by physical things.

When I have tried to explain this to people unfamiliar with our kind of work, they say: 'It is all very well that the Nuer use cattle to mediate all their meanings; we can understand that, but it must be different for us because we have such a wide variety, such richness of goods. Surely, we have got too much; surely if we went back like the Nuer and just had cattle, we would be able to cut down our lives and have all those meanings, and the world would be an easier place to live in?'

This is part of the argument against growth. The moralists take up my point about the Nuer very quickly, and say: 'Surely, primitive usage proves that we *are* senseless and irrational in our pursuit of more and more goods?' I do not think that that argument stands close scrutiny. A very modest life of subsistence contrasts with our own use of goods in, for example, the use of food. How would we be able to say all the things we want to say, even just to the members of our families, about different kinds of events and occasions and possibilities, if we did not make any difference between breakfast and lunch and dinner, and if we made no difference between Sunday and weekdays, and never had a different kind of meal when out friends came in, and if Christmas Day had also to be celebrated with the same kind of food? The same applies to space, and to clothing, transport and sanitation. Space is harnessed to the cultural process. As is well understood, its divisions are heavy with meaning. You do not need to be told that your housing, the size of your house, the side of the street you are on, its distance from other centres, all these spatial limits are there, publicly, visibly shoring up conceptual categories that would otherwise be very fragile.

Sense, meaning, rationality about goods, is the construction that is put upon reality. The reality is there, but it is only known in the way that we have constructed meanings in it. My friends say: 'Surely, though primitive people can be *seen* to construct their universe, naming the stars that they focus on and leaving others out completely, and filling their worlds with strange ghosts, animal familiars, witches, talking birds and the rest, surely *we* see the world as it really is? Surely, we passively receive meanings, we are not putting a construction upon it? We find what we find there, already.' But anthropologists cannot see the problem so simply. We too, like everybody else, use material things to mediate our own meanings to each other. We are engaged in an effort to make sense of the world, and especially the world that we have to relate to other people in. Sense needs a structure, from cradle to grace, as complete a pattern as possible. Admittedly, it is easier for people with a very stationary technology to erect a meaningful universe around them, just because they have got more time to think about the goods they have got. Technical change brings social change, you have to keep starting again. It is like scene-shifting. But we still have to make sense of the world. And the main basis of making sense is getting other people's agreement that what we think is there is really there. We have to use goods to get a shared information system. We use the goods to set up its boundaries and to send messages in it.

This is not to say that the messages are all good. This is not to say that envy and comptetiveness and cruelty and selfishness may not be part of the messages, but until we understand how goods are used for sending the messages and for interpreting them, we cannot make the real judgements that we should be making. By focusing on the goods instead of on the meanings that the goods are being used to express, we are really focusing on the surface, and not going deep enough to the real social problems which we are concerned to try to remedy. There is a procedure—this structural analysis of goods—which could map a subterranean field of choice, deliberately ruling out the distraction of the physical uses of goods. The process is analogous to what scientists do when they suspend everyday knowledge and create pockets of disbelief—physical objects are not chunks of stuff but are configurations of planet-like patterns of particles and forces and space. Like the scientists, we can suspend our knowledge that goods served bodily needs. We know it is true, but we can put it in brackets for the moment, and focus rather on the classifying project to which the goods are recruited.

We should treat the goods as markers—just the visible bit of the iceberg which is the whole social process. Goods are used for marking, in a sense of classifying categories. Marking is an appropriate word for it draws on all the meanings of the hallmarking of gold and silver, the signing of letters by people who are not literate by making their mark, marking boundaries, marking essays with alphas and betas ... the markers determine meanings, and with the markers, we are engaged in an effort to construct a rational universe. Goods are the visible part of the culture, and goods as we know them are arranged in vistas and hierarchies which give full play to the range of discrimination of which the human mind is capable. These vistas are not fixed, but neither are they randomly arranged as in a kaleidoscope. They are shifting, they are moving; ultimately, their structures are anchored to human social purposes. And these human social purposes may well deserve all the criticism and moralising that is generally given simply to the consumer's choice of goods. People's choice of goods should not be allowed to be a block to interpreting the human purposes which they serve.

Sense is the construction that is put upon reality—reality is there, but it is only known in the way that we have constructed meanings in it. But what is meaning? It flows, it drifts and is hard to grasp. Meaning that you attach to one set of clues transforms itself, and one person gets one pattern and another quite a different one from the same events. If you look back a year later, those events take on a different aspect again. The problem of social life is how to pin meanings so that they will stay still for a little while. And without some conventional ways of selecting and fixing agreed meanings, the very minimum consensual basis of a society is missing. As for tribal society, so the same for us. Rituals are conventions which set up visible public definitions. If you want meanings to stay still enough to be transmitted from one person to another, you have to try to make them public and visible and recognisable. The most effective rituals use material things, and the more costly those things, the stronger the intention to fix the meanings concerned.

In this perspective, goods are seen to be adjuncts to ritual.

Consumption of goods is a ritual process, whose primary function is to make sense of the inchoate flux of events. It is a short step from there to identifying the overall objective which rational beings, by definition, can be supposed to set themselves. Their own rationality must press them to make sense of their environment. The most general objective of the consumer can only be to construct an intelligible universe with the goods s/he chooses. How does this cognitive construction proceed? We should consider in more detail how goods become physical markers of social meanings.

First, let us take time, calendrical time: Christmas, New Year, birthdays, Sundays—the social universe needs a marked-out temporal dimension. The calendar has to be notched for periodicities—annual, quarterly, monthly, weekly, daily, and even shorter intervals. The passage of time can by itself, with these notches and markers, be laden with meaning. The calendar gives a principle for rotating duties, for establishing precedents, for review and renewal: another year passed, a new beginning. Twenty-five years—a silver jubilee, 100 years, 200 years—a centennial or bicentennial celebration. There is a time for living and a time for dying and a time for loving, and so on. Consumption goods are used for notching these intervals. Their range in quality rises from the need to differentiate through the calendar year and the life cycle. So think what would happen to our sense of time if we did without time-notching goods.

There appears to be a roughly inverse relation between the frequency of use and the value of the marking services which the object confers. Moreover, those marking services tend to vary directly with the number of people present. So it all can fit together quite neatly. Just imagine a household in a very simple, very stable culture. Suppose that they expect to own one set of glasses, cups and plates for everyday use, and a best set kept for Sundays, and the very best heirloom set stored on the top shelf wrapped in plastic bags for annual display at Christmas or New Year. Now, with those three sets of plates, this family can discriminate between events on a three-point scale. Finer discrimination can be signalled by food on a much longer range. Food can discriminate the different times of the day and the days from each other as well as the annual events, and it can also do justice to life-cycle events, such as weddings. We can also suppose that for each higher point on this scale notched by china, food and clothing, there is an increasing numerical factor for people sharing the event, and increasingly valuable marking service associated with being there. We should find that the rank value, then, of each class of goods varies inversely with the frequency of its use. The breakfast is taken separately, say, but more of the family and friends assemble for Sunday dinner, a still larger assembly collects for Christmas, a still larger one for weddings and funerals. The anthropologist sees necessities marking low-esteem high-frequency events, while luxuries tend to mark low-frequency events which are highly esteemed.

The periodicity of use not only sorts out the upper-class goods; it also serves to mark the differences between classes of people. At the king's court, as it were, it is birthdays and Christmas every day. So one thing we can say for sure is that there will always be luxuries in this sense, for rank must need to be marked or not exist at all, and all goods convey to some extent messages about rank. The class of pure rank-markers could be the high-quality versions of goods which serve no purpose, such as the best porcelain, the family heirlooms, the ancestral portraits. But it is not always easy to separate pure rank-marking from practical efficiency. Apparently, when Marshal Tito visited Buckingham Palace and admired the gold plate that was put out in his honour, Prince Philip said: 'Yes, it does look nice, and my wife finds that it saves on breakages.'

We are moving to seeing consuming goods as an act of joint production, with fellow-consumers, of a whole universe of values. Consumption uses goods to make firm and visible a particular set of judgements in the fluid processes of classifying persons and events. The individual needs compliant fellows if he is to succeed in changing the public categories. If he wants to reduce their disorder and make the universe more intelligible, he must have support. So his project of creating intelligibility for himself depends on fellows attending his rituals and inviting him to theirs. It is by their freely-given presence that he obtains a judgement from them that he has made a fitting choice of consumer goods for celebrating these particular occasions, and also on his own relative standing as a judge of such occasions and a contributor to that live action of developing the culture. He needs goods to give marking services and to get marking services. That is, he has to be present at other people's rituals of consumption, so that he can circulate his own judgement on the fitness of the things used to celebrate the diverse occasions. Each individual is himself in the classification scheme whose discriminations he is helping to establish. Goods perish or are consumed. But his is a small part of the total consumption process. In this information approach, it would seem very arbitrary to define goods, as pure economics does, by the itemised market transactions which deliver them into the house. Each item can equally well be perceived as a mere instalment, as part of a flow, like a little bit of paint which draws a whole line, the paint which goes into the construction of a classification system. This stream of consumable goods might be thought of as leaving a sediment which builds up the structure of culture like coral islands; the sediment is the learned set of names and names of sets, operations to be performed upon names, a means of thinking.

The demand for marking services always involves a demand for personal availability. You cannot attend two friends' consumption rituals at close intervals of time in two different places without speeding up travel. And a household cannot increase the number of friends attending its own consumption rituals without increasing the power for dealing with large quantities—without increasing space, without getting relief from time-consuming household processes. A rise in real income will tend, on this theory, always to be accompanied by a transformation of the frequency of ceremonial social events involving many fellow-consumers, a transformation from low frequency to high frequency. All this means interpreting an increase in real income as a potential increase in social inter-action. Conversely, exclusion from social interaction means real poverty, long before the level of food shortage is reached. And thus we can define luxuries as either grading signals— discriminators of rank, such as the best china which comes out when all the aunts descend on the family for a christening—or as the latest technological aid, those new capital goods which relieve pressure on available time and space and energy.

The anthropological approach, then, to the question of why people want goods, starts with the demand for marking services and concerns itself with two distinct properties of goods—their capacity to increase personal availability, and their capacity as rank markers. The first is technological, and the second is cultural, but the power to mark, and the power to increase availability of persons, can never be treated as independent of each other.

Man is a social being, and he needs goods for communicating with others, and for making sense of what is going on around him. This being so, his objective as a consumer can be summed up as a concern for information about the changing cultural scene, a concern to get information and to control information if possible. This means an effort to be near the centre of information transmission—and here the competition starts. It also means trying to seal off the boundaries of the system, so that other messages do not come in. On this theory of using consumption to mark an internal process of classification, the individual must therefore seek both scope and synthesis. S/he has to synthesise the information s/he gets. The wider the net which his/her classifications fling over the manifold of experience, the more difficult it is at first for him/her to relate all the different areas meaningfully to each other. But if classification proceeds peacefully, eventually there will be benefits accruing from the width of scope of the classification, for the meanings from one realm of discourse will play back upon the others.

In a finite social world, securely bounded, the meanings fold back and echo, and reinforce one another. Each new field that is added can be brought under rational control comparitively easily, by reason of these economies of effort which increased scope makes possible. But real economies of scale emerge when consumption is seen as part of an information system, and the consumer's main objective is seen also as gaining or keeping control of the sources of information, so that his/her own rational interpretations are secure. So now we are coming close to the competitive area that people refer to when they are talking about competitive consumption. We can understand the driving force behind demand.

The rational individual must seek as large a scale of operation as is needed in order successfully to hold together all s/he knows. S/he needs continually to maintain his or her synthesis, or adapt it in the light of rival views. The individual, the risk comes from some alien view that is more comprehensive in scope than his/her own, or appeals more to the people who s/he has engaged to support him/her in his/her own view. S/he risks the clues being changed to make no sense of his/her system, and a lot of sense in somebody else's. So an information approach to the question of demand implies that the individual is sensible to get the best information that is going, and even more sensible to get near its sources so as to be able to get the information reliably and quickly. But an even surer way not to have his/her own sanity overwhelmed by other people's contrary interpretations is to take charge of the information him/herself. Was it Malcolm Muggeridge who said, 'The point, my dear man, about television, is not to *view* it, but to get *on* it.'

I have cast my argument about goods in terms of access to information. Those who control that access often seek a monopoly advantage. Their strategy is to erect barriers against entry, to consolidate control of opportunities and to use techniques of exclusion. And for those excluded, the only two strategies are to withdraw and consolidate around the remaining opportunities, or to seek to infiltrate through the monopoly barrier. Since consumption is a primary field in which exclusion is applied, usurpation is attempted or withdrawal enforced by private individuals, one against another. An anthropological theory of consumption must focus upon these behavioural strategies. Any attempts to interpret the demand for goods which ignore these preoccupations about conserving power and privilege can only fall back upon consumer irrationality, and tell us that the consumer is a puppet, prey to the advertisers' wiles, jealously competing for no sane motive or rushing lemming-like, to disaster by greed. There is no serious consumption theory possible that avoids some responsibility for social criticism. Ultimately, consumption is about power. It is not a trivial matter. When we understand how commodities are used, then they themselves can become a beam of light focused on social policy.

To keep sane is the single, minimal objective which the individual must seek, by definition, as a rational being. The wish to participate in rational choice in an intelligible world is only a fair extension of the concept. Without this extension, all the other assumptions of economic rationality make nonsense. All other living beings organise their experience within a framework particular to their species, which limits the scope of possible messages and responses. But human rationality shapes the scope of the organising structures themselves. Human experience can flow into a vast variety of possible frameworks, for the rational human is responsible for recreating continually the universe in which choice can take place. The life project of making sense of the world involves interpreting the world as sensible.

This conceded, the moral question of why people want goods shifts away from the debunking of advertisers and from moralising about greed and envy. It shifts to moralising about exclusion, and the part that the choice of goods plays in defining and rejecting outsiders. 'Why can't we be content with what we have? Why not go back to the simple life?', we ask. Interestingly, the vocal critic of consumerism is usually rather well situated in the information system that is society, and I notice this in the complaints and prejudice that arise against the excluded. A much franker way of saying that there is too much envy and competitiveness in the demand for goods would be, 'Why don't they stop trying to get in?'

3

An institutional ecology of values

MARY DOUGLAS

Perception of dangers from technology, especially nuclear power, is a central issue for the social sciences. Much interesting work is being undertaken on risk perception. The dominant paradigm, as for most of psychology, is that of an isolated individual perceiver. My own task is to find a theoretical framework for studying perception in modern industrial society, not neglecting but taking proper account of social factors. In perception of risk this is likely to be particularly necessary, since any community tends to set standards of due care and to use indices of negligence or improper risk taking, so that it is not plausible to treat risk perception as an individual operation.

The background comes from an anthroprological approach to perception of danger which derives from 1940s and 1950s functionalist anthropology. Seen from an actor's perspective, the dangers that turn into disasters seem to hove in sight as unforeseen surprises. From the analyst's comparative perspective, they are not altogether unforeseen. Some prior perception of danger is incorporated into institutional structures. From long-accumulated experience, the culture has anticipated, labelled and listed the main hazards around; it has already alerted the members to early symptoms and drawn their attention to the moral defects which transform first signs into heavy damage. Dangers are culturally preselected for recognition and the people's response is fully coded in terms of appropriate procedures, enquiries, punishments and restitutions. The selection of dangers, the sustaining of attention and the appropriateness of blame are part of the institutional structure.[1]

These insights into stable cultures might seem irrelevant to modern society which is facing totally unprecedented dangers. They are irrelevant if the focus is on the danger, but that is the actor's perspective. They are conceivably relevant if the focus is on the institution, and that is the analyst's perspective. For the functional approach insists that dangers are instituionalised so that they stabilise and generally support the local regime. The analysis is exactly based on Durkheim's analysis of the social functions of crime. It does not much matter what the crimes are; even brand new crimes will be institutionalised to the same service. Likewise, one could expect that even brand new varieties of danger will get the same institutionalising treatment. Then it becomes urgent to ask what kind of institutional structures support what kinds of perceptions of danger. Such questions require some explicit assumptions as the basis for studying the institutional ecology of values.

1 Assume that institution-building and instituion-maintaining is a rational process in which individuals negotiate their goals and complex choices to reach some degree of institutional viability and coherence.

2 Assume that in so far as they agree at all on goals, the constituent members of an institution are also incorporating agreement on things to be avoided. Agreement on the specific kinds of losses to which they are averse is one of the topics of members' negotiations with one another. Consequently, some recognised risks are written into the constitution along with common goals.

3 Assume that institutions in their nature provide controls on curiosity as well as rewards for learning; the perceptual monitoring will not be random, but a function of the kind of organisation that is being achieved.

4 Assume that most institutions have some organisational problems which tend to be solved through public allocation of blame and that the nature of these problems and the blaming procedures vary according to the kind of organisation.

5 A machinery for renewing members' commitment to the institution's objectives is activated by the threat of disaster and this likewise corresponds to the type of institution.

Nearly a quarter of a century ago, Herbert Simon said 'the organizational and social environment in which the decision maker finds himself determines what consequences he will anticipate, what ones he will not; what alternatives he will consider, what ones he will ignore. In a theory of organization, these variables cannot be treated as unexplained, independent factors, but must themselves be determined and explained by the theory.'[2] The proper follow-up to this insight would be to classify the types of social organisation according to the way they blinker and focus the vision of the rational agent. I have searched far and wide for this development without success. Still less do I find (outside of anthropology) attention paid to the way that the organisation of society creates a feedback to the individual perceiver according to how moral concern is mobilised. The real disappointment is the poverty of sociological typologies incorporating perceptual bias. Discussion in sociology, organisation theory and decision-making analysis is confined to two main types: bureaucracy and market, developed by Weber and elaborated by many reflective writers from Parsons to Lindblom. The paradigmatic centrality of these two types explains why it is so difficult to transfer to modern society any insights whatever from anthropology. Market is the fundamental condition of industrial society. An bureaucracy is seen as the development (unwanted, maybe) of high culture. Combined, they are the point of reference which separates types of modern society from those technologically simple ones studied by anthropologists.[3] To bridge that impressive divide, a typology is needed that works at a higher level of generalisation, allowing distinctive social forms to be seen apart from the accidents of literacy and technology.

If anyone were to take de Tocqueville's interest in voluntary associations seriously, they would be dissatisfied with a typology that says nothing about them. According to de Tocqueville, nothing else in America deserves so much attention as the widespread habit of forming voluntary associations.[4] Though this form of organisation has been subsequently studied, little attention has been paid to the particular features which caught his eye.

1 He posited a close connection between associations and equality.

2 He observed that associations are specially needful for mobilising support in democratic societies, to make up for the absence of powerful private persons.

3 He noted that if an association is to have any power in these conditions, it has to have a large membership.

4 He also observed that this need to operate on a large scale posed difficulties.

5 Though he seldom used the word 'jealousy', he said much about the delusions, anonymity and frustrations of competitive striving in a condition of general equality.

Over the last decade I have been trying to work out a typology of social environments which could account for distinctive forms of moral and cultural bias.[5] The typology is generated along two axes of social control: one indicates the strength and number of regulations placed upon the individual's options (I call it grid); another indicates the exclusiveness and inclusiveness of the group boundary (I call it group). By comparing the structure of institutions according to these dimensions, we can identify several distinctive, persistent types of social organisation, each with its own supporting set of values. They include the society of competitive individualism (low grid-low group); the hierarchical, compartmentalised society (high group-high grid); and the egalitarian voluntary association (low grid-high group). I have had something to say about how these types of social environment provide distinctive perceptions of risk for the people who are actively engaged in supporting them. But without some help from outside anthropology and sociology, I had no comments to make on the connection between equality and voluntary associations which de Tocqueville specially noticed.

Help has come from an unexpected quarter: economics and the theory of public goods. De Tocqueville starts with the condition of equality and argues that it creates a political vacuum that gets filled by associations. I would rather put it the other way around and say that a power vacuum creates problems of organisation which are partly solved by adopting a principle of equality. According to de Tocqueville, equality is an uncomfortable position, full of discontent and lacking discipline. Equality means all being jumbled together in the same constantly fluctuating crowd, without recognition, honour or social standing, eyes coveting small prizes and resenting small inequalities. 'When everything is more or less level, the slightest variation is noticed. Hence, the more equal men are, the more insatiable will be their longing for equality.'[6] If we were to ask de Tocqueville why anybody should want to stay in that unhappy inchoate jumble, his answer would seem to be based on the positive value of equality, seen as a good in itself. He never argued that the experience of equality's disappointments might just as well lead to instituted differences rather than to associations. A very different approach to the question can be found in Mancur Olson's *The Logic of Collective Action*.[7] This book suggests indirectly that people put up with the disadvantages of equality only under special circumstances. What he actually says is that according to rational choice theory, the voluntary organisation that is not protected by coercive power and/or does not afford selective benefits for its members will not succeed in creating a collective good and will experience grave organisational difficulties. Markets and hierarchies flourish, thanks to the rational expectation of members that they will gain individual, selective benefits. The less that individual selective benefits are available, the more the organisation encounters problems of commitment, leadership and decision-making. According to Olson, when there is no coercion and no selective individual benefit, a group is going to be bothered by free-rider problems. Each member will expect to be able to enjoy the public benefits created by the others without anyone noticing whether or not he puts in his bit. If there is a difference between big and small stake-holders, the latter will tend to blackmail the former, threatening to withdraw and so gaining a paralysing veto power over the whole group. Leadership is thwarted; endless bargaining blocks the decisions of endless committees. Such a group has a problem even to raise funds for its minimum organisation costs and must be judged to be specially fragile and especially vulnerable to internal dissension.

The first step this kind of organisation needs to make when trying to collect contributions and prevent secessions, is to draw a clear boundary around members against the outside world. Second, it will need to make a rule of 100 per cent participation, so as to prevent any free-riding member from reaping unfair benefits. On this analysis, instead of starting with equality and moving to associations, we start with voluntary associations and see them forced to institute equality. Though this is as far as Olson takes us, it enables a great deal to be added to de Tocqueville's insight. When anthropology adds the distinctive social uses of danger to the typology, we can go further than Olson takes us.

First, I should strengthen the theoretical basis for identifying my three types and for going on with typologising. The new institutional economics has been busy identifying the sorts of social situations that underlie particular sorts of market imperfections and market failure. In the course of studying kinds of contractual relations, it was fairly straightforward to use rational choice theory to state the conditions in which pure market relations are less attractive than a relation of employment: uncertainty is reduced, the employer gains a more flexible service, the employee puts up with ambiguity and possible exploitation for the sake of security.[8] In this way the rational bases for distinguishing the origins of bureaucracy from market are laid. But we are interested especially in extending traditional typology to include some of the types of voluntary associations that interested de Tocqueville. These are cases which fit neither the specifications of bureaucracy nor those of pure market. The argument in economics about the definition and classification of public goods and the devices used to control free-riding has produced categories of 'exclusive public goods, snob-goods', 'coercive consumption' and 'crowd effects'. This literature leads to the development of the Club Theory[9] which is indeed very close to de Tocqueville's theme about the intentions of people forming associations and the institutional problems they face. Further, there is a small but significant literature on the market for superstars.[10] Within this typology there are three distinctive forms of social institution: the pure market in which no one firm can do anything to influence prices; the relations of employment in which are discerned the elements of bureaucracy; the superstar who can perform to ever-larger audiences without more cost to himself. In certain circumstances, his audience may suffer from lack of exclusiveness or crowding, so limited associations arise.

The explicit anchoring of the theory to the rational behaviour model and the effects of changes in market structure on the shape of institutions is marvellously relevant. Perceptual feedbacks from individuals to institutions and back again are traced through the assumed thought processes of the rational agent who finds that disadvantages in one kind of social environment can be corrected by small institutional changes. I have no plan to appropriate this discussion in economics or to adapt it to my theme. I merely signal it as providing a richer exercise in social typologising and one which happens to fit very snugly in many respects with the stable typology of society which keeps emerging from anthropological comparisions. It gives me confidence to go on trying to improve the typologies that relate values to their institutional matrices.

The anthropologist works on the assumption that when disaster befalls, each kind of social organisation will invoke a distinctive set of active powers in the universe to do three things: one cognitive, to explain; one political, to justify; one system-maintaining, to stabilise its own peculiar institutions. If we assume that a social type will only survive by the moral commitment of its members, the main task of cultural analysis is to examine the rhetoric of explanations, persuasions and excuses, looking for how it sustains the existing social system by the force of various appeals to active principles in the universe.

A stable constitution will pin blame for misfortunes on dissidents. Bureaucracy will blame those who breached its rules, or pin responsibility on the victim, so that disruptive blaming is checked. A row of punitive ancestors is an effective control in a society of a tradition-loving kind. To explain misfortunes it is plausible to all that the victim entered forbidden ground or violated an ancient edict and so brought his troubles on himself. No-one would be seen to do the adjudicating: the explanation of mishaps upholds authority obliquely, by the tacit consensus that authority is to be protected.

Nothing of this sort is acceptable in a society composed of competing superstars, their managers, rivals, patrons and clients, any one of whom could conceivably rise to stardom. This account comes close to the competitive, individualist society described for certain polities in New Guinea (and for the politicians' universe more generallly). Such a society will not persist unless an individual's freedom to contract is upheld. There is the temptation for the successful Big Man to dig in and institutionalise a bureaucracy or aristocracy around himself and his heirs. The system is kept fluid with room for new stars to arise by a special kind of explanation of disasters. Instead of seeking to blame, there is seeking to claim responsibility for what has happened. The favourite explanation refers to vast private resources deployed by the successful person. Let me class under the head of secret weaponry all these mysterious powers that an individual may claim to use, whether the power be innate, purchased or gifted. Each actor, pursuing his private ends, is busily joining or leaving coalitions: unsuccessful operations get driven down and out of the market, a few big ones emerge for a period of glory. If everyone is committed to the underlying principles, no-one will let it be said that a grave mishap was caused by refusal to abide by tradition. No-one is going to accept a coroner's verdict which implies that daring innovation, new forms of brokerage or free negotiation has attracted punishment. Some more morally flexible principle is needed. What I am here calling a theory of secret weaponry supports the successful person and sustains something like a market in superstar success. It justifies the changes in alignment that everyone needs to be ready to make. Wanting to leave Y who is growing old and to join X who is currently successful, they can justify the switch of allegiance because X has obviously got bigger battalions, better secrets, bigger guardian spirits, talent or luck on his side; and when X starts to fail, the same theory allows his supporters to drift away, saying that his technology has run down, his demon has deserted him or his luck has run out.

Turning now to associations, clubs, sects and communes, these are committed by internal political needs to make a virtue of equality. Voluntary organisation is also prone to factionalism. Faction leaders are a threat; a minor form of control is to accuse them of ambition; a major way is to accuse them of treacherous alliance with the stratified, unequal inhumane outside world. The more the internal crises heat up, the more it suits the latent goals of the organisation for everyone committed to it to stare at the horizon, spotting there the signs of conspiracy and cosmic disaster which can only be staved off if everyone converts to the egalitarian doctrine. In another case, the disasters on the horizon would justify expelling the unpopular faction leader. Lacking strong selective benefits to induce their members to bear the insults and tensions of living together, people in such associations use the accusation of treachery to solve their organisational problems. The term cosmic plot corresponds to ancestors and secret weaponry in our typology of active principles in the universe. The function of the witch or traitor in a society that sees itself at risk in a cosmic plot is diametrically opposed to that of the ancestor and to that of the superstar's secret weaponry. The latter claims his amazing powers explicitly and he thrives or fails according to his success in justifying his claim. The claim is an accelerator of his destiny.

The ancestor is too dead to claim credit himself, but the traitor has to be a live person visibly in the thick of the political scene so as to be the target of factional abuse. The idea of the ancestor is employed by the collectivity to suppress moral deviance, but the idea of the traitor is used for factional fighting. Each social type adimadverts differently at post mortems, inquests and other inquiries into disaster. Each uses distinctive moral principles to maintain itself. Real physical dangers are differently institutionalised in each case.

If this argument is convincing, the approach affords an improved lens. It is not an improved way of looking at dangers and deciding whether they are real or not. It is a way of looking at the way society deals with dangers. It is a way of bridging the gap between primitives and moderns, one which needs to be developed and tested with empirical research.

NOTES

1 Douglas, Mary, *Purity and Danger: An Analysis of Concepts of Pollution and Taboo*, (London, Routledge and Kegan Paul, 1966).
2 March, James, and Simon, H. A., *Organizations*, (New York, Wiley, 1958).
3 Douglas, Mary, 'The Effects of Modernization on Religious Change', *Daedalus*, Winter 1982.
4 De Tocqueville, Alexis, 'Associations in civil life', in J. P. Mayer and Max Lerner (eds) *Democracy in America*, vol. 2, ch. 5 (New York, Harper and Row, 1966).
5 Douglas, Mary, *Natural Symbols*, (London, Barrie and Jenkins, 1970); *In the Active Voice* (London, Routledge and Kegan Paul, 1982); with Aaron Wildavsky, *Risk and Culture* (Berkeley, University of California Press, 1982).
6 De Tocqueville, *op cit*, 604.
7 Olson, Mancur, *The Logic of Collective Action: Public Goods and the Theory of Groups* (New York, Schoken Books, 1965).
8 Williamson, Oliver, E., *Markets and Hierarchies: Analysis and Anti-Trust Implications*, (New Yorks, Free Press, 1975).
9 Williamson, Oliver E., 'Transaction-cost economics: the governance of contractual relations', *The Journal of Law and Economics*, vol. xxii., October 1979, 223–61.
10 Rosen, Sherwin, 'The economics of superstars', *American Economic Review*, December 1981.

4

The person in an enterprise culture

MARY DOUGLAS

FREE PERSONS

Setting up something called an enterprise culture is sometimes justified by the claim that it frees persons from constraints under which they should not be. The person in this context is said to be driven by self-interested motives. Community demands imposed by bureaucratic regulation inhibit the pursuit of freely-chosen objectives, and so infringes essential liberties of the person. The utilitarian case for the free market is transferred from economics where it can be tested, to psychology where it cannot. If the market for ideas is important at all there would have to be important arguments about the nature of persons as well as about their interests. However, although there is forthright political argument about the interests, on the nature of the person there is much dodging of the topic, skirting around or avoiding it. Every culture protects some matters from questioning by declaring that enquiry about them is impossible. Such avoidance is known as taboo behaviour. It seems that in our western industrial culture, knowledge of the person and the self is deliberately sunk into one of those areas of protected public ignorance.

The case for claiming that nothing can be argued about the self is maintained because the idea of self is heavily locked into ideology. The Frankfurt philosophers taught unequivocally that the self is ideology, and irredeemably enmeshed in political myth[1]. Trying to become emancipated from myth by the light of reason is vain: reason is the instrument of oppression. To the ear of the anthropologist to whom ideology is in some ways synonymous with culture, this is not the point to discard reasoning. On the contrary, recognising the ideological structure of the self is the right starting-point for an investigation.

The idea of the self driven by the self-regarding passions can be recognised as an ideological or a cultural construct, and part of the process of investigation is to identify other self concepts, responding to other ideological demands. The first task is to explain more fully why our learned conversations about the self are muffled, conflicting and inconclusive compared with talk about the nature of the self in traditional African societies that anthropologists study. The second is to start a more anthropologically sophisticated conversation on the subject, and then to work back from considering a variety of culturally-constructed selves to considering what the self has to be like to be able to operate in an enterprise culture.

The starting point is that claims to know about human persons are part of the rhetoric of political coercion. Westerners have taken to heart the idea that the self is an ideological construct. The blank space in our theoretical scheme has been constructed precisely to meet that understanding: better disallow anything that may be said in advance, rather than lend the notion of the person to political abuse. Confronted with Nazi theories about two kinds of human persons, Aryan and other races, Christianity had something to say, but its views rested on doctrine, not on knowledge that could be validated in the way of other disputed facts. A viable idea of the self cannot be entrenched by reference to religious doctrine, since the latter is not entrenched. Anyone who is ready to reject the authority of the church can be free of its doctrine. There is no immediate automatic feedback as there would be from denying the principles of gravity.

In earlier European history, Christian claims for orthodoxy invoked knowledge about persons being constituted with immortal souls; the claims to knowledge about the person justified forcible protection from the effects of sin and heresy. That this teaching allowed violent political coercion is one reason why the said doctrinal claims have lost their appeal: one doctrine confronting another doctrine needs more than loyalty in its defence. In Europe, witchcraft ideas were used to inculpate persons with the wrong constituent elements in their souls, or two persons allegedly inside one body, one controlled by the devil, or to restrain a person alleged not to be a full human being at all, but just a victim of demonic possession whom it would be kinder to put out of the way. Ideas about persons as witches and sorcerers have been used in the past to justify torture of marginals and deviants, and there would be no way in which the accused could rationally defend themselves. Biological-determinist theories of gender differences are also used to oppress.[2] Likewise, we could be fooled by the theory that the self flourishes in an enterprise culture and is stifled in a culture of hierarchy. Unless we can submit it to reasoned enquiry, this idea of the self could be just as coercive as any other. It matters a lot to be able to have a reasoned argument about the self's constitution and capabilities so as to be able to respond with reasons to arbitrary political coercion.

Isaiah Berlin was exercised by this very problem. His essay on two concepts of freedom distinguished one, which he regarded as legitimate: freedom from interference. The other concept, in his view illegitimate, was the idea of freedom to become or be a certain kind of complete, fulfilled person. He argued that the second is a contradiction of the idea of liberty. Who is going to define the fulfilled person and the person's completeness? Anyone else's definition of a person is apt to become an instrument of coercion.[3] To prevent the concept of freedom being put to coercive uses, it has been emptied of content. At the same stroke, the concept of the person was emptied of content. The liberal concern with freedom has put around this kind of knowledge a hedge of ineffability. The strategy is to insist that inside the person's physical appearance there is an inner self, the real person who is beyond knowledge. The strategy is to place the topic of personhood under taboo. A strong protective response (like taboo) prevents an articulated theory of the person.

However, it is not true that we live together without any exchange of ideas about what constitutes a person. In practical life, without being philosophers, we need to know what can legitimately be expected from other persons. Over the last three hundred years the self and the person have become separated in the discourse of our western civilisation. The category of self has been classified as the subject, inherently unknowable. The category of person has been filled by the need to meet the forensic requirements of a law-abiding society and an effective, ratonal judicial system. As pragmatically viable ideas, the self and the person are compatible and work. However, they are very weak as logical aids for arguing against theories of personhood with uncongenial political implications. If someone wanted to oppose the idea underlying utilitarian philosophy that the human being is motivated primarily by self-interest, there is no logically powerful argument in its favour to amend.[4] The case for an alternative view of the motives and satisfactions of persons would only be as strong as the gut reaction it could provoke in its favour.

THE INEFFABLE SELF

The problem in its modern form was posed by Hume who, like Locke, denied the existence of a 'self-substance', something underlying the episodic experiences we have of ourselves. The idea of a unitary, continuous, responsible self fell under the knife of his general philosophical scepticism. For lack of evidence, and for lack of reasoning to justify it, Hume concluded that the self's identity and unity are fictions. We are bundles of representations held together plausibly by the similarity of the experiences we have from moment to moment. There being no self-substance, our idea of our self arises out of the well-oiled grooves of mental associations; our remembered experiences, and the similarities between them, and other connections between them which we recognise, create relations between our ideas. These habits produce our idea of a continuous, rational, responsible self, which nothing else can justify. This is where he felt compelled to leave the problem, with much regret, and this is more or less where it still lies. Many distinguished philosophers have proposed alternative accounts of the self's existence, sometimes mystical, sometimes scholastic, sometimes idealist. The alternatives can serve well enough for anyone who rejects Hume's empirical philosophy. But if you stay with the problem in the terms Hume set for it, the belief in the unitary self is objectively unjustifiable: necessary and true, but founded on a great leap of faith.

For example, Heidegger suggested that we could get round the problem by assuming the self to be transcendent to all experience, its necessary ground. Sartre made nonsense of this attractive solution by showing a logical flaw: if the transcendent self is the ground of experience it cannot itself inspect itself, so how can it be known? What we know of the self is based on what we see of its activity of knowing, and we have no grounds for postulating some intrinsically unknowable self behind that

activity. Intuitively we want to side with Sartre in denying that
the self is something intrinsically unknowable, forever inaccessible. What follows below is in sympathy with the project for
knowing the self through its activities. In everyday encounters
the knowability of the self is heavily engaged. We claim with
confidence to know a lot about ourselves. But we cannot
validate our knowledge of selves except by our reliability in
prediction. As to persons, for public knowledge about personhood we are left without any agreed theory about when the
person starts, or ends; we stand in moral dilemmas about
transplant surgery, abortion, mercy killing, brain death. We
disagree, while lacking a way of airing our disagreements
coherenty.

Knowledge of God comes under the same disabilities. The
strategy of claiming ineffability did not work too well for the
defence of the idea of God against the European tide of
disbelief. But making God undefinable and unknowable might
prevent a plural community from trying to impose their idea of
God upon one another. Ineffability will do as much for the self.
However, the claim that it is ineffable is weak as an intellectual
defence. Ineffability blocks a certain kind of enquiry, but it will
not protect the self from arbitrary dictators with brand new
theoretical justifications for discriminating between us. The
only supports for the idea of ineffability are good will and
consensus. Suppose good will is absent and consensus has
failed? Suppose we ourselves, fickle to our principles, should
change our minds about the worthwhileness of those liberal
values which the ineffability principle is devised to save? The
idea of the ineffable self is just a blank space, a no-go area for
logical discourse. It gives no entry for reasoning and no hold in
rational debate against our own possible wishes to espouse
arbitrary, coercive theories of selfhood and personhood. It is a
peculiar cultural construct.

THE BODY/MIND LINK

The western culture, whatever we say seriously about persons
and selfhood needs to some extent to be compatible with what
a jury in a court of law will accept. This demand imposes a non-
negotiable link between the person and the person's living
body. Because of embodiment, we cannot claim to be able to be

in three places, or two, at the same time. For the jury the capacities of the self have to conform to the accepted constraints of space and time. This means that for us there are several philosophical problems about selfhood which other civilisations do not find problematical. First, the concept of the multiple self is absolutely objectionable. The jury room has no use for a concept of person with several constituent selves because responsibility must not be diffused. So there is no pleading for a criminal in the name of a theory of homunculi who take over different compartments of the self's choices and responsibilities. Second, the concept of the passive self is unacceptable. It is no good explaining in court that a person's actions are under the control of external agencies, such as furies, capricious gods, demons or personified emotions. It will not do to deny responsibility by saying that a sorcerer has turned the person into a zombie. For any of these versions of diminished responsibility to be accepted in the courts would entail a great deal of rewriting of the law books. For any of them to be philosophically accepted would make utilitarian philsophy even more difficult to maintain than it is now. But though we may not like them at the level of gut response, we are in a weak position for saying that they are wrong, since we have put the topic of the internal constitution of the self out of bounds. We cannot either say how those theories are wrong or how they might be right.

Other people's ideas about the self are stacked on anthropologists' shelves, ethnographic oddities not worth bothering about for a technologically superior western civilisation. The argument here is that the idea of a unitary self, because it concords so well with our legal and economic institutions, exerts on the dialogue a stranglehold like that of primitive philosophies. Fit with legal and economic institutions controls the possibilities of discussion. Thank God for the stranglehold. In the history of western jurisprudence this particular version of self, unitary and fully embodied, is the corner-stone of our civil liberties, a block against arbitrary defamation. We cannot accuse someone of doing harm by occult means in a distant place while there is good evidence that he/she was asleep in his/her bed. The impossibility of being in two places at once puts evidence based on visions and dreams out of court.

Approaching the self pragmatically by this external route

defuses the charge of political bias and gives us a way of comparing ideas of self with the legal institutions they uphold. On that impossibility, most verdicts of witchcraft would fail. The forensic uses of the self accord with the idea of the self as an ideological construct. The idea of the forensic self was proposed by John Locke to solve the philosophical problem of justifying the notion of a continuously conscious and responsible self. He tried to defend the idea on grounds of theological necessity. When we stand before the Judgement Seat of God at the end of our lives, he asked, how could we be expected to answer for our deeds if we have multiple or fragmented personalities? Therefore there must be a unitary responsible self.

Person, as I take it, is the name for this self. Wherever a man finds what he calls himself there, I think, another may say is the same person. It is a forensic term, appropriating actions and their merit; and so belongs only to intelligent agents capable of a law, and happiness, and misery. This personality extends itself beyond present existence to what is past, only by consciousness, whereby it becomes concerned and accountable, owns and imputes to itself past actions, just upon the same ground and for the same reason that it does the present ...

And therefore, conformable to this, the apostle tells us, that, at the great day, when everyone shall 'receive according to his doings, the secrets of his heart shall be laid open'. The sentence shall be justified by the consciousness all persons shall have, that they themselves, in what bodies soever they appear, or what substances soever that consciousness adheres to, are the same that committed those actions, and deserve that punishment for them.[5]

To anyone who believes in God's last judgement this may be an adequate justification of the unitary self lodged in its body, but it fails to convince anyone who does not believe in God and it should not weigh with one who believes in God, but doubts a day of judgement. The link between the self and its body is not an academic issue. Modern transplant surgery puts real-life pressure on the connection. The question of transfer of the self from one body to another becomes a practical issue which throws our habits of thought into disarray. It may become necessary to admit that it is neither logically absurd nor

practically irrelevant to conceive of transferable and disembodied selves.

Daniel Dennett has invented a story that illustrates the
weaknesses of contemporary thought on the body/mind link.[6]
In the story he has agreed to go on a dangerous mission,
leaving his brain behind. Surgery would completely remove his
brain, which would then be stored in a life-support system; each
input and output pathway, as it was severed, would be restored
by a pair of microminiaturised radio transceivers, one attached
precisely to the brain, the other to the nerve stumps in the
empty skull. When the hero has had the process explained he
says:

> At first I was a bit reluctant. Would it really work? The
> Houston brain surgeons encouraged me. 'Think of it', they
> said, 'as a mere *stretching* of the nerves. If your brain were
> just moved over an *inch* in your skull, that would not alter
> or impair your mind. We're going to make your nerves
> indefinitely elastic by splicing radio links into them.'

The operation was successful, and when he comes out of the
anaesthetic he is taken to see his own brain floating in a liquid,
and covered with little electrodes, circuit chips and other
electrical paraphernalia. To test whether it really is his own
brain, he hits a switch connected to it, and collapses from the
blow. When he comes round, he thinks to himself:

> Here I am, sitting on a folding chair, staring through a piece
> of plate glass at my own brain ... 'But wait,' I said to
> myself, 'shouldn't I have thought, here am I, suspended in a
> bubbling fluid, being stared at by my own eyes?' ... When I
> thought, 'Here I am', where the thought occurred to me
> was *here*, outside the vat, where I, Daniel Dennett, was
> standing staring at my brain. (p. 311–12)

Eventually he leaves his brain in the vat in Houston and goes on
his dangerous subterranean mission. At all times he can call
operation control and receive instructions. While he is working
underground on dismantling a warhead the cerebral links break.
He finds himself blind and deaf and dumb in a radioactive hole a
mile underground. It takes him some time to understand that
the realisation that his poor body is dead underground miles
away is taking place in his brain in the vat in Houston. But
where is he, really? Or which is he: the dead body, or his brain?
As the story goes on, having been disembodied, he is given by

the skill of the scientists a new body. Then all the problems of the legendary Hindu sages transformed into outcastes or kings, or of kings transformed into women, or of outcastes transformed into kings, are implicitly before us in our own vernacular philosophy. Dennett's funny story makes the point that personal transferability between bodies is not necessarily inconsistent with our space-time theories. So why do philosophers resist the implications of Hume's analysis? Why can we not accept a number of self theories, involving multiple selves, passive selves, invaded and possessed selves, each serving different forensic purposes? Are we to conclude that all other civilisations are wrong if they encourage notions of transfers of the self between one body and another? Philosophers cannot say that they are wrong, except on the forensic grounds that they would make society unworkable, but in fact many societies built upon these ideas work well. The objections we read are based more on morality and political acceptability than on feasibility. They argue that there has to be a unitary self, because the individual person has to be able to be held accountable. Thus is John Locke's religious argument secularised. Instead of the last judgement, the coherent, unitary self is validated by the demands of the secular law courts and by moral principles. Terence Penelhum waxes indignant on 'the moral trickery' of anyone who would represent his desires as external to himself.[7] Parroting Lockie in a secular vein, a unitary, responsible self-agent must be supposed to exist because it is intellectually, juridically and morally necessary. This is the prevailing forensic model of the person that best suits our culture.

INTENTIONAL SYSTEMS

The secular forensic model is an invitation to attend to the tension between self and the judges to whose penalties and awards the self is having to conform. The judges and jury are the other members of the culture, who have set up its standards and enforce them. If we could compare alternative ideas about the person we would be half way to getting past the intellectual block that prevents us from reasoning about selves in general. The forensic model of the person affords a possibility of setting up an external, empirical method of comparison. To this end, we look round for ideology-free, science-like descriptions of persons. The ultilitarian model of the self purports to be one such, but as we have shown, it is loaded with ideological assumptions. Furthermore, it has only one person, and no way of taking account of other persons except to make a simple aggregation of their satisfactions. It does not incorporate the results of politicking except by pushing into the negotiations the same analysis of costs and benefits which carry the burden of explanation for the selection of satisfactions. Being content with an individualist method is part of its ideological burden. Always focused on one actor, it can analyse human social behaviour as if all the other individuals were organised as a market, in other words as if there were no community. If we are looking for a culture-free approach, we have to bracket away the ultilitarian account of persons as a forensic model generated by a strong cultural bias. We want a method of finding alternative forensic models.

Daniel Dennett has proposed an all-purpose, minimal model of the person which he describes as an 'Intentional system'. The awkward language testifies to the effort to be free of adhering cultural bias. For lack of a better theory of the self he has had to invent a new way of thinking about the neuron pathways in the body to the individual brain, and about the pathways between the brain and the society, and he means the same model to do as well for thinking of the communication between communities. National states trying to calculate the intentions of other nation states and to infer from the intentions predictions useful for foreign policy count as intentional systems.[8] An intentional system needs three conditions: rationality, intentions, and a reciprocal stance towards and from other intentional systems.[9] Persons are rational beings whose actions are to be understood in terms of their intentions, these being construed from the logical relations between their beliefs and desires. Intentionality is a capability which persons attribute to one another. Since it works only in an environment of other persons this is radically different from methodological individualism. The 'intentional stance'[10] expects to predict how other persons are going to behave, and makes this knowledge the basis for strategies.

Prediction in terms of intentions is different from prediction in terms of physical laws. He uses the word intentions to include hopes, fears, intentions, perceptions, expectations, etc. We ascribe intentions to dogs and fish, or even to trees, so the intentional stance does not only include persons.[11] When he ascribes beliefs and desires to the computer chess player Dennett is not saying that the machine really has beliefs and desires, but that its behaviour can be explained and predicted by ascribing to it machine equivalents for beliefs and desires. Thus he can describe a computer in the same terms: it is much easier to decide whether a machine can be an intentional system than its is to decide whether a machine can *really* think, or be conscious, or morally responsible.[12]

A larger intentional system includes others, the community includes the person, the person includes the neurons. Dennett does not specify the relation between one level and the next. How is a level determined? The levels are supposed to connect and interact, but his model does not say how this happens. We can improve his model quite simply by incorporating the forensic process as the connecting medium and by giving cultural equivalents of person's beliefs and desires. Change his term 'beliefs' to 'theories' about the world; then change his term 'desires' to 'claims', so as to pay attention only to that part of intentions which enter the forensic process because they can be formulated as claims on others; then postulate that the claims invoke the theories in their support. These three slight adaptations give an abstract context of interaction between individual members of a community. Then the higher level or community can be presented as a system of claims sorted out by logic applied to negotiations and deals. Claims are the very substance of the higher level IS. At the community level the equivalent of individual claims are collective claims, or claims made on behalf of and in the name of the collectivity. The community equivalent of individual beliefs are collectively-held beliefs, public knowledge and generally accepted theories, or culture. Self-perception of a community will correspond to what its members think proper, and likewise, the knowledge of the self that is available to members will be limited by the forensic process.

CLAIMS

The project of this chapter is to find a way of evaluating the claims about the self in the enterprise culture. This involves noting the strong resistance to subjecting the idea of the self to reasoned argument, evidence if evidence was needed for its ideological embeddedness. The idea of the self is made to sit upon huge blank spaces of missing evidence. Admittedly this is the case for all ideas, so it is not the evidence that is missing but the theory that would indicate what would count as evidence in an argument. We have no such theory of the self because (for good reasons) we have deliberately put it into that inaccessible limbo that cannot be opened for theorising. A theory of knowledge based on claims does not intrude into that domain. It does not pretend to reveal anything about the inner experiences of the self, only about its uses in negotiation. A theory about claims made on the self has the advantage of not being grounded on an appeal to the transcendental. It is limited to knowledge that is made public, specifically to culture.

Transform, for the sake of argument, the judgement seat of God and the formal judgement seat of tribunals into the informal judgement of peers. In Dennett's terms they are intentional systems continually monitoring your behaviour and trying to make predictions about what you are going to do. The word 'claims' refers to demands that a person makes on the time or other resources of others. Acceptable claims at any point in time are equivalent to society. Claims includes all kinds of pretensions, requests, entitlements, expectations, demands. The gamut of claims runs from great confidence that an established claim exists and will be honoured, to a very tentative request for consideration. Disputes about claims on a person's time and property, if not quickly resolved, are always put to some testing of the condition of the world. Whoever can dispute a knowledge claim used as backing by his opponents can escape from the charges they seek to lay on him. As I have argued, the two kinds of claims, on persons and on knowledge, establish each other.[13] Dennett's model needs to insert the connection between responsibility and theories.[14] The gamut of theories runs from facts well established to very tentative hypotheses. Any pattern of claims can be sustained by any kind of knowledge.

If there is a sustainable pattern of claims it is a cultural system. Culture is the point at which claims and counter-claims come to rest and where authority is attributed to theories about the world. The context of claims and counter-claims sets up a pressure for consistency. Only a vigilantly maintained set of reasoned statements about the self will hold off the claims of others who will pounce on the least sign of contradiction, intellectual or moral weakness. To be able to invoke the self is an indispensable forensic resource for living in society.

INTERACTION BETWEEN INTENTIONAL SYSTEMS

Keeping a new concept free of content is a good strategy for starting an investigation at an abstract level. Dennett is careful not to be saying anything at all about the content of consciousness beyond the beliefs and desires and the power of inference. He never treads on the forbidden ground of subjective experience. His account is always from the outside, never risking a speculation on which beliefs or what kinds of desires could be found within. This is how he avoids importing unwanted metaphysical and political biases into his account.[15] A test of his theory about persons would have to be the same as the test that persons normally apply to their own theories about persons: predictive power.

Dennett's empty slots for beliefs and desires would be useful for predicting theories of the self if only the said beliefs and desires could be qualified a bit more. He does not try to assess the influence of the containing intentional system over its elements. He does not show how its internal relations are articulated. He cannot (and does not aim to) develop a critique of folk psychology, still less provide the basis for a critique of the self in the enterprise culture. But he does provide the beginnings of a model free of ideological adhesions that cultural theory can amend and use.

As a heuristic, set up four kinds of culture[16] each sustained by its members actively invoking a particular idea of the self. One of the four types will be the enterprise culture, one the hierarchical culture, one the culture of the dissident minority enclave. In each of these cultures power and authority are actively contested. The fourth is the type of culture in which the members are not involved in a dialogue about power. Each culture is carried in a community, an intentional system connected by claims with own sub-systems, the persons. Each culture produces, in the process of negotiating claims, its own compatible theory of the world and the self. It also calls forth desires from persons at the same time that it defines good and wrong behaviour. 'Society prepares the crime,' as Quetelet said,[17] and at the same time it defines the persons, as Durkheim said.

Consider hierarchy as one type of higher level intentional system. The test of a hierarchy is not stratified ranks but the overarching whole which contains them. It may be necessary to remind readers that every bureaucracy is not hierarchical; nor does every king reign over a hierarchy; not is a great industrial corporation a hierarchy if the chiefs whom Horkheimer calls 'totalitarian cartel lords'[18] treat its members as transient, dispensable resources. An individualist culture can have huge bureaucracies which make no moral claims on their own behalf, which are treated as private assets, stripped if possible by their members, treated as a kind of scaffolding or natural advantage which can be disposed of when it suits the individual member. Other bureaucracies, just as big, may be hierarchies according to the meaning of the term, that is, they contain units whose parts contribute to the maintenance of the whole and which never abandon responsibility for members. By definition this culture is maintained by claims accepted on behalf of the whole community; because claims overriding those of individual members are acceptable, authority can be exerted on behalf of the community; its member persons perform public ceremonials, invest in public goods and justify a high degree of organisation in order to strengthen the public claims they cherish. One result is that a well-run hierarchy has a lot to offer its members, and in consequence it is not worried lest they secede. Loyalty being secure, the main concern is that the up–down structure be not weakened.

In contrast, consider the dissenting minority enclave culture, which often tends to be sectarian. The main concern will be the fear of secession: anxiety lest the faithful leak away weakens authority and encourages a tendency to egalitarian organisation. Here, to be acceptable, claims should invoke the principle of equality. Third, the enterprise culture is distinguished from both of these by the weakness of the claims of the community over those of its members. Fourth, isolates who are not involved in economic or political or social competition, either having been forced out, or having chosen not to be involved, also have a typical culture characterised by absence of attempts to explain or influence events, and freedom from the ideological commitments which control so much of other persons' lives. It is as hard to find a pure hierarchy or a pure type of enclave culture as it is to find an extreme kind of enterprise culture or completely isolated members of the isolates' culture.

We look now for simple tests to show how incompatible cultures rest on distinctive, incompatible patterns of claims. One test should concern the claims that link the levels. How does a person become a member of a larger intentional system? It is easier to answer the question from the other angle: how does exclusion work? A second test should show the way the higher level system shapes individual desires conformably to its acceptable claims. A third test should show how the bundle of acceptable claims affects theories about reality, and particularly about the self. If we can develop a discussion on those lines, we can start to argue about persons in way that includes their ideological bias.

DOWNGRADING AND EXCLUSION FROM THE CLAIMS SYSTEM

The distinguishing feature of hierarchy is that every decision is referred to the well-being of the whole. A whole transcending its parts is what hierarchy means.[19] It is a claims system from which it is very difficult for anyone to be dropped. Everyone is there for ever, and everyone's claims are kept alive in some form or other. Inveterate disloyalty and unrepentant disobedience disqualify. Incompetence and infirmity do not. In the hierarchy the lobby of the weak is powerful since it is a good strategy to claim to represent it. (In consequence much distinctive regulation is entailed, for example, the protection of pension schemes will have priority over risky profits.) By what administrative arrangements is this result procured? This is achieved by maintaining the influence of distinct sectors in the overall decision process. Each person in such a hierarchy has to be enrolled within a recognised sector to have any claims at all, and the sectors have to be formally related to the whole. Since no-one can be eliminated, all have to be assigned places in the system, and the claims of the places have to be recognised. This type of higher level intentional system, the hierarchy, would be suffocated by mutually conflicting claims between lower level systems unless it had ways of grading and reconciling them. Inequality of status and inequality of claims is built in to the constitution. Successful claims are backed by reference to some expected good for the whole, and in this system, though some can claim more and others less, all have claims. The distinctive point is that people can drop down, but not out. On this issue there is little difference between a hierarchy and an enclave. In the latter, membership is theoretically for ever. Furthermore, it is generally an egalitarian claims system,[20] so there is no lower level for incompetents to drop down to. Disloyal traitors and subversive elements may be expelled from such a system of claims, but completely expelled. They will not be seen hanging around because neither incompetence not infirmity will have caused their exclusion, only political animosity.

In an individualist market-oriented society, incompetence disqualifies. The system tends to honour the person who organises effective networks. As exchange theory shows, there have to be failures in such a system, persons whom it is worth no-one's while to count as an ally. Falling into infirmity or otherwise showing weakness is a sure way of falling out of the network of worthy partners.[21] In the enterprise culture appalling black spots of poverty should not provoke surprise, especially in the face of immense private wealth. Though it needs to include the rising generation, and tries to reincorporate them into the competitive network, the claims of older failures and the demands for safety nets for the weak are incompatible with the doctrine of undiminished personal responsibility. The strength of the enterprise culture is the creation of wealth by a self-reliant meritocracy. Inevitably it has a large class of rejects. They are not the low-grade citizens of the bottom echelons of hierarchy, but derelicts who cannot be reincorporated into the system which excludes for poor performance.

DESIRES

As to desires, consider how consumerism has been misjudged. In all societies consumption is enjoyed, but consumerism, the unlimited private demand for commodities, is part of the individualist culture. Other cultural types impose restrictions on desires. The hierarchy certainly encourages conspicuous display, but requires that the show be on behalf of the community. The public affluence of palaces, cathedrals, law courts and public parks depends on the willingness of the taxpayer to fork out for civic benefits. The hierarchical person has been encouraged by all the devices which give a sense of belonging and loyalty to make personal desires subordinate to the claims of the community. Like the hierarchy, the culture of the enclave puts strong community constraints on spending. The idea of what is a suitable standard of living in an enclave is partly developed by opposition to those of the mainstream society, whether it is market-individualism or hierarchy: thrift is more elegant, more appropriate, than vulgar display. Consumerism is impossible in either of these types of higher level intentional system, and if a new habit of conspicuous private spending appears it can be taken as a symptom of a cultural shift.

The persons whose behaviour is condemned as consumerist are wrongly blamed if consumerism means private competitive consumption. They cannot help themselves; they are living in a social environment in which they must compete or risk being omitted from convivial lists, which will lead to being omitted from other important lists on which their livelihood depends. No-one really wants to get involved in a consumption rat race, but one person cannot put a lid on the pressure to compete with display of goods and hospitality. Only community disapproval can impose limits to competitive display, but this kind of culture is continually stripping the community. Persons in an individualist culture question authority, believe that censorship in all its forms is wrong, disapprove of sumptuary laws and other such controls on individual freedom of choice. The weight of their cultural consensus is thrown behind the work of liberation. It is part of the definition of the fully responsible individual to be sovereign in choice. For better or worse, consumerism rampages within the enterprise culture. It is inconsistent for its subscribers to berate consumerism and at the same time to subscribe unreservedly to individualist values.

THEORIES ABOUT THE SELF

Now we can return to those bizarre foreign ideas about the person. This chapter started out by explaining the kind of claims that are sustained by the theory of the unitary, rational responsible self. They are claims that are tested in law. The resulting idea of a forensic self is well adapted to a culture which

demands complete accountability from its members, the right
idea of the self for an individualist culture. If elsewhere zombies
and demonic possession and transfers of self are publicly
standardised ideas, we can be sure that they are also being
employed in the making and testing of claims. Folk psychology
is not just speculative, but used for predicting, explaining, and
preparing claims. This is the weakness of Daniel Dennett's little
story about the brain transplant; it has interesting confron-
tations but nothing about conflict of claims. Only by seeing
how the theory of the self is used in dealing with conflicting
claims can we have the rational conversation about persons and
selfhood that is so difficult in our western culture.

Start with a hierarchical culture where, as we have seen, the
claims of fellow members of the community cannot be rejected
out of hand. Each person belongs ideally to a sector that makes
effective claims on his/her behalf. In the enclave culture likewise
members are anxious to avoid a schism. The outsiders can carry
the full burden of responsibility for what they do, but insiders
are easily let off the hook. In both cultures, because of the desire
of members to honour the claims of the community, instead of
pressure to pin responsibility on individuals, there is pressure to
alleviate it. Pinning blame on weaklings will achieve nothing; so
long as they are loyal, they cannot be eliminated. When they
err, it is a better strategy to relieve them of too much
responsibility and work for them to be reincorporated. Split
personalities, passive persons, zombies, ghost-haunted, be-
witched and cursed persons may be theories that pass the blame
on to some other person, but they may also serve as kindly,
forgiving theories which show the sinner as a victim.

Side by side with the forsenic model, a therapeutic model of
the self develops. The therapist does not want the patient to
suffer from a sense of guilt or rejection. So he does not rub salt
into the sores by insisting on unambiguous personal accountability. He diagnoses misfortune as an attack on the unwitting
patient by a demon who can be fairly easily exorcised.[22] No-
one in the community is to blame, the misfortune was caused by
a capricious spiritual being. Or the patient learns that his own
self in a prenatal stage of existence chose trouble.[23] In this usage
the theory of the multiple self diffuses responsibility. A verdict
that the patient brought his troubles on himself means that
other people are not to blame, yet at the same time the patient

cannot feel too responsible since the self that made the bad choice was not himself as he is now.

GUILT AND RESPONSIBILITY

The context of therapy and consultation is more practice-oriented than the context of philosophical enquiry. Passive modes of conceiving the person permit the patient to join the therapeutic project as an independent agent. They distance him from moral responsibility but they do not nesessarily absolve him from responsibility in the law courts. Our own psychiatrists use the idea of the passive self, by way of not forcing blame. In his account of the language of psychoanalysis Roy Schafer criticised the overuse of what he called 'passive voice' language instead of 'action language'.[24] The analyst will say: 'Your chronic deep sense of worthlessness comes from the condemn-ing voice of your mother'; or 'You are afraid of your impulse to throw caution to the winds', both passive forms, allowing the patient to think of himself as a victim, without bearing responsibility for what he is.

In personal contexts where we want to evade blame, we also work happily with philosophically nonsensical ideas. We talk about being beside ourselves with rage, or out of our minds, objects slip away from our minds or enter them, as if the mind was a house with rooms. We are evidently quite able to entertain and to make everyday use of the idea of multiple personality. In other contexts, we are determined that each shall bear the costs of his actions. Accused by the traffic warden or the policeman in the patrol car, the sinner will do himself no good at all by citing his therapist's remissions of responsibility. The therapeutic model of the blame-free self works where the contexts of blame are segmented. The different selves are active ideas in different patterns of claims. For the context of healing, the law is peripheral. For the context of justice, healing is peripheral. There need be no problem about using the idea of multiple selves in one context and the single, continuous self in the other context, so long as the contexts can be distinguished. Thus far we have exonerated the foreign civilisations which operate with ideas of the self repugnant in our own. We are not more rational than they, and they are more forgiving than we. But that was a secondary objective for this chapter.

The first objective in taking seriously a range of alien ideas about selves is to complete Daniel Dannett's model by linking ideas about the self, through claims, with the larger intentional system. The latter is the community without which the self is meaningless. The community is the locus of ideology connecting the idea of the person to the culture which its members are making. It is interesting to compare the trade-offs for each cultural type. In economic terms the individualist (enterprise) culture raises the standard of living all round. The hierarchical culture is stronger on solidarity and stability. The enclave culture is good for pricking the conscience of both the other types[25] but not very good at raising the material standard of living. It tends to have a lot of worry about the loyalty of its members,[26] but the latter would seem to have a good opinion of themselves. There has been as yet no research combining assessments of cultural bias with psychological assessments of personality. In default, a guess suggests that the isolate would be most contented with his lot and least ridden with guilt, while the culture that tends to give its members a sense of irredeemable guilt and inadequacy is the enterprise culture.

It has long been recognised in psychoanalysis that modern industrial society is hard upon the person's self image. Perhaps for lack of a discourse in which self-concepts can be studied as aspects of culture, rather facile explanations of psychological stress have been proposed, such as consumerism, bureaucracy, inhumanity, fascism, industrialism. The barely articulated diagnosis is part of the thought style[27] of the enterprise culture. That the self-reliant, autonomous, responsible self should be its ideal is understandable, but cultural theory can give better explanations than psychology for why the ideal is so hard to achieve. First there is the burden of responsibility, often unfair. Failure to carry it meets with none of the kindly exonerations that failure meets in a hierarchy. The culture is so organised that incompetence and weakness cannot be compensated. Rewards go to performance and merit, there is less readiness to carry mediocrity, there is more failure, and punishment for failure is more severe. In the enterprise culture exclusion can be a silent process, almost imperceptible, by simple exit as in the market, not by complaining voice[28] as in enclave, or by formal edict as in the hierarchy. In the enterprise culture the person excluded need not know what has happened until some time after.

No-one else needs to notice either; the enterprise culture just waves a wand and its rejects become invisible.

In conclusion, the public idea of the self is part of a cultural commitment, and so varies according to the culture. Because of its active role in making the culture it is difficult to put the prevailing idea of self into a sceptical bracket. Our culture stalls on enquiry into the nature of the private self so as to protect the freedom of persons from ideologised coercion. But now we have entered the claims of the community into the account of the person the idea of the self turns out to be something which can be critically examined. Both self and community have to be examined together. Refusing to go into details about the ideological construction of the self is not the best way to resist the would-be tyrant's claims. Far safer to practise being articulate about the external and ideological bases of selfhood, because this leads to straight talk about the kind of community and the kind of culture we want to protect.

NOTES

1 M. Horkeimer, and T. W. Adorno, *The Dialectic of Enlightenment*, Transl. John Cumming, New York, Herder and Herder, 1972, edition quoted, Verso, 1979, original German, *Dailektik der Aufklarung*, 1944, New York Social Studies Association.

2 Stephen J. Gould, *The Mismeasure of Man*, New York, Norton, 1981.

3 Isaiah Berlin, 'Two concepts of Liberty', *Four Essays on Liberty*, Oxford, Oxford University Press, 1969.

4 Derek Parfit, *Reasons and Persons*, Oxford, Clarendon, 1984.

5 John Locke, *Essay Concerning Human Understanding*, 2nd edition, section 26, 1694. Cited in John Perry (ed.), *Personal Identity*, Berkeley, University of California Press, 1975.

6 Deniel Dennett, 'Where am I?', *Brainstorms: Philosphical Essays on Mind and Psychology*, Cambridge, Mass., Bradford Books, MIT Press, 1981, pp. 310–23.

7 Terence Penelhum, 'The importance of self-identity', *Journal of Philosophy*, LXVIII, 1971, pp. 670-2, quoted in Harry Frankfurt, 'Identification and externality', *The Identities of Persons*, edited Amelie Rorty, Berkeley, California University Press, 1976, pp. 238–51.

8 Dennett uses this abstract scheme to bridge the various sciences dealing with the mind, artificial intelligence, games theory, neurology, psychology and philosophy. It is meant to apply wherever the theorising is about the predictions that logical beings in a particular system are making about each other's behaviour from deductions about their beliefs and desires. A particular thing is an intentional system only in relation to the strategies of someone who is trying to explain and predict its

behaviour: Daniel Dennett, 1971, 'Institutional systems', *Journal of Philosophy*, 1971, 68: p.87.
9 Dennett, *Brainstorms*, pp. 268–9.
10 Daniel Dennett, *The Intentional Stance*, Cambridge, Mass., Bradford Books, MIT Press, 1988.
11 Daniel Dennett, in Rorty, *The Identities of Persons*, pp. 178–9.
12 Dennett, *Brainstorms*, p.16.
13 This argument is a development of that broached in Mary Douglas, *How Institutions Think*, Syracuse, Syracuse University Press, 1986.
14 Max Gluckman (ed)., *The Allocation of Responsibility*, Manchester, Manchester University Press, 1972.
15 B. Hannan, 'Critical notice, the intentional stance', *Mind* xcix, 1990, pp. 291–2.
16 Michael Thompson, Richard Ellis and Aaron Wildavsky, *Cultural Theory*, Oxford, Westview Publications, 1990.
17 Quetelet, quoted in Ian Hacking *Taming of Chance*, Cambridge, Cambridge University Press, 1990.
18 Adorno and Horkheimer, 1972, *op. cit.*: 87.
19 Louis Dumont, *Essais sur l'Individualisme*, Paris, Seuil, 1983.
20 Douglas, *How Institutions Think*.
21 An example of systematic rejection in an individualist world is given by Gerald Mars in a study of the society of longshore men in the Port of St John's, Newfoundland, Canada. See Gerald Mars, 'Longshore drinking, economic security and union politics in Newfoundand', *Constructive Drinking, Perspectives on Drink from Anthropology*, ed. Mary Douglas, Cambridge, Cambridge University Press, 1987, pp. 91–101.
22 Bruce Kapferer, *A Celebration of Demons*, Bloomington, University of Indiana Press, 1983.
23 Meyer Fortes, *Oedipus and Job in West Africa Religion*, with an essay by Robin Horton, Cambridge, Cambridge University Press, 1983.
24 Roy Schafer *A New Language for Psychoanalysis*, New Haven, Yale University Press, 1976.
25 Mary Douglas and Aaron Wildavsky, *Risk and Culture: An Essay on the Selection of Technical and Environment Dangers*, Berkeley, California University Press, 1982.
26 Douglas, *How Institutions Think*, chapter 3.
27 Ludwik Fleck, *The Genesis and Development of a Scientific Fact*, 1935, Translation 1979, Chicago, University of Chicago Press, 1935
28 A. O. Hirschman, *Exit, Voice and Loyalty: Responses to Decline in Firms, Organisations, and States*, Cambridge, Harvard University Press, 1970.

5

Citizenship in the enterprise culture

MARTIN HOLLIS

No cold relation is a zealous citizen ... To be attached to
the subdivision, to love the little platoon we belong to in
society is the first principle (the germ as it were) of public
affections. It is the first link in the series by which we
proceed towards the love of our country and of mankind.
These are the cadences of an old conservatism, rolled around
the tongue by Edmund Burke before the industrial revolution,
when the English oak was a symbol of the constitution rather
than a veneer for kitchen furniture. I take his words not from
their original context but from an article by the Right Hon.
Douglas Hurd MP, when Home Secretary, writing in the *New
Statesman* (27 April 1988). Hurd invokes Burke at a crucial point
in an argument about citizenship. The government, he declares,
is not about to adopt Hobbes as its patron saint. Underpinning
its social policy are three unHobbesian traditions—the diffusion
of power, civic obligation and voluntary service—which are
central to Conservative philosophy and rooted in British
history. By praying them in aid of a Thatcherite conservatism
he can conclude: 'Those qualities of enterprise and initiative,
which are essential for the generation of material wealth, are
also needed to build a family, a neighbourhood, or a nation
which is able to draw on the respect, loyalty and affection of its
members.'

This is a bold argument which attempts to combine the ideas
of enterprise and of culture and thus surmount a challenge
provided by Mary Douglas. Can an enterprise culture succeed
in blending individualism with public affections? I shall pose the
question with Mary Douglas's help, examine Hurd's optimism
on this testing bed and end with some thoughts about
citizenship.[1]

Anthropologists are often scornful of rational choice models, especially if a notion of economic or instrumental rationality is then claimed to unlock all the varieties of human culture. Is it not merely parochial to spy twentieth-century western market-eers at the core of human nature in all times and places from China to Peru? Mary Douglas's refreshing reply is that it is not self-evidently a mistake. All cultures must work out some way to relate individual aims to the common good and hence the theory of rational choice, although a twentieth-century idea, addresses a universal problem. Since the problem applies to small, face-to-face groups as much as to large, impersonal networks, it troubles traditional societies and does not vanish where there are strong local communities. Yet its solution depends on sacralising institutions, and so resists a theory of rational choice, because solidarity is a stumbling-block for economic-style individualism.

I take this line of thought from *How Institutions Think*[2]—a slim work in her large corpus but, she says, one which distills twenty years of reflection since *Purity and Danger*. The book offers 'a theory of institutions that will amend the current unsociological view of human cognition' and 'a cognitive theory to supplement the weaknesses of institutional analysis' (p. ix). These are two sides of a Durkheimian coin whose currency is to be understood by tracing the functions of a society's knowledge-system in giving meaning to its members' lives. Solidarity resides in institutions and how they 'think'. But she bids us go carefully. Institutions do not themselves think or feel or have purposes, and we should not be fooled by legal fictions to the contrary. The theory of individual rational choice is right to insist that thoughts, feelings and purposes can only belong in individuals. 'Yet, when it comes to the detailed analysis, the theory of individual choice finds nothing but difficulties in the notion of collective behaviour' (p. 9). Perhaps that is not surprising, seeing that 'it is axiomatic for the theory that rational behaviour is based on self-regarding motives', even though 'our intuition is that individuals do contribute to the public good generously, even unhesitatingly, without obvious self-serving'.

I do not in fact think it axiomatic for the theory that rational behaviour is based on self-regarding motives—a matter to which I shall return. But I entirely take the point that the analysis of institutions must set off down an individualist path, even though it turns out not to go all the way. The obstacle is intellectually interesting, yet exploring it is no mere ivory-tower pastime. If the enterprise culture has no way round it and thus frustrates the emergence of the common good, then any society inspired by enterprise alone will assuredly fail. 'Enterprise culture' would then be unmasked as a contradiction in terms, rather as its enthusiasts claim 'socialist freedom' to be.

To make it clear why the stakes are so high, I shall call on another eminent advocate of the enterprise culture to help identify the problem. On 21 May 1988 Mrs Thatcher addressed the General Assembly of the Church of Scotland on the theme of freedom and moral responsibility. Christianity, she argued, bids us work and use our talents to create wealth. Quoting St Paul ('If a man will not work he shall not eat'), she remarked that 'abundance rather than poverty has a legitimacy which derives from the very nature of Creation'. But there was a danger that 'making money and owning things could become selfish activities'; so there was a spiritual dimension which comes in in deciding what ones does with the wealth. She went on to say that although nothing followed directly about what kind of political or social institutions we should have, they must not destroy their own basis by taking away individual responsibility for one's own actions and for the exercise of mercy and generosity. 'Any set of social and economic arrangements which is not founded on the acceptance of individual responsibility will do nothing but harm.' So our institutions must encourage our best, most deep-rooted instincts—the basic ties of the family, the integrity of our faith and culture, a democracy which safeguards the value of the individual, and patriotism. She ended by spinning the threads together in the words of the hymn 'I vow to thee my country' with its mention of a second, unseen country of the spirit—'soul by soul and silently her shining bounds increase'. 'Not group by group or party by party or even church by church,' the Prime Minister commented, 'but soul by soul—and each one counts.'

The problem, then, is that wealth is a temptation to selfishness, especially if the motives to its creation are greed, display, status and other such egoistic impulses. Mrs Thatcher's hope is that Christianity, which is 'about spiritual redemption and not social reform', can both temper the motives and strengthen the will in the direction of mercy and generosity. The job of institutions is to encourage the hope but not to enforce it. In silent commentary, the *Observer* newspaper thoughtfully filled the flanking column of its front page with the results of an opinion survey showing that most people now find Britain a richer and freer but unhappier and more selfish place than ten years ago. Mary Douglas would add, I fancy, that mercy and generosity will soon vanish, unless supportive institutions reach deep into the lives of those not gripped like Mrs Thatcher by a strong Christian will. To put it more academically, Mrs Thatcher has a markedly unsociological view of human cognition, witness her celebrated remark that: 'There is no such thing as society. There are only individual men and women. And there are families.' Indeed she would probably think a sociological view a misplaced denial of human nature and moral responsibility. Can the fact and function of a sacralising culture be taken so lightly?

Meanwhile, Douglas Hurd has always been more worried that to encourage enterprise and initiative may be to undermine citizenship. There was a warning in a recent Mintel survey *Youth Lifestyle* which reported a 'new consumption and success ethic' among the young, 31 per cent of whom described money as a top constituent of happiness and only 17 per cent of whom described love as another—the 'I want it now' generation, as the survery summed up. That was bad news for a Home Secretary with overflowing prisons. It was also worrying for a minister in a government busily reducing the role of the welfare state, and needing to call on a spirit of public service and philanthropy to assume the state's duties of care. Unlike the Prime Minister, he has never fancied that the problem will solve itself as soon as the public-spirited motives, atrophied by excess government, grow to fill the gap.

The *New Statesman* article addresses the issues raised by *How Institutions Think* in a direct and interesting way. Were human nature Hobbesian, its goods positional and its tendency to invade for gain and glory, then the diffusion of power would be a mistake. The dangers of despotism and corruption would not be held in check by relying on Burke's small platoons and there would be no first principle of public affections in individuals. Conversely, if we are to subscribe to Burke's hope that the small platoon is the first link in the series by which we proceed

towards the love of our country and of mankind, then individualism must build a suitable first principle into human nature.
So Hurd declares in a simple but important sentence, 'Men and
women are social beings.' He credits them with 'affection and
allegiance for many collective organisations—from a soccer
club to a choral society, or even a political party'. 'But the
strongest loyalties are to family, neighbourhood and nation,' he
adds, as he leads into the quotation from Burke with which I
began.

This solution to the problem of combining freedom with
responsibility would, I think, do more to satisfy Mary Douglas.
It peoples institutions with men and women who are social
beings with the warm relations which can make them zealous
citizens. It takes a view of cognition—of the terms in which
men and women see their activities—which, if not exactly
sociological, is somehow communal. But there is still a snag,
which becomes plain if one contrasts the two quotations on the
opening page of this chapter. Where Burke speaks of attachment to the subdivision as the starting point, Hurd speaks of
'enterprise and initiative, which are essential for the generation
of material wealth'. Burke's 'little platoon' has been disbanded
until individuals have the enterprise and initiative to reform it.
The organically functioning world of eighteenth-century England has gone and, with it, the assumptions from which Burke
made the links to country and mankind. Indeed, Burke foresaw
the trouble in his *Reflections on the Revolution in France*. It is
captured in his denunciation of the new individualism—'the age
of chivalry is gone. That of sophisters, economists, and calculators, has succeeded; and the glory of Europe is extinguished for
ever.'

I do not mean that Burke is to be believed but I do mean to
deny Hurd a ready appeal to Burke. An eighteenth-century
organic conservative is a chasm away from a market individualist and cannot help with the central social problem of modernity. In Mary Douglas's terms, Hurd has failed to see that
'public affections' are not a natural stock but a public good,
whose existence is problematic. Even if they were well rooted in
Burke's England (which is questionable), they are not so in
ours. Indeed, current incentives to the individual creation of
wealth, aided by the promise of its individual consumption,
threaten to make the public good unattainable. Hurd has

no warrant to include respect, loyalty and affection in his model of human nature, nor to assume that they wil spring up with the creation of material wealth. He is trying to buttress one type of culture by borrowing from another type of culture. It is almost axiomatic for a cultural theory like Mary Douglas's, which identifies society and culture, that such borrowings will wither.

Mary Douglas is, to be sure, a stern umpire. Yet she is not necessarily a political opponent. For all I know, she may be as true a blue as one could meet. But no-one could read *How Institutions Think* without coming to reject any solutions to the problems of order and control which leave the hard work to human nature or to mere rhetoric. She is entirely clear that the collective goods involved in the emergence and maintenance of a social system run on private, profit-seeking principles cannot be ascribed to impulses in human nature or passed off as by-products of individual entrepreneurial activity. Human nature, she insists, is as institutions shape it. Market institutions are not self-sustaining, because they need 'the normative commitment to the market system itself, the needful fiduciary element sustaining prices and credit' (p. 42). Otherwise forms of cheating will destroy the free market as free-riders obey the logic of the n-person Prisoner's Dilemma. Commitment is the key to 'the needful fiduciary element' and it can be understood only by thinking deeply about the nature of institutions.

'Minimally, an institution is only a convention,' she remarks on p. 46, with an approving nod to David Lewis's treatment of institutions (including language) as deposited solutions to problems of co-ordination. An institution, she continues, is a 'legitimized social grouping', for example a family, a game or a ceremony, but not 'any purely instrumental or provisional practical arrangement that is recognised as such' (p. 46). The crucial difference is that an institution, even if mutually convenient, is legitimised only by means of 'a formula that founds its rightness in reason and nature' (p. 45). 'It affords its members a set of analogies with which to explore the world and within which to justify the naturalness and reasonableness of the institutional rules' (p. 112). Thus, although institutions, like purely practical arrangements, do serve to reduce uncertainty, they do so in part with the aid of a stabilising principle relating human conventions by analogy to something in nature. Such a principle is, *au fond*, a convention, but does its job only if not perceived to be one.

The philosopher notices Wittgensteinian parallels. The key notion is that of a rule, with some rules constituting the practices which they govern. Indeed, on one reading of Wittgenstein's utterances like 'the limits of my language are the limits of my world', the world too is somehow internal to the forms of life which mediate our relation to it. Further parallels follow for the chapters in Douglas entitled 'Institutions confer identity' and 'Institutions do the classifying'. When the mind groups things together, it is not registering a similarity but imposing one by applying a rule of sameness and difference. (How else could the camel, the hare and the rock badger be classed together in Leviticus as animals that chew the cud but do not part the hoof?) A taxonomy is not a discovery or even a hypothesis about natural kinds but the emergence of rules of, so to speak, 'grammar' which tell us how to go on.

I invoke Wittgenstein to offer Mary Douglas a philosophical ally, if her idea of institutions is challenged by philosophers (positivists, behaviourists or realists) thinking in terms of a given external world which includes humans among nature's objects. Wittgenstein's *Philosophical Investigations* gives an account of how our practices are constructed as we go along and yet tell us how to go on, which fits well with *How Institutions Think*. It includes humans in nature, while also insisting that 'nature' enters the account through the ideas displayed in our practices. At the same time, however, Douglas will not be content with merely philosphical support. When she calls for a *sociological* account of cognition, she means it; and invoking Wittgenstein is only a first step to seeing what more is involved in a sociological than in a philosophical account. This will become clearer if we pause to take stock of the emerging theme and pose some questions before returning to Wittgenstein.

A market system, then, *is* a culture, or, more precisely, will not survive unless it becomes one. It needs a *normative* commitment to the market, a fiduciary element sustaining prices and credit. It gets one if the goods traded acquire symbolic aspects and their consumption becomes a sustainable form of self-affirmation. A market is not a purely instrumental or practical arrangement but (or but also) an exercise in self-expression. Why do marketeers find the system right and reasonable? Well, although the enterprise culture has driven out the old magic, it has replaced it with a new magic. Analogies with the disciplines and selectivity of natural evolution connect the virtues of the capitalist entrepreneur and of the work ethic to the survival of the fittest. So self-regarding individuals can see themselves in terms which give them a self worth regarding; and, in the process, they give the market system the respect, affection and loyalty which it needs. Thus market individualists are institutional thinkers and, if they do not realise it, that is because 'the high triumph of institutional thinking is to make the institutions completely invisible' (p. 98).

I am not sure how this splendidly bold and imaginative solution to Douglas Hurd's worries will be received at Conservative Central Office. But, as Mary Douglas says, it should certainly please Durkheim with its account of individualism as the current form of the sacred and its theme that only institutions can supply the necessary cement of a society. On the other hand Durkheim sometimes exudes a pervasive determinism, for instance in his comment at the end of the *Rules of Sociological Method* that 'Individual human natures are merely the indeterminate material which the social factor moulds and transforms'. Douglas, by contrast, insists on 'the individual person's involvement in institution-building from the very start of the cognitive enterprise' (p. 67) and this more genuine individualism appeals more, at any rate to me. At the same time, however, it touches off a string of queries about the ability of active individuals to believe in the naturalness of their own handiwork. These reflexive questions may not seem troubling, given the richness of Douglas's account of how cultures organise to deflect them. But they trouble me and will, I hope, at least serve to put pressure on her notion of epistemology.

Can individualism serve as the sacred form of the modern age? Douglas's general line is that no society is viable unless it can sacralise the social bond between its members and that this is done through an 'epistemology'—a *conscience collective* able to make sense of life. This cognitive system relies typically on a presumption that the world embodies a moral order which, being both natural and right, sanctifies social placements and confers meaning on the lives of their holders. Individualism, however, seems to deny the sacredness of social positions. Its low grid-low group character apparently implies that the sacredness of the individual springs directly from the external moral order, without appeal to the naturalness or rightness of social forms.

That would not be awkward, were it not that the cognitive system is, according to Douglas, a construct in which individuals are involved from the beginning. In that case how can it have the holy power of an external moral order? That might be easily answered if Douglas let us distinguish between manipulators and dupes. A manufactured patriotism can bring real tears to the eyes of patriots and false consciousness can put a lump in the throats of the lumpenproletariat. But the supple manipulators at the Ministry of Propaganda cannot share the illusions which they create. As Samuel Johnson remarked sourly in *The Vanity of Human Wishes*,

> Our supple tribes repress their patriot throats
> And ask no questions but the price of votes

But Douglas insists that we are all party to the construction and yet also convinced by its constructed message that there is an external order. Is such collective self-deception possible?

Specifically, can principles of justice carry conviction when viewed in these terms? The social enterprise will fail, unless we accept its claim to embody true principles of justice. Otherwise we shall conform only for instrumental reasons and shall behave as free-riders when we can. Yet Douglas bids us agree with Hume that justice is an artificial virtue, a set of rules constructed for purposes internal to society. Unlike Hume, however, she does not believe that human nature is endowed with fixed and universal sentiments, like natural sympathy, which favour the artifice and perhaps give it some rational justification. So it sounds as if her account of justice and morality is relativist, making it impossible for her readers to believe that their local rules of justice are objectively natural and right.

She would not grant this difficulty. Recognition that ideas of justice have a social origin does not stop us judging between systems, she says on p. 121, since we can judge whether systems embody an objective view of human beings, a view which can be coherently organised for practical purposes. 'The way that humans are, the facts that they walk upright and cannot be in two places at once, are incorporated as part of any system of justice.' In recognising the social nature of cognition and judgement she hopes to avoid the destructive implications threatened.

She is walking a fine line. Admittedly her view does not commit her to a specifically *moral* relativism. But this is only because it is all of a piece with her account of other realms of cognition. Institutions confer identity and do the classifying not merely for what is right and reasonable but also for much, if not all, of the world's furniture, seen and unseen. Classifications are internal to their own systems of thought. She does say very firmly on p. 109 that she has no intention of letting us be caught in 'the circle of self-reference' and that she will provide a 'ladder of escape'. But the effect of her sociological account of cognition is, in general, to internalise objects, or at least social objects, to institutions. So, when one asks epistemic questions about the comparative merits of cognitive systems, the only objective answers appear to be ones which cite comparative success in solving the social problem of order.

Even if this amounts to an objective account of what is natural and right, it is at least a nuanced one and so unfit for public consumption by citizens who need to believe in the reality of their moral world. Douglas recognises this. 'How can we possibly think of ourselves in society except by using the classifications established in our institutions?,' she asks on p. 99 as she plunges into an intoxicating comparison of French and Californian vintnery to illustrate, among other things, how 'institutions veil their influence' (p. 103). But that merely underlines the difficulty. Her individuals are not the passive products of the cognitive system. They are involved in producing and sustaining it from the very beginning. Yet they will succeed in this enterprise, it seems, only if they do not see it for what it is—an exercise in passing off a human artifice as something external, natural and right. How can they, and indeed we, manage this cognitive dissonance?

These queries sum to one compendium question: how can we know what we are doing and not thereby fail to achieve it? Here I return to Wittgenstein, whose *Philosophical Investigations* are a aid to thinking along Douglas's lines. He offers an antidote to the kind of determinism which makes agents passive. Action is not the effect of desires and beliefs which have been caused in their turn by nature and nurture. To act is to follow a rule, which identifies the action and points to its likely motive. For instance, to castle in chess is not to shift small bits of wood under the stimulus of a mental or physical cause. It is to play a move, which can be made with stone or ink, in person or by telex, these being equivalent ways thanks to the rules of the game. The motive for castling, although usually not given by the rules directly, also relates to what constitutes the game and its strategies, winning by giving check mate. The difference between a chess player and a chess-playing machine is that the former understands the rules.

Games of various sorts, especially language games, are models for social interaction and for the symbiosis between people and institutions which Douglas portrays. Institutional games confer meaning on action and are external to each individual player. Yet they are constructed by those who play them and who decide by their practice what is the natural and right way to go on. Here is an account which offers to show how what is external to each can still be internal to all and can make us active, rather than passive, in doing what we have institutional reasons to do.

It is, however, an unmistakably idealist account in the sense of internalising everything significant to the world of the game. That creates a tension between what is often termed a third-person' and a 'first-person' point of view. Natural science works (or tries to work) largely from a third-person, spectator's angle, where the world is independent of our beliefs about it and the aim is to adapt our beliefs to our discoveries. Social science has often attempted this impersonal angle of vision, but persistently bumps up against the first-person view which individuals take of themselves. The contrast is most acute for ethics, where the social scientist is wont to offer cool third-person descriptions of the variety of moral beliefs and how they function socially, whereas the first-person standpoint is usually premised on claims to the objectivity of values and on the irreducible character of moral responsiblity. But it is a general contrast, applying wherever the spectator's third-person account is at odds with what actors, speaking in the first-person, claim is animating them. Idealists tend to favour the first-person; but the spectator often sees more of the game.

Wittgenstein's resolution (arguably, at least) is to prefer the first-person, but in the plural. The individual 'I' is replaced by the collective 'we'. But, whatever its merits in making inter-subjectivity trumps, it transfers much of the tension to the relationship between 'I' and 'we'. Individualism stubbornly insists that *my* choices are mine, not ours. Here, I fancy, Mary Douglas prefers the intersubjective. Like Durkheim, she regards an atomist view as a contemporary form of the sacred and one which relies on an illusion, a fictive abstraction from the interaction of groups. Yet *How Institutions Think* is not intended to be a celebration of her membership of an institution. It uses the plural 'we' but it expresses a point of view intended to be hers. She hopes to persuade us—meaning each of us individually—that we should join her one by one or soul by soul. It simply cannot be as distanced from the first-person singular as it claims that the *truth* about institutions requires. In other words, much as I enjoyed her use of finger-print powder to dust the invisible institutions, neither I nor she can be content to absorb the pair of us into institutional thinking. The tension remains.

Meanwhile the moral significance of the games of social life cannot be wholly internal to the games. Institutions, which provide aims for their members, also make the members feel good about pursuing the aims. If that were all there can be to justification, then the annual reports by Amnesty International become tourists' guides to the quaint variety of moral customs under the sun. Without scope for external leverage, the enterprise culture becomes morally closed, an exercise in institutionally abetted greed without responsibility for casualties. Mary Douglas's comment is, I think, that institutions lay claim to legitimacy by means of analogies with nature which can be challenged. But, as she points out herself, the character of nature is not a brute fact. If it were, brutal institutions could be anchored in the brutalities of nature. As Voltaire remarked sardonically in *Candide*, 'natural law teaches us to kill our neighbour and accordingly we find that practised all over the earth'. Nature and human nature are to be read symbolically in the making of the legitimising analogies, and hence internalised in their turn.

This threat of relativism can be resisted for a while by embedding small games in larger ones. Burke's image of 'the little platoon' is of soldiers bound together not merely by membership of the platoon but also because they and the platoon belong to a larger heirarchy of companies, battalions, regiments and divisions. The little platoon is not self-contained and can be judged by how well and justly it carries on within its wider context. This is not an ultimate measure, since it may be that the army is corrupt in its turn. But Burke's links proceed from the subdivision to 'the love of our country, and of mankind'—a final reference group embracing all of humanity, which may be wide enough to allay relativist anxieties.

On the other hand, mention of 'mankind' sounds like a rhetorical flourish and one more in the universalist style of the Enlightenment than Burke can allow himself. Douglas Hurd's corresponding flourish speaks of the qualities needed 'to build a family, a neighbourhood or a nation' and stops there. International institutions, such as they are, do not much command our 'respect, loyalty and affection', he might have added. Citizens of a nation are one thing, citizens of the world quite another. Relatedly an army is a misleading image for what Burke was talking about, since it suggests a simple heirarchy of platoon, company, battalion and regiment, or a simple nesting of self within family, within neighbourhood, within nation. But Burke's links are organic (witness his mention of the germ of public affections), not chain-of-command. So the problem remains that *whatever* can function healthily is, it seems, thereby reasonable and right.

Furthermore Burke's 'public affections' depend on, to use his terms, 'prejudice' as opposed to 'reason'. Mary Douglas will agree, I fancy. At any rate, although she speaks of institutions as monitors of what is 'reasonable', she nowhere suggests that affections are *rational* and she is clear that no theory of rational choice can account for them. The light of reason destroys the shade of prejudice and so destroys whatever needs that shade to grow. This is (partly) why Burke deplored the age of sophisters, economists and calculators and hence why champions of the enterprise culture cannot invoke him to bless their speeches about economic efficiency.

My compendium question was: how can we know what we are doing and not thereby fail to do it? Its point is not that the circus artist cannot walk the tightrope if he looks down, or that the centipede that stops to work out which leg it moves first can no longer move at all. Self-consciousness is not always a disaster and Wittgensteinian knowledge of 'how to go on' can often include self-monitoring. The point is more specific. How can the conjurer be fooled by his own magic? The enterprise culture needs the respect, loyalty and affection which belong to a less individualist world. It conquers through *die Entzauberung der Welt*, in Weber's diagnosis, but needs to restore enough magic to make its culture sacred. To see this as a functional problem is to disbelieve its solution. So the culture presumably consists after all of conjurers who make magic with detachment, and of 'citizens' whose membership depends on being fooled.

This is a colourful way of putting an entirely serious problem, not only for citizenship in a world without magic, but for philosophy at large. It is perhaps plainest in ethics, where it troubles the standard hopes of a universal moral philosophy to answer the Socratic question of how one should live. Moral philosophers as different as Kantians and Utilitarians have long tried to hit on some universal standpoint for deciding moral dilemmas. The Categorical Imperative and the Felicific Calculus are rival attempts at an impersonal view, detached from every particular place and time—a view from nowhere, one might say. Yet the very idea of a view from nowhere seems instantly suspect, a neat epitomising of what surely must be wrong with the whole Englightenment project of human morals without superhuman magic. At any rate this is the theme of Bernard Williams's *Ethics and the Limits of Philosophy*,[3] which I mention for its provoking thought that 'reflection destroys knowledge'. Ethics, he suggests, cannot be fully reflective because the agent needs to take something of his context and his place in it for granted. Members of an established culture know how to go on in their moral relations but only while they do not reflect fully on their situation. Reflection destroys this knowledge and there is no going back.

Williams connects this line on ethics and the need to keep it partly closed to philosophy with the failure (in his view) of Descartes' attempt to find an absolute standpoint for all human knowledge. Not even pure science can achieve the detachment with which God would see things as they really are. We cannot even in theory be so self-effacing. If he is right, then the modern search after truth, conducted by the light of reason, yields to the post-modern conviction that the search must fail. Every epistemology is vulnerable to cultural shifts in assumptions which, even if it is aware of them, it cannot eliminate. Mary Douglas is using 'epistemology' in this post-modern way to identify a functioning system of beliefs without endorsing any claims to their objective and eternal truth. Although she is in good philosophical company, witness my references to Witgenstein and Williams, there are awkward implications for the idea of citizenship, especially in an enterprise culture.

Citizenship is 'no cold relation', to quote Burke again. It is not a merely instrumental membership, as if of a motorists' association. Citizens are incorporated into a body which claims their loyalty when it exercises its right to make life-and-death decisions. This loyalty stems partly from a cognitive acceptance that the polity is natural and right, and partly from what Burke called public affections. It is, in some sense, a moral bond cemented by moral sentiments. But this is a difficult use of 'moral'. It goes beyond the idea of morality as personal commitment to one's intimates, since many of one's fellow citizens are strangers. It stops short of the idea of morality as universal relations between all human beings, since states do not love their neighbours as themselves when it comes, for instance, to the relief of poverty or waging of war. This middle distance between personal and universal morality is difficult ground both for cognitive acceptance and for public affections.

That makes the scope of citizenship contestible from two directions. From a personal standpoint, why are the successful committed to concern for the unsuccessful and how far does such concern extend? On the one hand Mrs Thatcher's view is that 'any set of social and economic arrangements which is not founded on the acceptance of individual responsibility will do nothing but harm'. On the other, spiritual leaders of the Church of England do not agree with her that Christianity, being about spiritual redemption, is not about social reform. They have been arguing that redemption and reform go together and that public affections need caring institutions as much as private good will. At the same time, however, Christianity teaches that everyone is one's neighbour. That is an attack from the universal standpoint and, were it accepted, it would undermine the patriotism and sense of British tradition which is the cement of Mrs Thatcher's idea of British citizenship.

This debate about the character and standing of nation-sized loyalties continues. For instance, the House of Commons set up a Commission on Citizenship in 1989, whose first report calls

for a new 'fourth dimension' to complement the present notion
of citizenship as 'political, civil and social entitlements and
duties within a framework of law'. A fourth dimension 'would
involve the ideal of public good and civic virtue which finds its
expression in the largely voluntary contribution to society of
citizens acting either as individuals or in association with one
another'. With Mary Douglas's help, we see at once that this
cannot possibly be a new dimension, since the political, civil and
social framework could never have functioned unless already
animated by the largely voluntary contribution of citizens. But
the question about the well-springs of citizenship is real and
urgent, especially in a modern culture whose spirit of enterprise
is not congruent with its ideals of public good and civic virtue. I
hope that some answers will emerge from a volume inspired by
Mary Douglas.

Meanwhile, I shall end with a word about the place of reason
in the attempt to ground the rightness of political institutions in
reason and nature. Douglas was quoted earlier as saying that 'it
is axiomatic that the theory of rational behaviour is based on
self-regarding motives'. If so, 'reason' in the formula 'reason and
nature' cannot be what is referred to by 'rational behaviour'. Yet
once reflection has destroyed knowledge (if we follow Bernard
Williams), what else can 'reason' be?

Douglas holds (rightly) that a cognitive system supplies
reasons for action which are not based on self-regarding
motives. Yet, by her account, such reasons can move us only if
the system succeeds in blocking questions about their objectivity, because the dangerous truth is that they have none. In
that case, when individuals 'contribute to the public good
generously, even unhesitatingly, without obvious self-serving',
they seem to be under an illusion. Conversely those who
behave in accord with the theory of rational behaviour seem to
have what reason there is on their side. I wish to challenge this
presumably pragmatist view.

Confronted with individuals who contribute generously to
the public good, the theory of rational behaviour has two
moves. One is to regard them as irrational. The other is to credit
them with other-regarding preferences, so that they are still
egoists but in a blander sense which can include seeking the
satisfaction of seeing others flourish. The latter move seems
more promising but has the snag that it makes the theory

almost vacuous. An obvious counter is to call for a notion of rational preferences, thus invoking the sort of reasons for action which a cognitive system depends on legitimating.

That would accord with much of what Douglas wants to say except that it will not work in her terms, if those who must believe the magic of objective reasons come to spot the sleight of hand. Yet is it sleight of hand to maintain that there are truths about human life and moral reasons for action to go with them? Douglas thinks so, because of her view that all claims about reality are finally internal to some web of belief. I agree that every reasoned belief involves judgement and that we cannot step out of our collective heads. But, as she says herself when speaking of justice, we can still judge between systems. The only way to produce a consistent view, which recognises interpretation to be pervasive and yet insists on objectivity, is to maintain that there can be true interpretations.

It can then emerge that the enterprise culture does not rest on one of them. It sets about sacralising the social bond by putting the standard theory of rational behaviour into the heads of citizens, who then unsurprisingly cease to believe in the sacredness of social responsibilities. I look to Mary Douglas for the antidote. But it will need to lay claim to truth.

NOTES

1 I would like to thank Mary Douglas warmly for her helpful comments on an earlier draft.
2 London, Routledge & Kegan Paul, 1987. All page references are to this edition, unless otherwise stated.
3 London, Fontana Books, 1985.

6

Entrepreneurship, enterprise and information in economics

SHAUN HARGREAVES HEAP

INTRODUCTION

In this chapter I argue that economics needs Mary Douglas's cultural theory or something like it. When Mary Douglas first tried to interest economists in culture, with her discussion of consumption, she did not exactly receive a rapturous welcome. Indeed, she was largely ignored, albeit in the manner that passes for politeness amongst economists. But matters are rather different today because there is a growing recognition of a problem in economics which her work directly addresses. The problem concerns 'entrepreneurship'—broadly understood as the activity which propels an economy away from one equilibrium and towards another. Mainstream neoclassical economic theory has notoriously little to say about entrepreneurship. It is one of the scandals of orthodox economics and, for the most part, we prefer not to mention it. However, the 'problem' of entrepreneurship has recently begun to surface in economic theory in a new and more worrying form and it seems it can no longer be ignored.

I provide below a brief explanation of how the problem of entrepreneurship has recently surfaced with the issue of equilibrium selection when there are multiple equilibria. The general problem is introduced and located as one of 'entrepreneurship', and then follows a survey of those areas in economics where multiple equilibria have become commonplace. Subsequently I sketch the potential contribution of Mary Douglas's cultural theory. This is largely an exercise in language translation, showing how ideas in cultural theory relate to the ways that economists, particularly game theorists, perceive the problem of equilibrium selection.

I only claim that the linkages between cultural theory and

discussions of equilibrium selection constitute a potentially useful research agenda. However, I would like to offer something more in support of that contention than a translation of terms. Consequently I offer an account of how culture fits into the explanation of the rise of the Japanese corporation. This explanation turns on a discussion of how cultural factors predispose different corporations to solving the problem of 'trust' in economics in different ways. In particular, I shall argue that Japanese mechanisms for creating trust were particularly well suited to the new problems of trust that were created by the rise of what is sometimes referred to as flexible specialisation or post-Fordism. This is a matter of some significance because a theory of entrepreneurship ought to help explain why some economies have been more enterprising than others, and if it does it ought to throw some light on the contemporary call to enterprise. Thus, I conclude with some reflections on the contemporary call to enterprise which are born of the Japanese experience.

THE NEW 'PROBLEM' OF 'ENTREPRENEURSHIP'

Traditionally, entrepreneurship has been associated with the discovery and processing of new ideas or new information by perspicacious individuals. The entrepreneur sees or imagines new possibilities for what were hitherto unrealised and yet beneficial trades between individuals. Thus, the entrepreneur helps to propel the economy from one equilibrium position towards another. In this sense, all economies where there is change must have entrepreneurship in some form or another. Accordingly, I shall use the term to describe whatever actions and processes are responsible for this movement and I shall not confine the discussion in the traditional manner to the actions of particularly talented, creative individuals. Following on from this usage, I will refer to those economies which are more successful at creating and seizing these opportunities for beneficial change as more 'enterprising' than those that are less successful.

Neoclassical economics deals in equilibrium states of one kind or another and so it is perhaps not surprising that it has had difficulty coming to terms with an analysis of what goes on out-of-equilibrium. Indeed, it is easy to appreciate the difficulty posed for neoclassical economics by out-of-equilibrium theorising. The neoclassical equilibrium concept turns on a particular model of rationality (an instrumental version): the economy is in equilibrium because no agent, given this definition of rationality, wishes to alter behaviour. Hence, by definition, out-of-equilibrium behaviour for the economy is not consistent with rational behaviour by all agents in the economy. Consequently, any attempt to theorise and explain out-of-equilibrium behaviour is never going to be a simple addition to, or extension of the neoclassical canon. It will have to include some foundational work on expanding the notion of (rational) behaviour.

This, of course, does not justify neglect. But, there used to be a respectable line of argument which licensed a certain amount of amiable hand-waving at the problem by neoclassicals as they moved on to crank-out another comparative static result. Namely, so long as there is one equilibrium to which the economy is moving, then how we might get there is not nearly so interesting as the properties of the equilibrium itself since we can reasonably assume that we will get there one way or another.

Over the last decade this line of defence has become less and less tenable. There are an increasing number of models of the economy with the property of multiple equilibria and path dependence and when there are multiple equilibria, no amount of hand-waving will turn out-of-equilibrium behaviour into a second order concern. Quite simply, how agents behave in disequilibrium in these settings becomes crucial in the explanation of how one equilibrium is selected.

Let me give a rather famous illustration from economic history to bring out the point. There are doubtless a variety of different ways in which the keys of a typewriter or the keys on a computer keyboard can be arranged. Perhaps some arrangements will favour some sorts of writing over others. But given the costs of learning one arrangement, the small inconvenience of using the arrangement on activities for which it is not optimal, and the costs of producing a variety of configurations, there will probably be strong incentives towards a universal arrangement. Consider, for instance, the cumulative process; firms will increasingly opt for machines with an arrangement which ties in with the keyboard skills of the labour force as this will maximise the potential pool of qualified labour available to the firm, and the labour force will, in turn, acquire skills for arrangements which have the most widespread use as this will maximise their opportunities for work. The two combine powerfully to produce a single arrangement that all employers purchase and all workers learn.

So there are potentially many arrangements which might satisfy our needs, but only one is likely to be used. How does it get selected? The actual history is interesting and highlights the importance of diseqilibrium behaviour (see David, 1985, for the full details). A Wisconsin printer called Sholes perfected the four-row configuration and alphabetic arrangement as a technical solution to a particular problem which he had encountered: the avoidance of typebar clashes on an up-stroke machine. The manufacturing rights were sold to Remington and they made some changes to the alphabetic arrangement. In particular, as a sales gimmick, the top row assembled all the letters necessary for a sales person to type, apparently effortlessly, the brand name of the Remington machine: Type Writer.

Over the next thirty years the Remington arrangement came to dominate the market, such that an equilibrium of near-universal use had been achieved by the turn of the century. Thus, the particular idiosyncracies of the disequilibrium history, the problems with the up-stroke typebar clashes, and sales gimmicks, contributed significantly to the eventual equilibrium. Of course, this would only be of passing interest to economic theorists, if one of the multiple potential equilibria (keyboard arrangements) was much like another. But, as is often the case when there are multiple equilibria, their characteristics vary considerably. For example, the Remington Type Writer is typically beaten by other keyboard arrangements in speed trials and it is the Dvorak and Dealey keyboard which holds most of the world records for speed typing. Thus, in this instance, the disequilibrium history is particularly interesting because it has left us a keyboard arrangement which is in many respects grossly sub-optimal. Or, to put the matter slightly differently, the activity of entrepreneurship matters because not all entrepreneurship is as enterprising as it might be.

THE INCREASING OCCURRENCE OF MULTIPLE EQUILIBRIA

In this section, I present a brief survey of those areas in economic theory which have generated important multiple equilibria results in the last decade (for a more extended discussion of these results and their implications for economics, see Hargreaves Heap, 1989). The reader who has no interest in the details of this and who is happy to accept that there is a growing incidence of multiple equilibria can safely fast forward to the next section. However, it may be helpful for all readers, in making the connection with Mary Douglas's work, to say something general about the cause of these new multiplicities before I list the details.

The general source can be traced to a growing realisation that information in economics cannot be treated as 'just another commodity'. It has long been recognised in economics that individuals typically do not have perfect information and so must acquire information to form expectations about future events and the like before they can decide what is the best course of action to undertake. However, for a long while mainstream economics treated this activity as a purely mechanical one, analogous in most respects to the production of any commodity. Search theory is perhaps the clearest example of this approach. Individuals collect information up to the point where marginal benefit equals marginal cost, just as a firm might employ a factor of production up to the point where marginal revenue (the benefit in this case) equals marginal cost. But, equally, the traditional reliance on the mechanical adaptive expectations rule fits well with this same picture.

This treatment of information makes sense when forming an expectation about some external event like the weather. But it makes much less sense when the expectations relate to events which will be influenced by the behaviour of other agents in the economy. The processing of information here takes on a different character. The weather is there, no matter how we form expectations about it. But expectations about the behaviour of others depends on how they form expectations because their expectations will influence their behaviour. The acquiring and processing of information in these circumstances is not like the accumulation of more and more facts about the weather, rather it is more akin to working out whether there is a fixed-point to the process of thinking about how others form their expectations, given that they are forming expectations about how you form expectations, and so on.

Keynes made much of how expectation formation in these circumstances depends on the prevalence of social conventions that have no special economic foundation but which provide a guide to the fixed-point for everyone. But paradoxically it is the raional expectations revolution in economics which has been responsible for highlighting the Keynesian character of expectations: that is, that they involve solving a problem of interdependent decision-making. This is paradoxical because the rational expectations revolution was originally thought to weigh-in on the side of those who argued against Keynes. However, this association was typically premised on early arguments in favour of unique rational expectations equilibria, whereas the later literature has revealed the prevalance of multiple rational expectations equilibria. The existence of multiple equilibria reinforces Keynes's early analysis of the problem of expectation and opens this door to the same line of argument with respect to the role of social conventions.

At the same time as the rational expectations revolution has been helping to turn information acquisition and processing into something which is a tricky exercise in interdependent decision-making rather than the simple production of 'just another commodity', the formal analysis of interdependent decision-making in game theory has been proceeding apace. In particular, the developments in game theory over the last decade have also been pointing to the increasing likelihood of multiple equilibria. Thus, the pure theory of interdependent action has been signalling multiplicity at a time when the insights of this pure theory are thought to apply to an increasing number of settings as a result of the intervention of the rational expectations revolution into the discussion of information acquisition.

Developments in game theory

Repeated games. Several Folk theorems have been proved for games which are repeated. These theorems demonstrate that there are an infinite number of perfect equilibrium strategies in such 'super' games. The perfect equilibrium concept is the development of the Nash equilibrium concept to these dynamic games. A Nash equilibrium is defined by strategy pairs which are best replies to each other, and a perfect equilibrium consists of strategies which specify actions for each sub-game which are a Nash equilibrium for those sub-games.

These theorems were first proved for infinitely repeated

games, and it is not hard to understand how they arise because one can imagine ever-more complicated forms of conditional/ punishment strategies being developed when there is an infinite horizon. The same insight holds with respect to games where there is always some probability that they will be repeated again. But one might suppose that it would not be consistent with a finitely repeated game because any punishment strategy must be consistent with the rational end-play of the game, and punishments that are costly to enact will not be undertaken at the end of the game when there is no future play which they can effect. If punishment strategies will not be played at the end, then backward induction will tend to rule out punishment strategies in earlier plays. However, there is a Folk theorem for such games, albeit one that has some controversial features (see Fudenberg and Maskin, 1986).

One-shot games. There have been two developments in the analysis of one-shot games which are worth mentioning in this connection. One concerns the claims to uniqueness of mixed strategy equilibria when there are multiple equilibria in pure strategies. The other relates to the role of extraneous information in games when there are unique mixed strategy equilibria.

When a one-shot game has multiple Nash equilibria in pure strategies, it often has a unique mixed strategy equilbrium (a mixed strategy combines the pure strategies probabilistically). In these circumstances, it has sometimes been argued that rational players will not face a dilemma of equilibrium selection because the unique mixed strategy equilibrium will commend itself to both players. But this argument has recently been attacked because there is no account of why individuals should be motivated to play the mixed strategies which form the unique Nash equilibrium. The precise probability combination in a mixed strategy equilibrium leaves each player indifferent between playing either pure strategy, and thus one might plausibly expect the player to randomise between strategies. But this is not an argument which explains why the player chooses to randomise in the particular way (i.e. the precise probability combination of the mixed strategy equilibrium) which produces indifference for the other player (see Varoufakis, 1991).

Many games, like the crossroads game discussed in Chapter 1 above which have unique mixed strategy equilibria, can have commendable multiple pure strategy equilibria when agents condition their beliefs on extraneous information. This is the case, for instance, in the crossroads game when two players use a convention; there are any number of conventions which will serve to co-ordinate behaviours. The convention is based on extraneous information, but it yields Nash equilibria which pareto dominate the mixed strategy equilibrium. So, when such one-shot games are played repeatedly between different players in an evolutionary setting, one might expect a convention to emerge (see Sugden, 1986).

Bargaining games. Bargaining games involve dividing up the gains from trade. Nash offered an axiomatic approach to such games when they are played co-operatively. It lists axioms which are thought to encapsulate desirable properties for a solution to the division of the cake and then sees what solutions satisfy them—so it should not be confused with the Nash equilibrium concept for non-co-operative games which looks for strategy pairs which are best replies to each other. Nash's axioms yield a unique solution for all such games. For instance, in the case of identical players, it recommends an equal division of the cake. This may have some desirable normative properties, but unless the axioms will obviously command the agreement of all rational agents then it is unclear why one should expect the Nash solution to obtain. Indeed, one of the axioms, the independence of irrelevant alternatives, has attracted criticism because it is not obvious why it should command assent among rational players (see Varoufakis, 1991).

For this reason there have been a number of attempts to explain how the unique Nash co-operative solution (or something like it) might emerge from the bargaining game when it is played non-co-operatively (see for instance, Rubinstein, 1982). Unfortunately it seems that uniqueness in these non-co-operative games has only been achieved through the introduction of further and usually controversial assumptions concerning the rationality of belief (see Sugden, 1990, and Varoufakis, 1991).

Instead, when rationality of belief is treated weakly, as implying only that beliefs are confirmed by experience, then any number of conventions based on extraneous information will yield beliefs about the division of the cake which, when acted upon, are confirmed by the play of the game. Thus, for instance, if both players' beliefs are based on a convention that

the taller person gets 60 per cent and the shorter person gets 40
per cent, then the taller person will demand 60 per cent, the
shorter person will demand 40 per cent and there is agreement;
of course, there are any number of equilibria which can be
constructed in this manner.

The rational expectations revolution

Game theory has an obvious applicability to decision settings
where interdependence is transparent. This is often the case in
many micro situations: the analysis of oligopolies, the co-
ordination of work within teams, the relations between buyers
and sellers of highly differentiated products, between a bank
and an important customer, and so on. Accordingly, the
problems of multiplicity and equilibrium selection have increasingly and unsurprisingly surfaced in microeconomics. What is
perhaps rather more surprising is that the same problem has
moved to the forefront of macroeconomics. The reason is the
rational expectations revolution.

The rational expectations hypothesis suggests that individuals' expectations about future events/variables should only
suffer from random white noise errors. If an expectation-
generating device produces systematic errors then, in principle,
the individual can learn about the source of the systematic error.
And since he or she will profit by removing such errors, we can
expect that only white noise errors will remain.

Formally, this has the effect of forcing agents, implicitly or
explicitly, to recognise their interdependence at the macro level
whenever it exists. This happens explicitly when the process of
agent expectation is formally analysed and it is assumed that
they use all the available information of the economy, including
economic theory, to form an expectation. Economic theory
forces agents to recognise their own interdependence. They are
playing an expectations game with other agents in the economy
and so the earlier insights of game theory become directly
applicable.

This also happens when one slides over how agents actually
come to hold a rational expectation and one considers only those
expectations which will satisfy the condition of white noise
errors. The rational expectation is given by the Nash (or perfect)
equilibrium in the expectations game. To appreciate this, notice
that when each agent expects the others to play the Nash

strategy, then each agent will play the Nash strategy as the best reply to the Nash played by others, and thus the Nash strategies provide a set of self-confirming and rational expectations.

In this way, game theory comes to the fore again, and with it the increasing liklihood of multiplicity. The following list gives some important areas in macroeconomics where multiple rational expectations equilibria have been diagnosed, sometimes with explicit reference to game theory and sometimes not.

Unemployment and 'animal spirits'. There are several models where agents can hold a variety of rational expectations about the future, in the sense that each expectation, when widely shared, is confirmed by experience, and where the outcomes for the economy in terms of employment are very different depending on which rational expectation is selected by agents. Overlapping-generations models are a rich source for such multiplicity, and their origin is easy to understand because of the recursive structure of these models which makes them similar to speculative bubbles (see below, and see Azariadis, 1981, for path-breaking work and Geanakoplos, 1987 for a survey). But even without the intergenerational effects which produce this recursive structure, one can understand how such multiplicity can arise from a simple trading game. Suppose each individual decides how much to produce depending on how likely it is that he or she will sell that output. Further suppose that the likelihood of making sales depends on how many other people come to the market and how much they bring. Then, since how many others come to the market and how much they bring depends on their decisions to produce, which in turn depends on their expectations regarding likely sales, we have the possibility of multiple equilibria. For instance, low expectations of sales leads to low production which means there will be low levels of activity in markets, whereas the expectation of high sales means high production which means lots of traders in the market (see Diamond, 1982).

Unemployment and demand management. A corrolary of the multiplicity mentioned above is that any change in a policy variable, like the money supply, will have indeterminate effects. Since the new money supply can be associated with a range of new equilibria, the effect of policy cannot be determined without a specification of how equilibrium selection is achieved. Interestingly, both Hahn (1980) and Geanakoplos and Polemar-

chakis (1986) demonstrate in very different types of models that when individuals condition their beliefs on extraneous information in the form of simple Keynesian or monetarist beliefs about the way the economy works, then these beliefs will select an equilibrium which confirms those beliefs.

Speculative bubbles. There are now several models for the pricing of assets, from equities to foreign currencies, which yield multiple equilibria. One of these equilibria is usually stationary in terms of economic fundamentals, and the rest are explosive paths. The explosive paths can occur because an expectation of future price rises will produce higher current prices, and the expectation of future rises will be rational provided prices in the future rise, and they will rise provided there are expectations of rises beyond that, and so on. At first it had been thought that these paths could be dismissed since explosive behaviour cannot occur for any significant period of time. However, later models have demonstrated that a stochastic explosive equilibrium can be constructed which leads one to expect bursting bubbles for asset prices (see, for instance, Blanchard and Watson, 1982).

This is a brief survey. It is designed to convey that equilibrium selection has become a central issue in economics. This is important not only because it means that entrepreneurship, broadly understood, is high on the agenda of economics now, but also because it helps to explain why economics may be more receptive to Mary Douglas's ideas now than it was when she first wrote for economists in the 1970s. Those views on consumption remain extremely relevant (see Chapter 2 in this volume), but when they first appeared mainstream economics was not especially troubled by consumption. It had a variety of theories and no stark anomalies which needed explanation. Thus, Mary Douglas was contributing to a subject at a time when economists had no special reason to listen. Today, matters are very different. There is a well-recognised problem and, as I hope to sketch in the following sections, Mary Douglas's cultural theory is well placed to contribute to its removal.

THE CONTRIBUTION OF CULTURAL THEORY

In this section I offer a translation of terms between economics and anthropology to show in a general fashion how Mary Douglas's cultural theory can contribute to explaining equilibrium selection.

When there are multiple equilibria of the kind that I have described above, the problem of equilibrium selection amounts to a problem of co-ordination. This is clear in games which are explicitly co-ordination games, but it is also the case for any game where there are multiple equilibria. Suppose the equilibria are distinguished alphabetically, {a, b, c ... }, then [a] will be the equilibrium which is selected provided all agents believe that [a] will be the equilibrium, or likewise [b], [c], and so on. An equilibrium will be 'the' equilibrium provided everyone recognises it as 'the' equilibrium, and this is a matter of pure co-ordination.

The question then becomes how to describe the process of co-ordination? How do agents decide together that [a] or [b] or [c] or ... is to be the one? Since this co-ordination problem is solved in a decentralised manner, it is tempting, and this is the line of argument which has been pursued by economists, to argue that agents condition their beliefs on some set of prevailing circumstances which can be observed by all players in the game. Provided all players share the same rule for forming belief based on circumstances and observe the same circumstances, then they will co-ordinate their beliefs in a decentralised fashion. But by definition, if belief is conditioned on the circumstances of the game by itself, then there is nothing in the circumstances which will distinguish one equilibrium from another. Thus, the circumstances upon which agents condition belief must include features which are not related to the game itself. This idea has been captured in economics by the thought that agents condition their beliefs on 'extraneous information' and it has led to the idea of 'sunspots equilibria' (see Aziariadis, 1981). The sources of distinction in the co-ordinated version of the crossroads games are a good example of extraneous information. Equally, the shared extraneous information could be something like sunspots activity and then the equilibrium which is selected will vary with the level of sunspots activity.

The question for economics then becomes what extraneous information do agents use? And this is where Mary Douglas's cultural theory comes into play. As far as economics is concerned, it affords a theory of 'extraneous information'. She is suggesting that the sources of 'extraneous information' can be systematically related to where the transaction takes place in her grid/group framework. Individuals operating in markets with low grid and low group will not use the sames types of 'extraneous information' as individuals operating in an organisation which is high-grid and high-group. Consequently, Mary Douglas would not expect individuals in different organisational settings to react in the same way when confronted by the same event requiring them to select new actions. I provide an illustration of how culture affects equilibrium selection along these lines and which has direct bearing on the degree of enterprise in an economy in the next section.

TRUST

The question of trust arises in almost all economic relationships and solving the problem of trust is one of the keys to an enterprising economy. Contracts, that specify exactly what each agent should do in each circumstance and which can be publicly enforced, might seem to obviate the need for trust in economic relationships. But it is not easy to write such fully contingent contracts when the future is uncertain. Nor is it easy to enforce contracts when many aspects of an activity cannot be monitored publicly. The parties to contract may know whether there has been poor performance because they are directly involved in the activity but enforcement necessitates that independent third parties (courts) should also be able to judge performance.

These difficulties frequently arise in the relationship between employers and employees and they can cause a sub-optimal set of exchanges. For instance, consider the case captured in figure 6.1. Here, employers trade wages for labour provided by the employees. The pay-off to each party of each wage offer also depends on the effort expended by the workers once they are on the job. The employer earns more profits when workers expend high effort and are paid a high wage than when workers expend low effort at a low wage. Likewise, workers prefer the high wage-high effort bundle to the low wage-low effort bundle. Unfortunately, effort cannot be monitored and so they will not agree to the high wage-high effort bundle. The difficulty is that workers prefer high wages and low effort to high wages and high effort, and the employers, realising this and the impossibility of monitoring effort, prefer the low wage-low effort bundle to the high wage-low effort one which they expect to result from a high wage offer.

Employer pays

		High wage	Low wage
Employee works with	High effort	3,3	1,4
	Low effort	4,1	2,2

Figure 6.1

This particular facet of the exchange between workers and employers puts the onus of trust on workers. If only the employers could trust their workers not to pursue their self-interest in such a strict and ruthless manner, and to follow the spirit of an agreement to work hard for high wages, then the pareto superior outcome could be obtained. But the problem of trust typically also attaches to employers in this exchange. To complicate the exchange only slightly, suppose employees must decide whether to acquire a skill that makes them more productive but which is specific to the firm and has no market value outside the firm. Suppose further that employers prefer workers with this skill who are paid a high wage to workers without the skill who are paid a low wage. Figure 6.1 plausibly describes the payoffs to both parties when workers face a choice now between acquiring the skill (= high effort) and not acquiring the skill (= low effort). The difficulty now is that workers realise that once they have acquired the skill they become prey to the self-interest of employers which is to pay a low wage in those circumstances. Accordingly, they prefer not to acquire the skill and be paid a low wage rather than to acquire the skill and be paid a low wage. Here, if only workers could trust employers not to pursue their self-interest, then they would acquire the skill and the pareto superior outcome would become available.

In short, one can expect Prisoner's Dilemmas to arise in exchanges of this sort, and unless there is trust in the relationship, the co-operative and pareto superior outcome will not be achieved. Thus we can conclude that one of the factors which will influence the degree of enterprise in an economy is how successfully it solves the problem of creating trust in these relationships and thereby obtains the pareto superior outcome.

The economics literature has suggested broadly two ways in which this 'trust' problem might be solved. One involves repetition of the game and the other entails changing the preferences or motivations of agents. Repetition helps to unlock the Prisoner's Dilemma because it makes both parties attend to the long-term consequences of their actions. In this context it can make sense to forgo the short-run gain from 'cheating' on an arrangement because this will ensure better long-run returns from playing the game co-operatively. This occurs in two rather different conceptual ways depending on whether the game is repeated finitely or indefinitely/infinitely. In the latter, punishment strategies become credible and individuals forgo the short-run gains from behaving nonco-operatively because they fear the long-run punishment (see Axelrod, 1981). In the former, it makes sense to behave co-operatively because this fuels a reputation for co-operative behaviour which enhances the long-run prospects for playing the game (see Kreps, Milgrom, Roberts and Wilson, 1982).

This is the type of solution that is commonly found in hierarchic corporations, where employees have extended career ladders which they can expect to climb if they perform their duties satisfactorily at each rung. In effect, the career ladder can be thought of as the institutionalisation of a punishment/reward strategy; and for it to operate in this way, the duties must be well specified at each rung. Otherwise, it is difficult to monitor performances and unless performances can be monitored cheating cannot be well detected and the stick/carrot of repetition will be rather weak.

By contrast, the type of solution that works through altering preferences or motivation is much more straight-forward. In one way or another, individuals have to take the common interest which everyone has in the pareto superior outcome into their own calculations. There are a variety of ways in which this might be formally achieved. Individuals can be given some moral physchology, say like Kant's, which leads them to act differently on these preferences, or they might respond to calculations of extended sympathy, or directly to the benefit of the group. However, it is done, the basic point is that group returns have been made to count in the calculus of individual decisions and this is what overcomes the Prisoner's Dilemma.

Successful societies must solve Prisoner's Dilemmas, otherwise they will be at a competitive disadvantage. So we can expect all societies to generate mechanisms/institutions for solving these sorts of Prisoner's Dilemmas, but, since there are at least two ways in which the dilemma might be overcome, we should not expect all societies to use the same mechanism. Rather, to signal connection with Mary Douglas, along the lines sketched in Chapter 1, we might expect the different cultures of different societies to make one or another solution seem salient to the members of that society. For instance, it will be plain that the solution that turns on altered motivation/preferences will complement and be facilitated by a culture which has the values associated with what Mary Douglas refers to as high-group, where people feel loyalties to the group. Equally, this is clearly not the kind of approach which will sit easily with a background culture of individualism since the connection between individual interest and action must be severed in some degree.

By comparison, the repeat/hierarchic strategy is much better suited to individualistic cultures because although the individual must submit to the authority of the hierarchy, the individual chooses to do this as a result of individual interest. There is no commitment here to the hierarchy as part of some greater commitment to the group with this solution. We can also note that repeat/hierarchy sits most comfortably with individualism when the hierarchy is created around differences in job or activities within the organisation. Pay is thereby connected to job, different jobs require different skills and so the difference in pay becomes a reflection of differences in individual skills.

Given the stylised differences between, say, North American and Japanese culture, one might expect that North American and Japanese companies would tend to favour respectively the use of the repeat strategy and the preference/motivation change strategy in the design of their internal organisation. So much is probably uncontroversial.[1] However, I want to go further than this and suggest that although there are formally a variety of ways of solving the Prisoner's Dilemma problem, they are not all equivalent. In particular, some methods are better adapted than others to the solution of some forms of the Prisoner's Dilemma. Thus, as the economy changes, and with it the type of Prisoner's Dilemma, so some economies will be better able to adjust to the new challenge than others, and thus culture affects the degree of enterprise.

To be more specific, we have seen a slow but discernible shift, over the last ten to twenty years, away from the techniques of mass production to techniques which are sometimes referred to

as flexible specialisation (the switch is also sometimes characterised in terms of moving from Fordism to post-Fordism: see
Milgrom and Roberts (1990) for a recent formal discussion).
This is not the place to develop the reasons behind the switch.
Technological change has been one of the causes because the
micro-electronics revolution has enabled the cost economies
which were hitherto associated with mass production to be
increasingly reaped by techniques of batch production. The
emphasis on quality, which depends crucially on consumer
perception of what is quality, has been another factor behind
the change. The point is to notice that the new emphasis on
'flexibility' and 'quality-as-response-to-consumer-needs' has
created a new form of specific human capital within firms.

This new form of specific human capital has created new
problems of trust for corporations throughout the world. The
nature of this trust problem is such that it has been easier for
corporations which have solved the trust problem in the past by
changing the structure of preferences/motivation with a background high-group culture to adapt to the new problem than it
has been for corporations which have relied on pure repetition
and a background individualist culture. Thus I hope to explain
the contribution of culture to the recent success of Japanese
corporations as contrasted with their North American
counterparts.

This is the argument in a nutshell. It draws heavily on Aoki's
(1988, 1990) discussion of the Japanese corporation and this can
be consulted for further detail. I shall attempt here to put just
sufficient flesh on the argument to give it some plausibility. The
traditional hierarchic organisation, where information flows
vertically and where plans are formulated at the apex and
instructions are codified and sent down to lower levels, is not
well placed to respond to continuous incremental changes.
They are very good at activities which do not change very
much. The apex can then plan a sequence of actions which are
best able to achieve the goal and encode these actions in a series
of routines for each level of the hierarchy. By contrast,
incremental change requires continuous adaptation of plans and
this overloads the planning capacity of a hierarchic organisation. As soon as one set of plans has been worked out, events
change and a new set is required. In these circumstances, it
seems that the planning department can only sensibly produce

indicative plans and the detailed application and implementation of those general goals must be left to the actual departments and shops undertaking the action. They must be free to respond to events as they arise. However, if this is to be a viable strategy, then there has to be some mechanism for ensuring that there is co-ordination between the various different departments and shops. If the planning department is no longer dealing with the detail and thereby ensuring co-ordination, something else must be.

Aoki argues that Japanese corporations have responded to this challenge. They have become more flexible by leaving discretion to departments and shops, and co-ordination is achieved through continuous horizontal flows of information between departments and shops. These flows arise through person-to-person contacts. Such daily contacts permit co-ordination and they are potentially much more efficient as channels of communication than the codified ones of a traditional hierarchic organisation because a complex piece of information can be conveyed relatively easily in a face-to-face encounter between people who know each other well. Furthermore, the participation of ordinary workers in production planning in this manner helps to unlock the implicit knowledge of workers which is often thought to be crucial in realising the objective of high-quality products. This system of co-ordination does rely for its success on some very specific human capital. Workers have to have the communications skills to deal with their co-workers in the organisation and they must have a reasonable understanding of the production process as a whole; otherwise there can be no presumption that any two shops will decide to co-ordinate their activities in ways which are helpful to the organisation as a whole.

The response to flexibility through horizontal co-ordination creates a new sort of specific human capital and a new trust problem which successful corporations must solve. It is not a problem that the archetypal North American hierarchic corporation seems well placed to solve as compared with the Japanese corporation for two reasons. Firstly, there would be enormous difficulty with codifying the performance of a specific human capital skill like face-to-face communication: the essence of this skill is informal and evolving, and this counts against the use of the repetition strategy for solving the Prisoner's Dilemma. By

contrast, the strategy of creating trust through preference/
motivation change is not handicapped by the informality of the
skills. And Japanese companies, with a background high-group
culture, were more able to draw on this strategy and thus adjust
to the challenge of flexible specialisation than their North
American counterparts. Secondly, in so far as the repetition
strategy is still used then the stick/carrot of reward/punishment
cannot operate in the manner in which it does in traditional
hierarchies. There is an advantage in job rotation under these
conditions because it helps to generate the knowledge of the
production process as a whole and it works against the
tendency, that can arise under a system of horizontal co-
ordination, for shops and departments to develop their own
interests against those of the company. But if there is to be a
rotation of jobs and there is to be a hierarchy of rewards to
motivate trust under the repeat strategy, then the hierarchy
cannot operate on differences in the job. The hierarchy of
rewards will have to be independent of the jobs through which
workers rotate. This is, in fact, the case in Japanese companies
where there is a rank hierarchy. Each worker belongs to a broad
category of workers, white-collar, blue-collar, which has a
number of ranks associated with it. The individual worker
obtains a rank through promotion which he or she enjoys in
every job. A similiar solution is available to North American
companies but the point is that the culture of individualism is
not as conducive as the background Japanese culture. Pay can
no longer be related to an individual skill in some job in the
manner which sits easily with individualism. Instead, the worker
is rewarded as a result of demonstrating loyalty to the firm and
this blends more easily when the firm, as the group in this sense,
is taken as a source of value. Furthermore, it is made relatively
easy to do by the Confucian influence in Japanese culture that
affords a ready support for rank hierarchies which cut across
occupations (see Morishima, 1982).

CONCLUSION

Plainly, the contribution of culture should not be overstated
since many of the 'typical' features of Japanese companies can
be found in successful North American ones. However, few will
probably need persuading that culture has something to do
with economic performance. What I hope to have done is

provide a sketch of how culture makes this contribution. This is consistent with my argument that Mary Douglas's cultural theory will be helpful to economics because it can explain equilibrium selection.

I shall conclude with some brief reflections on the contemporary call to enterprise, based on the discussion of 'trust' in the last section. Firstly, let me raise a question with respect to the call in the UK. Does not the attempt to enthuse us with the cultural values of low grid and low group look somewhat strange in view of the move towards flexible specialisation and the experience of Japan? To be more specific, Japanese corporations seem to have combined elements of low grid (for instance, lots of informal and unscripted communication between workers) with features of high group (for instance, lifetime employment and company provision of services). Mary Douglas's analysis suggests this is a hard combination to hold. In Japan, it seems that job rotation and a rank hierarchy play an important role in maintaining the combination. So on this reading of events, while the contemporary call to enterprise may be on the right track with respect to low grid, it is missing the high-group dimension, and one might suspect that the commitment to greater inequality based on market valuations runs against its creation.

Secondly, there is a general point about the conscious choice of new institutions which has a special relevance now for the discussion of the transformation of the economies in the USSR and Eastern Europe. If culture helps to select equilibria, then any new institution there will work more or less well depending on the support it receives from the background culture of society. This ought to be taken into account and it is probably wrong to think of a single institutional blueprint for these economies because they cover very large numbers of people with very different cultural traditions.

Finally, the Japanese experience also suggests that the designers of institutions in Eastern Europe and the USSR need to pay attention to the way that different institutions fit together. Thus, for instance, Aoki argues that the internal organisation of a Japanese firm fits well with the close control of corporations by banks. An equity-based financial system would not blend as well because it gives too much latitude for companies to underperform, and when they do underperform the market processes which come into play typically involve bankruptcy or takeovers and reorganisations or shake-outs. This would not complement the internal organisation of the Japanese firm with its firm loyalty and jobs for life because such a system will only seem attractive so long as there is some guarantee that the company will perform adequately. By contrast, close bank control provides workers in the company with insurance against the risk of the company underperforming.

There are two mechanisms through which 'fitness' in the economy as a whole can be guaranteed: via the process of market selection where the weak get weeded out, and through internal regeneration whenever underperformance is detected. The market selection mechanism cannot guarantee jobs for life within a company and so the system will only fit well with an internal organisation of firms in which workers can avoid the risk of underperformance in some other manner. They typically do this in North America by maintaining skills which are marketable in a number of places. Thus capitalists avoid risk by diversifying their equity holdings and this meshes with a system where workers minimise risks by acquiring general rather than specific human capital skills, thus enabling their inter-firm mobility. By contrast, capitalists avoid risk in Japan through close bank scrutiny of company behaviour and this complements the system of lifetime employment because it insures workers against the risks of acquiring specific human capital.

NOTE

1 In case the ascription of high-group to Japanese culture sounds like Eurocentric prejudice, it is worth noting that it is a feature of Japanese culture which is recognised by indigenous commentators. For instance, Morishima (1982) suggests that: 'the Japanese are strong believers in the importance of the family and of kinship; they are nationalistic and believers in the importance of race; they are warm towards their own circle, but cold towards anyone from outside. It is true that the view of how far one's circle extends has changed over the years, but it has remained the case that there are two quite different yardsticks governing the behaviour of the Japanese, one applied to those within one's own circle, and another applied to those outside it' (p. 197). This seems to fit Mary Douglas's definition of high-group well! Morishima traces these distinctive beliefs to the particular brand of Confucianism found in Japan.

REFERENCES

AOKI, M. (1988) *Information, Incentives and Bargaining in the Japanese Economy*, Cambridge, Cambridge University Press.

AOKI, M. (1990) Towards an economic model of the Japanese Firm, *Journal of Economic Literature*, March, 1–27.

AXELROD, R. (1981) The emergence of co-operation amongst egoists, *American Political Science Review* 75, 306–18.

AZARIADIS, C. (1981) Self-fulfilling prophecies, *Journal of Economic Theory*, 25, 380–96

BLANCHARD, O and WATSON, M. (1982) Bubbles, rational expectations and financial markets in P. Wachtel (ed.), *Crises in the Economic and Financial Structure*, Lexington, Mass.: Lexington Books.

DAVID, P. (1985) Clio and the economics of QWERTY, *American Economic Review*, Papers and Proceedings, 75, 2, 332–7.

DIAMOND, P. (1982) Aggregate demand management in search equilibrium, *Journal of Political Economy*, XC, 881–94.

GEANAKOPOLOS, J. (1987) Overlapping generations model of general equilibrium, in J. Eatwell, M. Millgate and P. Newman (eds.), *The New Palgrave*, III, 767–79, London: Macmillan.

GEANAKOPOLOS, J. and POLEMARCHAKIS, H. (1986) Walrasian indeterminacy and keynesian macroeconomics, *Review of Economic Studies*, LIII, 755–79.

HAHN, F. (1980) *Money and Inflation*, Oxford: Basil Blackwell.

HARGREAVES HEAP, S. (1989) *Rationality in Economics*, Oxford: Basil Blackwell.

MILGROM, P. and ROBERTS, J. (1990) The economics of modern manufacturing: technology strategy and organisation, *American Economic Review*, June, 511–28.

MORISHIMA, M. (1982) *Why Has Japan 'Succeeded'?*, Cambridge: Cambridge University Press.

RUBINSTEIN, A. (1982) Perfect equilibrium in a bargaining model, *Econometrica*, 50, 97–109.

SUGDEN, R. (1986) *The Economics of Rights Co-operation and Welfare*, Oxford: Basil Blackwell.

SUGDEN, R. (1990) Convention, creativity, and conflict, in Y. Varoufakis and D. Young (eds.), *Conflict in Economics*, Hemel Hempstead: Harvester Wheatsheaf.

VAROUFAKIS, Y. (1991) *Rational Conflict*, Oxford: Basil Blackwell.

7

Convention and legitimacy: how artificial is justice?

ONORA O'NEILL

'Tho' the rules of justice be *artificial*, they are not *arbitrary*': thus David Hume in *A Treatise of Human Nature* (1739). Mary Douglas, who calls Hume 'the anthropologist's philosopher' (Douglas, 1987, p. 113) agrees. She argues that the social conventions that constitute a society's system of justice are far from arbitrary. A system of justice must meet a complex set of constraints. Although there is no unique system of justice, justice is a matter, not of arbitrary, but of legitimate convention. Legitimate conventions must be coherent, non-arbitrary and sufficiently complex as well as practicable. Mary Douglas claims in *How Institutions Think* that concerns about relativism can be dispersed by such considerations. However, what worries most critics of relativism is not the thought that relativists may regard just any arbitrary rule as a principle of justice, but that they say too little about the constraints of justice. The question to be asked is not whether justice is or is not artificial but more precisely, *how* artificial it is or *how* it is artificial. Nobody is likely to dispute that some aspects of justice are artificial. However, without more detailed investigations it will be uncertain whether the artificiality of justice sustains the communitarian positions towards which Mary Douglas gestures (Douglas, 1987, pp. 116–18, 125–7) or the (evidently artificial!) liberal constructivist approaches to justice which she dismisses (Douglas, 1987, pp. 126–8). A more detailed enquiry might begin by distinguishing various understandings of the claim that justice is artificial.

IS JUSTICE FRAGILE OR ROBUST?

One, perhaps superficial, understanding of the thought that justice is artificial might be that justice is a fragile and delicate artefact which can be produced and sustained only in rather special circumstances. Just as artificial intelligence and artificial sun tans need high technologies and their elaborate institutional setting, so we might think that justice needs rather special circumstances. If justice were artificial in this sense, institutions of justice would be too fragile for hard times, when they would either collapse or have to be suspended.

If this is what it means for justice to be artificial, it is important to identify the 'circumstances of justice' within which institutions of justice remain possible and whose absence makes justice unsustainable. Hume suggested that these circumstances hold quite generally, since they consist simply of the commonplace facts of moderate scarcity and limited altruism: "tis only from the selfishness and confin'd generosity of men, along with the scanty provision nature has made for his wants, that justice derives its origin' (Hume, 1739. p. 495). In dark times, such as famine or war, the thought is that justice would break down, while in golden ages when benevolence was unlimited or scarcity abolished justice would be useless (Hume, 1739, pp. 494–5).

John Rawls, the leading contemporary advocate of a liberal constructivist account of justice, follows Hume, but identifies a longer list and divides it usefully into subjective and objective circumstances of justice (Rawls 1971, pp. 126–30). The objective circumstances of justice are, roughly, features of the normal human condition. They include the cohabitation of many individuals who are mutually vulnerable under conditions of moderate scarcity. The subjective circumstances are, roughly, given by an account of human nature. They include not only limited altruism, but cognitive limitations and the fundamental diversity both of individuals' life plans and of philosophical and religious beliefs.

In his more recent work, Rawls makes it clear that he thinks this pluralism of fundamental values *within a given society* is characteristic specifically of modernity (Rawls, 1985). He now presents his theory of justice as one that articulates the underlying beliefs of a certain sort of liberal, western society in which (allegedly) there is no generally recognised account of the good for man, but which converges on ideals of equality and democracy. In short, he accepts that his principles of justice are those of a restricted range of cultures. In making this (quasi-) communitarian turn, Rawls in effect accepts certain points that Mary Douglas makes not only about his work but about other

liberal individualist accounts of justice such as those of Alan
Gewirth and Brian Barry (Douglas, 1987, pp. 116–17, 125–7).
Rawls stresses that he has always argued only for one of many
possible conceptions of justice. Since he now explicitly starts his
argument from the outlook of citizens of a liberal polity who
accept the ideal of democracy, his conception of justice remains
liberal in content, but renounces traditional liberal claims to
universal scope. What we get is liberal justice in one country,
and in some other similar countries.

Since Hume and Rawls both include moderate scarcity among
the circumstances of justice, it is not clear what either would say
about rules of interaction in conditions of extreme scarcity or
abundance. These conditions are simply excluded from the
scope of their arguments. Mary Douglas draws on the anthropological record to make a stronger claim about the scope of
justice, which she believes will in fact survive beyond the classic
circumstances of justice. Justice, she argues, is not fragile. It is
not artificial in the sense that it falls into abeyance outside
limited circumstances. Even in circumstances of dire scarcity,
principles of justice are followed. Emergencies may displace
some of the niceties of justice, just as they may erode the niceties
of courtesy, but much remains intact. She points out that even
during famines, principles of social hierarchy and precedence
govern food allocation decisions. She concludes that these
principles are not artificial in the sense that they survive only in
very limited circumstances (Douglas, 1987, pp. 122–3). In
emergencies we are likely to discover just how robust can be the
duly sacralised principles of justice of a society. Those who
count as legitimate victims accept their suffering, even their
death; those who eat or take what could have kept the victims
alive can live with what they do, and do not judge it unjust. We
should not be misled if systems of justice seem fragile in
emergencies which undercut or destroy all social context;
neither the behaviour of those whose social world has been
destroyed, nor thought experiments about behaviour in hypo-
thetical 'lifeboat' situations, shows that the standards and institutions of justice embedded in actual social systems are fragile.

IS JUSTICE CONVENTIONAL OR NATURAL?

A second and more central way in which we might think justice
artificial is that it varies with and is the product of particular

societies. There is no such thing as justice in the abstract; there are only specific conceptions of justice. Contemporary constructivist attempts to identify universal principles of justice are just mistaken. We must always ask *whose* justice is at issue. Mary Douglas takes it that justice is artificial or conventional in this sense: it is not fragile, but it does vary between societies. Principles of justice are just whatever rules a society constructs to regulate interactions. Some conceptions of justice may be recognisably liberal, based on some version of equal respect for individuals. Others are hierarchical. Each society sacralises a determinate conception of justice; none can be vindicated beyond the domain in which it is established. Justice may not be fragile, but it is nevertheless artificial in the sense that it is socially produced and variable. Moral realism, whether naturalistic (justice is inscribed in human nature) or transcendent (justice is known by some 'non-natural' faculty of intuition), is to be rejected because it denies that justice is artificial. The idea of justice is 'Fabricated precisely for the purpose of justifying and stabilising institutions ... it is founded on conventions ... no single element of justice has innate rightness: for being right it depends upon its generality, its schematic coherence, and its fit with other accepted principles' (Douglas, 1987, p. 114).

Like Hume, Douglas thinks justice can be artificial without being arbitrary. However, her reasons are quite different from Hume's reasons. Hume believes that the principles of justice cannot be arbitrary because he has a rather determinate view of human nature, which includes a view of human needs and interests. The artifice of justice is constructed upon the realities of human nature, which are the same in all ages and nations. These provide the vindication for principles of justice for any human society:

> We have now run over the three fundamental laws ... *stability of possession ... its transference by consent and ... the performance of promises.* 'Tis on the strict observance of those three laws, that the peace and security of human society entirely depend ... Society is absolutely necessary for the well-being of men; and these are as necessary to the support of society ... those laws, however necessary, are entirely artificial and of human invention; and consequently ... justice is an artificial, and not a natural virtue (Hume, 1739, p. 526).

For Hume justice is artificial because it is not among our natural passions; but his account of justice is safe from arbitrariness because it is based on a naturalism which enables him to identify a single set of principles of justice as suitable to the human condition. Like other human artefacts, justice, the artificial virtue, depends on and has to fit with human nature.

The conception of justice which Hume derives from his account of human nature is rather specific. It differs in part from the conception which Rawls derives from the ideals of a liberal democratic polity: more emphasis on property, less on equality. Hume not merely thinks that the artefact of justice is not arbitrary; he thinks that its shape is fairly well fixed by our nature and circumstances. It is evident why artificiality does not entail arbitrariness. However, the fixity of human nature does not fix the form of all human constructions. Archaeologists do not find it hard to identify artefacts of daily use such as arrowheads or needles, but they often have trouble with cross-cultural identification of more rarified items, which they are driven to classify as cult objects. Is Hume to be believed that justice is more like an arrowhead than a cult object?

THE CONSTRAINTS OF JUSTICE

Mary Douglas's claim that justice is neither arbitrary nor a reflection of human nature leaves various possibilities open. In particular, she might represent justice either as reflecting specific cultures, or as demanding allegiance to universal principles. In fact her position is something between the two. Although she insists that a system of justice must be culturally embedded and intelligible (Douglas, 1979 and 1987), she also demands that it meet certain formal constraints (Douglas, 1987, pp. 121–2).

A system of justice must be internally coherent. It must not involve a large 'amount of arbitrary rules' but rather provide abstract principles that could be used to regulate behaviour. It must be comprehensible and hence not too complex. It must lend itself to practical and efficient administration. She concludes that 'it is as straightforward to study human systems of justice objectively as it is to measure the length of human feet from heel to toe' (Douglas, 1987, p. 121). These critera are not uncontentious. For example, is a system that embodies large elements of arbitrariness, such as the wisdom of Solomon or the Nazi *Führerprinzip*, by definition not a system of justice? How is practicality to be understood? Does not the criterion of efficiency presuppose the ideals of a society which sees human action as decomposable into 'options' for whose evaluation some metric is available?

However, these seem to me minor issues. The more interesting point at stake here is how well the view that justice is artificial, in the sense of being the construction of actual societies, can survive detachment from Hume's (or another) account of human nature without ending up in relativism. Douglas shows convincingly that the quasi-formal constraints she lists can work, particularly when they are conjoined with an uncontentious account of the human condition, i.e. of the objective circumstances of justice. For there are imaginable sets of social institutions that fail these tests, so could not count as systems of justice.

Douglas gives two examples. The first is that a system which denied that two-thirds of the population were human would not be a system of justice. This example seems to be ambiguous. If the denial is a matter of mistaken biological belief or other defective cognition, the deficiency does not lie in the system of justice. This is the way in which Douglas appears to take the issue, for she suggests that this example really shows a defective capacity to distinguish reality from illusions. I am less sure, however, how she would view the example if it were taken as denying that two-thirds of the population have moral standing. Would she conclude that we were dealing with a defective conception of justice, with a system of rules that is not a system of justice at all, or with a different conception of justice? Plenty of stable and legitimated sets of social rules have gone a long way towards denying the moral standing of large sections—even of two-thirds—of the population. Would Douglas hold that a system of rules which assigned slave status to one section of the population and denied them rights of redress was a system of justice? Did the *ante bellum* South have a system of justice? Are systems of rules that institutionalise the subjection of women systems of justice?

Douglas's second example of a system of rules which would not count as a system of justice is one in which people are punished for what they are alleged to have done in others' dreams. Again, it is unclear how to take this. Is a society which takes dreams as good cognitive evidence bound to be too arbitrary to meet her formal criteria for social rules to count as elements of a system of justice? The very argument Douglas uses to remind us that identities are socially constituted might suggest that dreams of others' offences need not be wholly random and unreliable. If so, could they have a role in a system of social rules that she would classify as a system of justice? (Or are 'reliable' dreams only projections from more ordinary procedures for adjudication, so epiphenomenal rather than due process?)

In spite of difficulties with these two examples, it seems plausible that Mary Douglas is correct in claiming that the formal criteria she lists will constrain systems of social rules. If the constraints are justifiable, she has established that justice must be artificial (in the sense that it reflects no moral reality), yet not arbitrary; some systems of social rules could not constitute systems of justice. Only an intelligible, non-arbitrary set of rules that meets certain formal constraints would count as a system of justice.

RELATIVISM AND JUSTICE

Can this argument defuse the worries people actually have about relativism? Often these worries are fuelled, not by the thought that a system of rules that is unworkable or incoherent or wholly arbitrary might constitute a system of justice, but by the thought that an entirely intelligible, workable, highly efficient, deeply legitimated system of rules should not automatically count as just. We should be able to ask whether such systems of rules are just or unjust. Even if 'systems of justice' is tied extensionally to systems of coherent, workable, legitimated rules of interaction, we should still (according to anti-relativists) be able to conclude without paradox that a 'system of justice' can be unjust. Anti-relativists are likely to think that the judgement that Nazi institutions were unjust is not on a par with a Nazi judgement that liberal institutions are unjust. Nazi institutions would apparently count as a system of justice by Mary Douglas's criteria. Despite some odious rhetoric, the Nazis did not deny that the Jews were human beings; the whole abominable system assumed that the categories of administrative, economic and medical activity, which apply only to human affairs, would apply to those who were exterminated. What the system denied was their moral standing. Having denied this, it applied rules that were coherent, workable, efficient and not too complex.

Anti-relativists who share this worry will not generally want to reject the formal constraints that Mary Douglas lists. They are likely to think that her list is not strong enough to demarcate just from unjust systems, and that she does not escape relativism. However, it does not follow that all anti-relativists will seek to offer an account of the construction of justice that identifies a unique set of just institutions for all times and all places. It is surely quite imaginable that there may be a range of conceptions of justice which excludes some (or many) imaginable stable and efficient systems of rules. In short, even if judgements of justice may differ at different historical stages, there may be more to justice than Douglas's form of non-arbitrariness.

However, if Douglas's approach cannot avoid the worries that anti-relativists actually have, and the Humean route needs the unvindicable assumption that we can frame everything in a neutral account of human nature, what route can anti-relativists who accept that justice is artificial travel?

THE SCOPE OF JUSTICE.

So far we have reached a sort of dilemma. On the one hand we might take a view of circumstances of justice which includes subjective and objective components. In that case the subjective components will include a view of human nature or perhaps an ideal of the person which can be used to construct a rather determinate conception of justice, which will hold only for societies whose members match that conception of the person or of human nature. Alternatively, we might take a view of the circumstances of justice which includes only objective elements. In that case it seems that we must reach some version of Mary Douglas's conclusions: there are many well-formed conceptions of justice, which provide stable rules for regulating interaction and for shaping the identities and desires of persons. Justice is indeed not arbitrary, but its principles are socially relative.

Could any construction of justice offer more if it assumed only the objective circumstances of justice? It is at least possible to sketch an account of justice which is more Kantian than Humean, in that it does not rely on so definite a view of human nature and does not rest on claims about the means to or components of human happiness or well-being. (I do not know whether Kant could count as an anthropologist's philosopher. Standard readings make him sound umpromising because his approach is formal and his examples are culturally myopic. On the other hand, Kant lectured on anthropology for over twenty years and was well aware of cultural and specifically religious diversity. I claim only that this sketch is Kantian, not that it is Kant's, and that the label should not make anthropologists fear the worst!) (O'Neill, 1989).

The first matter to consider is the scope of principles of justice. Suppose that the objective circumstances of justice are simply that a plurality of agents—or of potential agents—shares a world. This starting point might be justified as follows. Without a shared world there is no potential for interaction, hence justice would be redundant. Without a plurality whose action is at least partly unco-ordinated there is no potential for conflict, and again justice would be redundant. Neither the problem of order nor the need for a system of justice will arise unless a plurality is a geniune plurality of agents; if we assume that co-ordination is guaranteed by means of a pre-established harmony provided by God, the central planners or a strong theory of human nature, we have simply assumed that the circumstances of justice do not arise. The point of the traditional insistence that justice is a *political* virtue is to stress that it has no place among those who are too isolated to interact, or among those who are too integrated to act (to some degree) separately. (Neither the men and women of Rousseau's earliest state of nature, nor the planned denizens of *Brave New World*, live in circumstances of justice.) On the other hand we need and should assume no implausible ideals of autonomy or rationality.

An account of justice that is appropriate for such an interacting plurality must at least include some principles that can hold for all its members. Putative principles of justice that were not universal in this sense simply exclude some from the domain of justice. (Those excluded might be viewed as insulated from others' claims ('above the law') or from the possibility of making claims against others ('outlaws') or from both ('isolates').) In each case exclusion portends not merely exclusion from justice but from reciprocal social constraint—in short, from society. Principles of justice must then at least be universal in the sense that their writ runs throughout a domain of interacting agents.

The claim that principles of justice must hold universally among all members of an interacting plurality is often disputed on the grounds that it appears to exclude certain presumed accounts of justice that allow for or demand hierarchy and differentiation. However, this is a mistaken conclusion. To claim that principles hold universally is to make a point about their scope. It would be a further matter to claim that they demand uniform treatment and action. Uniformity is a matter of the application, not the scope, of principles. Universal principles may be compatible with differentiated treatment. For example, the principle of 'to each according to his need', or of graduated income tax, or of equal opportunity in a differentiated labour market are universal in scope but demand differentiated treatment. No questions are begged against traditional or hierarchical visions of justice by the demand that *principles* of justice apply to all. On the contrary, principles that did not apply to all could hardly assign to each a place in some hierarchy.

UNIVERSALITY WITHOUT UNIFORMITY

If the basic principles of justice are to hold universally among some interacting plurality, they must take account of the implications of interaction. Any principle regulating interaction becomes a background constraint on the way others can act. No universal principle can constrain in ways that undercut action on that principle. Once more, there is no covert shift from universality to uniformity; we may assume that universal principles have highly differentiated application, but not that differentiation (self-defeatingly) goes so far that some are made into victims rather than agents, so disabled from acting on (any interpretation of) that principle. For example, universal principles of coercion or violence or deception could not be among the basic principles of justice for any interacting plurality, since each is a principle whose universal enactment creates victims who cannot (not merely do not, or do not want to) live by the principle. Universal coercion or deception or violence cannot be basic to any system of justice that is to hold for all members of a plurality. Correspondingly the rejection of coercion, violence and deception are basic principles of justice.

All this is stated abstractly and briefly. In actual human societies neither coercion nor deception nor violence can be wholly eliminated. It is only the deep principles of a system of social organisation that can renounce them. The actual institutions of a society may have to incorporate elements of coercion, deception, violence and differentiated social roles and relationships. But that does not show that the basic principles of social organisation are not universal. Coercion may be used to enforce law, but law itself may be designed to prevent coercion from being an underlying principle of social organisation. Deception may be unavoidable in processes of legitimation, but social bonds may themselves be designed to prevent rather than secure deeper forms of deception. It is not true that 'moral philosophy is an impossible enterprise if it does not start with the constraints of institutional thinking' (Douglas, 1987, p. 124), but only that it is an incomplete enterprise if it does not take account of these constraints.

Principles of justice do not and cannot include algorithms for their own implementation. That is always a matter for social and political debate. The fundamental debates of politics can be seen as debates about how the limitation of coercion and deception could be institutionalised in workable institutions and rules within a particular society. Modes of institutionalisation will no doubt vary for differing economic conditions and for different sorts of agents; it is one thing to institutionalise non-coercion among the robust and prosperous, and another thing to do so among those who are marked by a long history of subjection and intimidation. The assumptions that we need to draw on in political debates are not, however claims about the traditional subjective circumstances of justice. We do not need to make claims about human nature in all ages and nations. We need to rely on claims about the actual social world and its inhabitants at an actual time in their history. It is in this task, rather than in identifying principles of justice, that Douglas's work on institutions is of great importance. Many arguments about limits to and democratic control of state power, education and freedom of expression and communication can be seen as asking how principles of non-coercion and non-deception might be institutionalised for societies and people as we actually find them. Such debates need not deny—they may insist—that institutions matter in part because they can transform identities and preferences.

Nothing in the argument I have sketched suggests that there is a unique set of institutions of justice. The principles of justice we can construct on Kantian lines underdetermine the institutions of justice. These principles cannot show that the institutions of justice are the same for all times and places or that they are archetypically liberal institutions of justice. They cannot even show that every hierarchical society is unjust; the claim is only that those systems, hierarchical or otherwise, which depend in principle on victimising some are unjust, because their fundamental principles cannot be followed by all members of a plurality who find themselves in objective circumstances of justice. Hierarchies that define positions of relative weakness without compensating security are *likely* to constitute social arrangements that institutionalise fundamental coercion, violence or deception. They are likely to be unjust. But only those hierarchies that secure not just positions of differing weakness and strength, but positions of ineradicable vulnerability or of unchallengeable domination, are unjust. Those that differentiate social roles without securing oppression or victimisation may not be unjust. Equally, societies that do not differentiate roles much, but weaken individuals by isolation and lack of social coherence, may institutionalise a high risk of coercion and so may be unjust.

Principles of justice constructed in this way could provide no more than guidelines for institutions that embody justice. Institutions that embodied these principles would not only be intelligble and non-arbitrary in the senses that Mary Douglas lists, but could be defended against the criticism of relativism. We need not accept that every system of well-formed, action-guiding rules that can be efficiently instituted and socially legitimated is a just system. If we can identify certain principles that cannot coherently be rejected by any plurality who find themselves in circumstances of objective justice, we can offer reasons for thinking that some coherent and stable systems of rules are monstrously unjust. Anti-realists, who see justice as an artificial construction, can also be anti-relativists, yet they need not deny that diversity of culture and circumstances both sanctions and requires diversity of institutions of justice. If these considerations are plausible, the artificial virtue of justice is not only robust and non-arbitrary, but provides a reasoned basis for assessing the justice of distant societies and institutions and for rejecting the paralysis of relativism, while respecting the diversity of institutional embodiments of justice.

ACKNOWLEDGEMENT

I wish to acknowledge the support of Wissenschaftskellog zu Berlin while writing this chapter.

REFERENCES

DOUGLAS, M. with ISHERWOOD, Baron (1979) *The World of Goods*, New York: Basic Books.

DOUGLAS, M. (1987) *How Institutions Think*, London: Routledge & Kegan Paul.

HUME, D. (1739) *A Treatise of Human Nature*, L. A. Selby-Bigge (ed.), Rev. ed. 1958, Oxford: Clarendon Press.

O'NEILL, O. (1989) *Constructions of Reason: Explorations of Kant's Practical Philosophy*, Cambridge: Cambridge University Press.

RAWLS, J. (1971) *A Theory of Justice*, Cambridge, Mass.: Belknap, Harvard University Press.

RAWLS, J. (1985) Justice as fairness: Political not metaphysical, *Philosophy and Public Affairs*, 14, 223–51.

8

Environmental risk management in an enterprise culture

TIMOTHY O'RIORDAN

PUTTING RISK IN ITS PLACE

Environmental risk is not a new phenomenon, but it has acquired a new meaning. People have died and suffered from environmental hazards since time immemorial (Royal Society, 1987) The shortness of life expectancy in Neolithic cultures attests to that, as does evidence of sinusitis in skulls of cave-dwellers condemned to breathe in fire smoke during long winter nights (Brimblecombe, 1987, pp. 3–4). In mid-Victorian Britain, the chance of death for a child in the poorer parts of London was one in five, an intolerable statistic today, while the probability of a coal miner catching the delibitating lung disease pneumoconiosis was 1 in 500, again an unacceptable risk today (Royal Society Study Group, 1983).

In the past, therefore, the risk of dying before old age was always far greater, between ten and one hundred times greater, than it is today. Yet as medical science advances and disease-related death recedes for most of the world's affluent peoples, so concern over health-related risk is growing, even when the probabilities of suffering illness or injury may be below one in a million, or a factor of two hundred less likely than dying of a common ailment such as bronchitis (Health and Safety Executive, 1987, p. 23)

Why is this the case? Four reasons interconnect:

Participatory risk assessment

A demand exists to be better informed and to have more effective personal influence over events that could endanger health and from which there is no ready means of escape. This is a feature of a more politically active society generally, as well as a sign of a loss of faith in official regulatory bodies. Formerly such bodies were awarded with the willing trust of the vast majority. No longer is this the case. The intricacies of new risks, the greater awareness of the tendency for the regulatory official to be 'captured' by the client, and the lack of funding available to recruit and retain staff have all influenced the way in which the informed public judge the effectiveness and independence of regulators (see Council for Science and Society, 1977; Hawkins, 1982).

A distrust of paternalistic expertise

In areas where probabilities are unquantifiable and potentially catastrophic events can only be imagined, expertise no longer carries the special status of scientific rarity that it once enjoyed. People want to be their own risk assessors: they do not trust automatically the supposedly superior judgements of others (Kasperson and Pijawaka, 1985). This means that technical risk assessors have to make even more pessimistic assumptions over safety margins than they regard as necessary, and that they have to incorporate additional safety features to cover people's 'fears' in order simply to retain some credibitility in their expertise (O'Riordan *et al.*, 1987). Indeed it is nowadays the case that the 'second order' or 'post-normal' science of the beliefs and demands of the affected public, demands that are stimulated by lack of trust, inadequate communication, and a sense of injustice and powerlessness, are becoming ever more important in determining the tolerability of risk (see Funcovitz and Ravetz, 1990).

'Blame' on disliked or misunderstood management and regulation

When a risk creator, normally a chemical corporation or nuclear establishment, considers any new investment, or when a company in such areas experiences a serious accident at one of their plants which injures and kills many innocent local people, then the frustration of powerlessness becomes translated into social criticism of corporate power. Risk aversion becomes a metaphor for anti-corporate prejudice and hostility to the dominance of capital. This point is forcefully made by Mary Douglas in her book *Risk Acceptability According to the Social Sciences* (Douglas, 1987).

Failure of communication

A sense of alienation is created when there has been a failure of communication about the nature and likelihood of environmental peril. Unless that communication is meaningful, not just in words, but via arrangements that effectively draw the public into the hazard management process, a sense of distrust emerges even when safety measures may be more than adequate. Risk communication is not a matter of language or even symbolic concepts. It is about extending hazard management into the everyday worlds of all those who have to live beside a hazardous installation or who are expected to handle a potentially dangerous substance. This void of miscommunication is left unfilled by the media who by and large fail to appreciate their important responsibilities for informing people about risks. Media coverage of risk events has been remarkable for its ignorance, it pejorative language and its irresistible temptation to symbolise and to stereotype. In recent years, as Peltu (1989) reports, coverage of risk issues by the media has improved a lot. Scientific familiarity amongst journalists has become more commonplace, and many sub-editors are willing to provide more space to allow fuller coverage of argument. Nevertheless, the problem of poor communication remains, largely because of the failure to bridge the conditions that create the division and misunderstanding between first-and second-order science mentioned earlier. All of this adds to the sense of alienation and widens the gulf of mistrust between risk creators and risk receivers. The latter begin to concentrate on the dangers without fully contemplating the associated benefits of risky activities.

This problem of risk miscommunication is beginning to plague both industry and government. Writing in the ESRC Newsletter in February 1987, William Waldegrave, former UK Minister of State for the Environment, Countryside and Planning wrote:

> One of the most important tasks facing government is to inspire a devlopment process which takes into account not only the nature of any environmental risk, but also the perception of that risk by the public who must suffer its consequences. We cannot always agree but we must at least create the circumstances and the means to discuss the risk

in terms that both risk assessors and the public understand before irrevocable decisions are taken.

Waldegrave was voicing two fears. One is that government cannot handle the political difficulties of siting hazardous installations, over which there is deep public anxiety, without running into political hostility. This is particularly the case for radioactive waste disposal facilities, and is becoming similarly a problem for toxic waste incinerators. That trouble manifests itself in lengthy disputes, costly public inquiries and much resentment. The net result is a further tightening of the regulatory screws adding further costs and delays to industrial production. For certain chemical plants, all nuclear installations and many toxic waste disposal sites, these have become serious issues. The fear is that the economic future of the biotechnology industry, with its propensity for creating new genetic formulations, could be jeopardised. To date, however, carefully-thought-out provisions are being taken in advance of the full-scale development of this industry, to ensure that the science of genetic manipulation is adequately scrutinised.

THE CONTRIBUTION OF MARY DOUGLAS

Mary Douglas has cast the fresh eye of the seasoned anthropologist on the risk debate via two books, *The Culture of Risk* and *Risk Assessment According to the Social Sciences*. In these publications she has argued that the spate of social psychological research into risk perception that began in the mid 1970s is misguided. The missing dimension is the degree of cultural adjustment or non-adjustment to unusual phenomena that may in themselves be frightening or alienating or simply unwanted.

'The public reception for any policy for risks,' she wrote (1987, p. 5) 'will depend upon standard public ideas about justice. The more that institutions depend upon personal commitment rather than upon coercion, the more explicitly they are monitored for fairness.' A sense of fairness means that people must be allowed to interpret the nature and likelihood of danger in their own terms, but also in conjunction with the risk creators. This collegiate feeding of co-operative endeavour means that people have to be enabled to make their own judgements about the link between the dangers and benefits of risky technologies. They also require points of reference in their own community to assist them in communicating their concerns and their responses to proposals and events emanating from particularly risky installations and products.

Danger is not an abstract phenomenon. It is coded into real events affecting known people—family, neighbours, fellow-citizens. It is not possible to hide behind the statistical abstractions of anonymity. The Chernobyl aftermath has laid that to rest, as has Bophal, though the trauma of the latter particularly distressing event would have been far more shocking if it had affected wealthy people in a developed nation.

'The engineering contribution,' wrote Mary Douglas, 'consists of isolated independent invididuals who naturally behave like engineers. They want to know the facts and these facts, once clearly presented, will convince them of the safety or riskiness of a proposal ... understanding will lay fear to rest' (1987, p. 21). Mary Douglas is concerned to remove the anonymity of risk assessment techniques and the conventions of treating value of life as a common denominator, in a depersonalised form.

Mary Douglas is right. This approach has not worked: hence the government's dilemma. The more that risks are communicated in the symbols of probability or outcome, the less risk receivers will be convinced of the meaningfulness of the evidence. For certain kinds of environmental risk we are now entering a new kind of participatory culture. To be succesful, the enterprise culture will have to take this into account.

RISK MANAGEMENT IN THE ENTERPRISE CULTURE

To provide a definition of the enterprise culture, it is probably best to list a set of assumptions most closely associated with an enterprise culture, namely:

(i) individual initiative and entrepreneurial spirit collectively leading to increased well-being;

(ii) voluntarism and self regulation producing a form of internalised accountability;

(iii) competition and market-place economics leading to efficiency and least-cost outcomes;

(iv) diminished public sector involvement and intervention being desirable for the better regulation of human affairs.

Note that these are propositions only. In fact, as we shall see, there is a growing tension in the risk arena, between a wish for tough self regulation, based on a strong social conscience, and a fundamental desire to see independent, authoritative *external* regulation to ensure consistency and quality control in risk management. The two are potentially compatible, but do not always mix in practice.

Into this paradox stepped Mary Douglas with her vision of two meditating cultural approaches to the management of risk, which can be outlined as follows.

The opportunist culture stresses the role of the socially responsible individual who calculates quite carefully personal payoffs and social losses of his/her actions, but who regards the 'risk world' as neutral, i.e. not so structured as to mean that dangers are externally imposed. For the opportunist culture, risks are regarded as self-selected so should be self-managed. Also in such cultures there is little enthusiasm for risk-sharing strategies or for any upgrading of societally controlled coercive regulation acting in the so-called public interest.

The hierarchical or sharing culture on the other hand does recognise the need for social management of public responsibilities. This culture understands risks as an outcome of powerlessness and injustice, so sets risk boundaries on private initiative to develop a sense of socially imposed self-regulation. Risk sharing becomes institutionalised via voluntary associations, consultative devices and compensatory mechanisms. The sharing culture also creates dangers, but recognises its social responsbilities to ensure that nobody suffers unduly as a result.

For Mary Douglas these two cultures are mutually exclusive. Indeed she sees society as being riven by tensions caused by the gulf of non-comprehension that separates out cultural norms which bind her grid–group categories. 'Each kind of society,' she writes in her recent piece 'Cultural variation and the concept of the individual' (Douglas, 1988), 'is stabilised in a uniquely specialised normative order. Its principles cannot be borrowed by either of the others without grave inconsistency.'

For Douglas, the enterprise culture operates on the basis of few restrictions on individual transactions, geared for the movement and for the improvement of the individual. The self-regulation referred to above acts only as a brake on excesses that might harm the future well-being of the agent in question. It is a self-centred notion, not notable for its degree of altruism.

In the risk framework, such a position is not tenable. The risk creator cannot be in a position to act selfishly. To do so would endanger not only the reputation of the organisation, be it a public or private company. It would also bring into disrepute the very purpose of the risk–benefit calculus, thereby threatening political and economic support for the activity itself. This has already taken place in the nuclear industry, now heavily burdened by external regulation and facing an uphill struggle in gaining public and political acceptance for the disposal of radioactive waste (see Openshaw, 1988). It now faces the biotechnology industry as it observes growing public suspicion regarding the release into the open environment of genetically manipulated organisms (see Royal Commission on Environmental Pollution, 1989). Increasingly, the debate over such technologies and their promoting economic agents in the form of research institutes, commercial industry and regulatory agencies, is whether the net gains of the new produce are really worth the dangers and anxieties. A false step by one of these promoting agencies could tip the balance against the public acceptance of their very existence.

Industry is nowadays well aware of this dilemma. A recent survey by the *Economist* newspaper (Cairncross, 1991) found that industry generally recognised that risk reduction was a necessary feature of their modern public relations and marketing strategies. A company knowingly contributing to environmental danger or public hazard would soon suffer from loss of shareholder confidence.

Thus it is difficult to support Mary Douglas's claim for an exclusivity between the enterprise culture and the sharing cultures. It is probable that some sort of fusion is necessary if both are to survive. The growing current interest in charging for environmental damage and putting a price on environmental values such as cleansing, shielding or absorbing cannot be left to the extended market alone. Even the most market-supportive economists accept that an element of regulation, externally imposed and funded from the public purse, is necessary if fair treatment amongst polluters is to be guaranteed (see for example Pearce *et al.*, 1989).

The enterprise culture, when it comes to risk reduction, essentially has to follow an amalgam of motives involving self-centredness, co-operative practice and an element of altruism. This suggests that the motivations of the economic agent, normally a low-grid, low-group enterprise in its culture, have to be mixed with the interests of the same agents acting as citizens and moral agents—where an element of higher-grid and higher-group cultural norms begin to dominate. The following trends are indicative of this amalgam, though the transition process is far from complete.

International risk regulation

International risk regulatory institutions with a desire to ensure consistency and comparability in safety regulation across national borders are in the process of being formed. They will be armed with a 'foresight' capacity to anticipate and plan for dangers before they actually occur. Already the world-wide nuclear and chemical industries have adopted this posture and it is evident that the major national risk regulatory agencies are collaborating in a much more effective manner. This is particularly evident in the European Community already. It will be more so once the Community has formalised its single market beyond 1992 (see Haigh, 1989). International regulation could provide the safety and public trust framework within which self-regulation will flourish. As the European Community becomes a single market in 1992, so the strength of centralised risk regulatory agencies will grow. This may not be entirely popular, as some national governments will resist the growth of uniform standards with their penchant for more inflexible policing methods.

Self regulation

Self regulation will also become far more significant as a risk management strategy. Big firms will build in their own captive risk assessment teams who in turn may provide a unified consultancy service for smaller interconnected firms. Internalised risk assessment could become more homogeneous in approach. This could spell danger as it might lead to 'cook book' risk reduction measures that fail to account for the vagaries of technology and social acceptance.

In addition, big companies are steadily taking on a 'green capitalism' image. They need to know the scale of consumer acceptance or resistance to new products in risk and other environmental testing. To do this they will increasingly have 'green' marketing specialists who will sense out opinion or product trends. This should develop a much greater corporate sensitivity to good environmental practice and product design, though one imagines that there will be leaders and followers and that there will be no great uniformity in all of this.

Thirdly, big corporations with the capital and the incentive will turn to captive agencies i.e. wholly owned insurance subsidiaries designed to provide liability cover for the aftermath of accidents or product mishaps. This has been encouraged by the growing trend of independent insurance companies, in the wake of Bophal, Seveso and Three Mile Island, not to provide base cover for environmental risk protection. To save their skins, companies are having to develop their own insurance arrangements. That necessarily means more self-regulation and tighter internal codes of good practice. Here is where the opportunist and the sharing cultures meet, but note that only the capital-secure companies will be able to benefit. In the risk enterprise culture, the rich and successful are most likely to be the ones that thrive.

Independent regulatory agencies

In this brave new world, the risk regulatory agencies might be freed from the strictures of civil service payrolls and monetarist policies towards budgetary planning. In short, they could be freed to charge for these services and to pay their officers appropriate salaries according to experience and ability. Three scales of fees might become available.

(i) *a cost recovery charge*, namely a pure administrative charge based on the costs of providing the service and issuing a licence.

(ii) *a social charge* where the payment reflects the residual, i.e. post-regulated, risk that still creates concern and anxiety. This would be based on a scale of 'loss of peace of mind'. Companies could reduce the burden of that charge by establishing comprehensive community risk-communication offices in the local area through which people could negotiate compensatory arrangements.

(iii) *a foresight charge*, namely an additional payment to cover the cost of providing a research and development capacity, possibly in league with other agencies in other countries, to monitor for environmental danger and to assess likely outcomes of possible new products or formulations. In the monetarist version of the enterprise culture, public money is becoming less and less available for this vital service.

The danger of all this is that the powerful will be able to protect themselves but the weak will either go to the wall or be forced into illicit 'cowboy' antics that could clandestinely endanger people and wildlife. This is a real concern so there may have to be mechanisms to provide 'blind' liability funds to assist the weaker to be better self regulators and to upgrade the general state of surveillance.

The other danger is that in an enterprise culture as presented here there is the possibility that the traditional 'watchdog' groups that normally exert public-interest pressure on government and industry will be more muted. This is either because they will be isolated, or because they will become incorporated as advisers to corporate-controlled risk regulation. Either way the intervener groups could lose their traditional sceptical and probing roles, without which self-policing cannot maintain its credibility. There is no easy answer to this dilemma. Any imaginable solution carries with it difficulties and inconsistencies. Possibly the best arrangement is to ensure a degree of incorporation and independence via sister groupings of watchdog groups, yapping together from both the inside and the outside.

Can the enterprise culture really bridge the opportunist and hierarchical cultures and make risk management more credible and effective? The conditions are ripe for exploration, experimentation and careful independent monitoring and evaluation. There is no reason why it cannot work so long as adequate safeguards are built into every innovation that is developed, and that both the state and the people the state represents recognise the need for such safeguards. If the enterprise culture is to succeed, this must be a minimum condition.

REFERENCES

BRIMBLECOMBE, P. (1987) *The Big Smoke: A History of Air Pollution in London Since Medieval Times*, London: Belhaven.

CAIRNCROSS, F. (1991) *The Environment: Costing it Out*, London: The Economist Publications.

DOUGLAS, M. and WILDAWSKY, A. (1983) *Risk and Culture*, Berkeley, Calif: University of Berkeley Press.

DOUGLAS, M. (1987) *Risk Acceptability According to the Social Sciences*, Chicago: Russell Sage Foundation.

DOUGLAS, M. (1989) Culture and collective action in Morris Freilich (ed.) *The Relevance of Culture*, New York: Burgin and Garvey.

FUNCTOVITZ, S. and RAVETZ, J. (1990) *Second Order Science: Risk Assessment and the Global Challenge*, London: Council for Science and Society.

HEALTH AND SAFETY EXECUTIVE (1987) *The Tolerability of Risk from Nuclear Power Stations*, London: HMSO.

KASPERSON, R. E. and PIJAWAKA, K. (1985) Societal response to hazards and major hazardous events, *Public Administration Review*, 45, pp. 7–19.

O'RIORDAN, T., KEMP, R. and PURDUE, H. R. (1987) On weighing the gains and investments at the margins of risk regulation, *Risk Analysis*, 7 (3), pp. 361–9.

PELTU, M. (1989) Media reporting of risk communication uncertainties and the future, in H. Jungermann, R. E. Kasperson and P. M. Wiedermann (eds.), *Risk Communication*, Jülich, Germany: KFA, pp. 11–32.

ROYAL COMMISSION ON ENVIRONMENTAL POLLUTION (1989) *Genetically Manipulated Organisms*, Thirteenth Report, London: HMSO.

ROYAL SOCIETY (1987) *Living with Risk*, London: Royal Society.

9

A social animal

ANGUS ROSS

For Mary Douglas, all social institutions are artificial constructs, conventions, albeit conventions that are legitimated, in the eyes of participants, by a parallel 'cognitive convention' that enables them to be represented as natural. As part of its effort to legitimate its institutions, each society constructs its own view of the world and man's place in it, seeking to represent those institutions as uniquely natural and therefore right. If Douglas is right, a society's account of the nature of its institutions and, more broadly of man and his relationship with nature must, it seems, be viewed with a certain suspicion, for those accounts will not be unmotivated. There is a familiar strand of liberal thought that at first sight seems to constitute a counter-example to this general thesis, but which on closer inspection illustrates it rather nicely. The image of a founding social contract is intended to convey precisely the thought that society is *unnatural*, an artificial construct, erected to serve interests that individuals possess independently of their membership of society. Thus no form of social order can claim the legitimacy that comes with naturalness. However, it is possible to see some forms of social order as less unnatural than others. The best society, it may seem, is the minimal society, the society which places least constraint on the natural liberty of the individual.[1] This is not the only way of defending liberty as a political ideal, but the thought that society is something unnatural to us plays a sufficiently prominent part in liberal mythology for it to be worth asking whether it is true.

It is not entirely obvious how Mary Douglas would have us answer this question. She tells us firmly that social institutions are conventions, but she also stresses that man is a social being, rejecting the familiar economist's picture of the individual as a pure rational chooser whose fundamental nature and concerns can be specified without reference to the fact that he lives in society. In part, Douglas is emphasising the fact that our *situation* is a social one, and that our concerns are for that reason social concerns. She is also, I take it, making the familiar point that our nature is shaped and moulded by the society in which we live and cannot be understood in abstraction from it. But none of this amounts to the claim that society is natural to us in the sense that social contract theory denies. What is at issue is whether we are to regard the shaping and moulding effects of society as something imposed *against* the grain of nature, so to speak, or whether, on the contrary, society provides the conditions essential to the full flowering of our natural powers, much as soil and water are essential if a plant is to grow and flower. Freud's writing provides an example of the former view; our natural, biologically-given instincts are such as to render civilised social life impossible if allowed unfettered expression. The individual is the seat of a constant struggle between the forces of civilisation (i.e. society) and the forces of nature. But the question of the relationship between our biologically-given instincts and society is one that needs to be addressed within the context of an account of human evolution, and any reflection on what we know, or must assume, about the evolutionary history of our species suggests a rather different picture.[2]

All the evidence points to our ancestors having lived a social way of life for many millions of years. Prior to the emergence of what the anthropologists call culture, which in evolutionary terms is a relatively recent development, a social way of life must have been natural to our ancestors in just the sense, and for just the same reason, that it is natural for a fish to swim in the sea. Before we acquired the capacity to learn and to pass on new skills and new ways of seeing things, before we acquired the capacity to construct new and more elaborate social institutions, our ancestors must have been predisposed towards a social way of life because that was the way of life for which natural selection had fitted them. Their innate skills, sensitivites and concerns would have been those of social beings. This must have been so, if only because the capacities and predispositions needed to sustain culture only make sense within, and could therefore only have evolved within, a way of life that was already (naturally) social in character. It is true that as we acquired the capacity to learn, our behaviour would have become more flexible, less rigidly determined by instinctual responses, but there is no reason to suppose that in acquiring the capacity to sustain culture we shed all the innate characteristics which had hitherto predisposed us to a social way of life. There is no reason, that is, to suppose that in acquiring culture we ceased to be social by nature. On the contrary, it is likely that at least a part of the framework of natural responses within which culture first emerged is necessary to its continued existence. In any case, our acquisition of the skills appropriate to life in a cultural environment itself constitutes an adaptation to a particular kind of social life. We are fitted by nature for the distinctively human form of social life. There is no paradox in the thought that we are by nature a cultural animal. Just as it is natural to us to speak a language, though not of course any particular language, so, it is natural to us to live within institutions of our own devising.

The claim that we are social by nature is usually seen as supporting a communitarian political ideal. Many utopian thinkers, Marx included, have taken it to mean that, given the right conditions, i.e. those which allow our true nature to reveal itself, social co-operation will come easily and naturally to us, without the need for constraining institutions. Before we can assess the political implications of the present line of argument, we need to be more specific about what is involved in being adapted for life in society. There is, after all, more than one way of being naturally social. In the case of the social insects, for example, it would perhaps be right to say that social co-operation comes easily. Each individual is innately predisposed to play his or her pre-ordained part. In the higher animals, however, social life is characterised to a greater or lesser extent by conflict between individuals. On the assumption that it is the existence of co-operation that makes a way of life social, it is hard not to see conflict as a sign of a less than perfect adaptation to a social way of life. It is hard, indeed, to avoid seeing the ant colony as representing the ideal society. Alternatively, faced with the sheer variety of forms of life which are referred to as 'social', we may be tempted to abandon the term altogether.

Ants, we can say, are adapted to the ant way of life, rabbits to the rabbit way of life, and we, presumably, to the human way of life, and that is that. However, there is a way of thinking about what makes a way of life social which avoids taking the ant colony as our paradigm and which still enables us to see significant parallels between human and animal society.

Let us focus, with Mary Douglas, on one of the preconditions of co-operation, the existence of a shared way of seeing things. Up to a point, the existence of a shared way of seeing things is guaranteed by membership of the same species, but only up to a point. Among the higher animals at least, social life requires a greater degree of agreement than can be guaranteed in this way, and thus arises the need for communication. The notion that communication is central to human social life, and that its purpose is to secure agreement on how the world is to be understood, is a central theme of Douglas's work,[3] but the point applies equally to other species' attempts to live together in social groups. Disputes over position in a pecking order, access to mating partners, possession of territory, are primitive examples of attempts to secure agreement as to how things should be seen, and all can be seen as involving communication. Indeed, disputes over how things should be seen are not confined to social animals, though it is above all in social groups that it matters to one individual how other individuals see things. (Where this is not so, as in the case of shoals of fish or herds of cattle perhaps, we would not want to describe the groups in question as *social* groups.) It is usually in the interests of all the parties involved in such a dispute that there should be agreement, but in the absence of a pre-established harmony of views it should be no surprise that agreement is not always easily reached. A concern with how others see things and a desire to secure agreement is in itself a potential source of conflict. How much conflict actually occurs in a given society will depend, *inter alia*, on what mechanisms exist, natural or artificial, for securing agreement without recourse to open conflict, but we have here a form of conflict that is endemic to, and to a large extent peculiar to, social life.

If we see the role which communication plays in securing an agreed way of seeing things as a central part of what makes a way of life social, at least in the sense in which we apply that term to the higher animals, then *Homo sapiens* is of course the

social animal *par excellence*. Our species has developed the skills
of communication further than any other. In part this is a fact
about our cultural achievements, among which must be num-
bered the various human languages, but it is also a fact about
our biologically given nature. Most obviously, we are born
with the mental equipment and predisposition to learn a
language, but it is worth remarking that our natural propensity
to see meaning in things and actions goes well beyond
language in the usual sense. The writings of anthropologists like
Douglas are eloquent testimony to the fact that we are, as
Cassirer puts it, an *animal symbolicum*. It is also worth remarking
that the 'natural' expressions of the emotions are more highly
developed in our species than in any other. I want to focus on
an aspect of communication that is most evident in connection
with expressions of emotion but which is in fact present in all
forms of communication. To be a communicator, I will argue, is
to be both sensitive to and disposed to react to others of one's
kind in certain characteristic ways. To possess a sufficiently
developed capacity for communication is, in fact, to possess just
those sensitivities and dispositions that dispose one to a social
way of life. To understand social life, we need to understand the
implications for the affective side of our nature of the fact that
we are communicators.

Consider for a moment one of the simplest and most primitive
of all forms of communication, the simple alarm call, as found,
for example, in many species of bird. There is, of course, no
question of attributing to the bird that emits such a call the
intention of warning others of the presence of danger. What
qualifies it as an example of communication is the fact that it is
the biological function of that call to make other individuals
aware of the danger perceived by the individual who emits the
call. For us to be able to attribute this function to the call, it is
necessary, firstly, that those individuals who utter the call tend,
by and large, to do so when and only when they perceive
themselves to be in danger. Secondly, at least some of those
who hear the call must be disposed, on hearing it, to assume
that danger is present, as evidenced, say, by the fact that they
break into flight or take cover. Only where both of these
dispositions are present can we say that the call serves to
transmit the information that danger is present from one

individual to another. To put the point more generally, it is a condition of our being able to see the emission of a sound or other perceptible signal as a case of communication that the individuals concerned possess two complementary sets of dispositions. On the one hand, there must be a certain reactivity, in that individuals are disposed to react to certain perceived states of affairs by emitting the sound in question. On the other hand, there must be a certain sensitivity to the sound, in that on hearing it individuals are disposed, other things being equal, to assume that the corresponding state of affairs obtains.[4] Consider a community of individuals who possess such dispositions in respect of a number of different sounds, each serving to convey a different item of information. We can think of each of these individuals as possessing two more broadly specifiable dispositions, corresponding to two sides of its nature as a communicator. On the one hand, given the function of the sounds in question, we can see each individual as possessing a disposition, not just to emit certain sounds, but to give expression to his/her view of things in so far as he/she is able (i.e. within the limits of his/her powers of expression). On the other hand, given the character and function of the sensitivity which each possesses to the sounds emitted by others, we can see this sensitivity as a sensitivity, not just to the sounds, but to the corresponding beliefs and perceptions of those who emit the sounds. It amounts to a disposition to share the beliefs and perceptions of others in so far as they are given expression. It amounts, in fact, to that sensitivity to the perceptions of others that Hume called 'sympathy'.[5]

It is not difficult to see that some forms of human communication, most obviously the natural expressions of the emotions, follow this pattern, but the point has a much wider application. Note firstly that it is not necessary to the argument that the dispositions in question be innate in origin. Wherever dispositions of this form are found we have communication, though admittedly if that is *all* we have, it will indeed be a primitive form of communication. How far they reflect an innate expressiveness or sensitivity to others and how far they are the product of training or conditioning is a further question—though it is worth remarking that human infants do seem to have an innate urge to express themselves, without which it is unlikely they would ever learn to speak. Admittedly, adult speech is very different from a simple ejaculation like a cry of alarm. It is a complex and above all conscious form of communication, informed by complex intentions, but that is quite consistent with it also being the subject of pre-reflective impulses or inclinations. We often speak of wanting to say something or feeling that something needs to be said, and much of our response to what is said by others is equally a matter of unreflected disposition or habit. That such dispositions are an essential part of what it is to understand a language can be seen from the inadequacy of accounts that attempt to do without them. Attempts to say what it is for sounds to constitute a meaningful use of language by appealing to the speaker's intentions[6] put the cart before the horse. The ability to form and recognise complex communicational intentions is something which language makes possible, not something that can be appealed to in an account of how it works. David Lewis's account[7] of what it is for sounds to constitute a meaningful use of language has the merit of focusing on the need for certain regularities in their use and in our response to their use (his 'conventions of truth and trust') which correspond closely to the two dispositions identified above. But Lewis's suggestion that we observe these conventions out of a rational recognition that it is in our interest to do so as long as others do the same fails for much the same reason that the Gricean appeal to speaker's intentions fails. The kind of rational appraisal of what to say and believe to which Lewis appeals presupposes an awareness of belief, both in ourselves and in others, which once again puts the cart before the horse. A grasp of language and a capacity to give expression to our beliefs is itself a condition of the possibility of an awareness of belief, both in others and in oneself. At bottom, understanding a language is a matter of being disposed to use and respond to its use in systematically appropriate ways, and these responses cannot have their roots in a rational appreciation of their consequences.

That said, it is clear that a full mastery of language involves much more than the two dispositions we have identified as minimal conditions of communication. To a first approximation, we can think of a mastery of language as built up in layers, like an onion, with each layer presupposing the one beneath. As a speaker learns to respond to the situations he/she faces in increasingly discriminating ways, those dispositions which correspond to a very early stage in his/her acquisition of language become overlaid, though never altogether extinguished, by other, often conflicting dispositions. At the centre of the onion, our argument seems to suggest, will lie a disposition to give expression to one's own view (i.e. a disposition to utter words appropriate to our beliefs or feelings) together with a Humean sympathy with the expressed views of others (i.e. a disposition to respond to the words one hears by embracing the appropriate view). However, it would not be plausible to think of the first of these dispositions as a disposition to give expression, constantly and indiscriminately, to *all* of one's beliefs or feelings, or even to all the beliefs or feelings one is capable of expressing. (That would not be so implausible in the case of an utterer with very limited powers of expression, e.g. an utterer only capable of expressing the belief that danger is present.) What the argument requires is that we be able to see a grasp of language as consisting, in the first instance, of pre-reflective dispositions which *in some way* engage the full range of the speaker's powers of expression. That requirement is met if we can suppose that, for each belief or attitude the speaker is capable of expressing, there are circumstaces in which, a context of communication in which, he or she *would* be disposed to express that belief or attitude. An individual of which this is true can be said to be disposed to express his/her view on those matters which he/she sees as being of importance, public importance, in the context in question. I do not mean that we can attribute to such an individual the conscious thought that what he/she says is of public importance. The point is simply that to be disposed to express one's view on a certain question in certain contexts, but not on other questions or in other contexts, is to manifest, in the most direct way possible, the fact that one takes that question to be of public importance in those contexts.

To return for a moment to the dispositions which we have said constitute minimum conditions of the possibility of communication, it is not hard to see that these dispositions are sufficient, in principle, to generate a shared way of seeing things within a given group of individuals. Note, however, that in their most primitive manifestation, as in the example of a bird's alarm call, they imply no interaction between individuals of a kind we could call social. Utterers of an alarm call react to the perceived danger, not to the presence of other individuals, of whom they need not even be aware. The same is true of individuals that respond to such a call. They are *sensitive* to the call in that it has altered their perceptions. They too now assume that danger is present and react appropriately. But their reaction is a response to the assumed danger, not to the utterer of the call. In itself, their reaction manifests no awareness on their part of the utterer of the call.

The situation is different where the utterer is disposed to express views on, and only on, those matters seen as being of public importance in the situation in question. Such an utterer discriminates between situations. Sometimes s/he is disposed to express the view that P and sometimes s/he is not, not because s/he has changed his mind about P but because sometimes s/he sees it as 'needing to be said' and sometimes s/he does not. Perhaps it is evident that everyone is already aware (or accepts) that P. Take the case of an utterer of alarm calls who is disposed to cease the calls when they elicit the appropriate response and to redouble efforts when they fail. In varying his/her expressive activity in this way he/she manifests an awareness of whether the message has got through. He/she manifests an awareness, albeit limited, of the hearer's state of mind. Another obvious situation in which a message may 'need saying' is that in which one's hearers are actually expressing a contrary view. An utterer who is not disposed, other things being equal, to redouble communicational efforts in such a situation is one who has failed to recognise it for what it is. In being disposed to express his/her own view with particular vigour when confronted by the expression of a view s/he takes to be incorrect, in being disposed, that is, to challenge those s/he disagrees with, s/he is once again manifesting an awareness of the views of others. In its simplest, most primitive form, communication is a wholly unconscious affair, involving no awareness of the views of others. It is only when a communicator is disposed to focus expressive activity upon particular others that s/he can be seen as manifesting an awareness of others as possessors of views that may differ from his/her own.[8]

Note too that a communicator so disposed is one to whom it *matters* what view others take of things. Such a concern with how others see things is clearly a potent source of conflict, but it also manifests itself in ways we would not immediately think of as involving conflict. For example, to comfort those in distress is to seek to alter their view of their situation, to seek to convince them that things are really not that bad, by means of the expression of a contrary view. To be disposed to comfort (as distinct from assist) those in distress is to manifest an awareness of their view of things as one that needs correcting. It is to manifest an awareness of, and of course a concern with, distress as a subjective state.

In short, to possess a grasp of language or any other communicational skill is not *just* to possess a skill. It involves being sensitive to, and inclined to react to, others of one's kind in certain characteristic ways. Minimally, it means being inclined both to express one's own view of things and to be influenced by the views of others. But if there is to be communication that manifests an awareness of the views of others, and thus anything that could count as social interaction, there must be a positive inclination to challenge those with conflicting views. It is evident that the dispositions we are describing will not always coincide with the dictates of reason, but it is not seriously possible to regret the fact that we possess them, if only because they are conditions of the possibility of the development of precisely that capacity for independent, reflective judgement and self-control, by contrast with which we find our more primitive responses wanting.

As we have said, in talking about the implications of being a communicator we are talking about the necessary characteristics of any social animal. Let us ask how far the picture that has emerged chimes with Douglas's anthropologically inspired picture of a social being. Take the question of the place of conflict in social life. On the present account, to be social by nature is to be prone to a kind of conflict peculiar to communicating beings, a kind of conflict that not merely *arises* from the existence of different ways of seeing things but is actually *about* how things should be seen. Some social species seem to be more prone to this type of conflict than others, but the greater the extent to which a species' way of life depends on a degree of agreement in ways of seeing things that is not guaranteed by nature, the more reason we have to expect a readiness to challenge conflicting views to be a feature of its make-up. The fact that we are adapted—and, the presumption must be, well adapted—for life in society implies no guarantee that social harmony will be easily achieved, even in the small, face-to-face communities within which we must have spent the bulk of our evolutionary history. Thus the claim that we are social by nature offers no encouragement to the view that if only we could abolish capitalist exploitation, or cleanse society of some other corrupting influence, human nature would reveal itself as essentially good, and social co-operation would come easily and naturally to us without the need for constraining institutions. But equally, it offers no support to the view that our difficulties are to be blamed on a recalcitrant or badly designed human nature. Our quarrelsomeness must not be taken as a sign of an imperfect adaptation to social life, or as a hangover from some earlier stage in our evolution that is no longer appropriate in our present state of social development.

In discussing how we escape the Prisoner's Dilemma and achieve social co-operation (*How Institutions Think*, ch. 2), Douglas is surely right to insist that appeals to human nature provide no easy answer. She is right to focus, instead, on the difficulties intrinsic to the task of institution building, which is to say, the difficulties intrinsic to the task of securing the necessary agreement in ways of seeing things. The present approach does, however, imply a slight shift in the onus of explanation relative to that suggested by Douglas's discussion. She is quite properly anxious to avoid taking agreement for granted and emphasises the way in which differences of interest act as a source of disagreement. It would be wrong, however, to leave the impression that our nature is in itself simply a source of disagreement. There must be a general presumption in favour of agreement arising from our disposition to accept the views of others. Unless *most* of the time we were disposed to accept the views expressed by others there would be nothing we could call communication, the sounds emitted would have no meaning for they would serve no function. (Compare the thought that unless promises were generally kept, the act of promising would have no meaning.) A shared way of seeing things is a state of affairs to which our nature as communicators inclines us. It is the persistence of disagreement that calls for explanation, though there is admittedly no shortage of available explanations.

The real problem, as Douglas's discussion makes clear, is to understand, not the possibility of agreement as such, but the possibility of the kind of shared way of seeing things that makes genuine co-operation possible. Many shared ways of seeing things offer only limited possibilities of co-operation because they also bring men into conflict with each other. We might also note that, since a measure of agreement is itself a condition of the possibility of communication, what requires to be explained is how an initial area of agreement can be extended, thus making possible the emergence of richer forms of communication carrying a greater load of information. In discussing the emergence of the institutions and modes of thought that make co-operation possible, we are, *inter alia*, discussing the evolution of the institution of language.

It is in her discussion of consumption behaviour that Douglas is most explicit about her assumptions concerning human nature. The central idea is a familiar one, that of human rationality, but the use she makes of it is strikingly original. When the economist employs the idea of consumer rationality, the consumer's utility function over the various goods and services available is simply taken as given. Douglas sets out to illuminate precisely those consumer preferences which the economist is forced to regard as having no rational basis. She focuses on what she sees as a precondition of all choice that can claim to be rational, the ability to 'make sense' of the world. Making sense of the world may not be a problem peculiar to our species, but it is *more* of a problem for us, and we tackle it in a distinctive way:

> All other living beings submit their experience to a species-specific organising framework which limits the scope of possible messages and resposes. But human rationality does not submit. It negotiates the organising structures. Human experience can flow into a vast variety of possible frameworks, for the rational human mind is responsible for continually recreating a universe in which choice can take place . . .
>
> The most general objective of the consumer can only be to construct an intelligible universe with the goods he chooses.[9]

The conclusion is striking, with the promise of application far beyond the field of consumer behaviour. (The motivation of political activity is surely a case in point.) But the argument Douglas offers is brief and elliptical, so it may be worth trying to spell it out more fully, focusing as before on the implications of being a communicator.

It helps to keep in view not only the contrast between the human and the non-human, to which Douglas appeals in the above quotation, but also the contrast between a social animal and a non-social animal. For any social animal, the problem of making sense of the world is greatly complicated by the fact that in order to know where it stands it must assess the implications of the various messages it is receiving from others. A simple sensitivity to how others see things of the kind discussed above will not be enough, for these messages may be conflicting or ambiguous, and the individual needs to arrive at a coherent overall picture. At the same time, s/he will, as we have seen, feel the need to give expressiion to his/her own view of things, his/her own way of making sense of things, and in that way to exercise some control over the way others see things. This is true of all social animals, even those for whom the basic framework within which they seek to make sense of their experience is fixed and limited. In her more recent writing,[10] Douglas has shown considerable ingenuity in exploiting the insights of the orthodox theory of rational action, with its assumption that individuals are engaged in the rational pursuit of interest, but her discussion of consumption behaviour employs a very different conception of individual motivation. Expressive activity that arises directly from the individual's need to give expression to his/her view of things is not to be construed as an instance of the conscious selection of the most efficient means of furthering his/her interests. The main point of consumption, Douglas tells us, is to get some agreement from our fellow men and women,[11] but this is not, I take it, an activity we engage in because we are aware that it furthers our interests—though no doubt it usually does. It is simply an enterprise to which our nature impels us.

To return to the idea of making sense of the world, the fact that human beings are cultural animals, capable of employing 'a vast variety of possible frameworks', makes the task of making sense of how others see things both more formidable and more urgent. All communication implies a degree of cognitive interdependence, but among the things a human being needs to learn from others is which framework, which categories, he should employ in seeking to make sense of his experience. The fact that we are cultural animals also makes it more urgent to give expression to our own view of the sense of things, both in that a richer set of classification is at stake, and in that the categories themselves are potentially subject to dispute. Thus we must expect natural selection, in equipping us for life in a cultural environment, to have endowed us with a particularly high degree of alertness to the meaning of what others are doing, of which our language-learning capacity is just one aspect. At the same time, we must expect natural selection to have endowed us with a particularly strong urge to give expression to the way we see things, both linguistically and in other ways.

To see how this involves us in the project of 'constructing an intelligible universe', we need to introduce a further aspect of the contrast between the human and the non-human, or to be more precise, between language and more primitive forms of communication. The linguistic unit of communication is the sentence, and unlike a primitive cry of alarm, the typical sentence is made up of words in combination. Its meaning depends not only on which words have been combined together but on the particular way in which they have been combined. Looked at from the other direction, language is a *system* whose basic units, words, can be employed in a variety of combinations to convey different meanings. Moreover, as Saussure and Wittgenstein have helped us to see, the meaning of each word is a function of its place in the system. The meaning of any given word is a function both of the way it is capable of being combined with other words and of the set of contrasts generated by the existence of other words whose use it excludes. Beyond a minimal level of complexity, it is inevitable that not *all* combinations will convey an intelligible message; not all combinations will make sense. In fact more combinations, selected at random, will not make sense. This kind of lack of sense is something a competent speaker will, other things being equal, seek to avoid. To be disposed to express one's view linguistically is to be disposed, *inter alia*, to employ meaningful combinations of words and to avoid meaningless combinations. It is to be disposed to make, to create, sense and to avoid nonsense. The expression 'make sense' here takes on a new meaning. Making sense is no longer just a matter of interpreting the world; it is a matter of changing it, a matter of actively constructing combinations that make sense. These two kinds of 'making sense', interpretation and construction, are distinct, in that the first could exist without the second (in other animals, for example). But where the second exists, there is necessarily a close connection between the two. The sense we express with the words we employ will normally be our view of things, and our view of things is, of course, our interpretation of the world. In the central case at least, the sense we seek to construct is the sense we interpret the world as having.[12]

Douglas's suggestion, of course, is that the business of making sense with words is only one example of a more general concern with making—in the sense now of constructing—sense. In furnishing a house or deciding what to wear, in choosing what food or drink to serve at a meal, we are saying something about ourselves or the occasion and helping to define our relationship with others. In dividing up space and time in certain ways, in creating a certain spatial or temporal order, we express a view as to the proper ordering of activities and relationships and in so doing help to create or reaffirm a certain social order. It is no exaggeration, then, to say that we are engaged in an effort to construct an intelligible universe, [13] and success is vital, for 'to continue to think rationally, the individual needs an intelligible universe, and that intelligibility will need to have some visible markings'.[14] As with words, the meaning of each item, each 'visible marking', is a function of its place in the whole scheme, and there is the ever-present possibility of our efforts failing to make overall sense. This time, however, failure can mean the loss of the intelligibility, not just of a single message, but of the whole framework which gives meaning to our choices and actions. Though it is clear that we are to see this as a universal human concern, Douglas suggests that it is more pressing in some societies, and in some social positions, than in others. For example, in low-grid social environments like our own, where inventiveness and creativity are particularly highly valued, 'the problem of controlling or disseminating information is made more difficult by continual change in the information stock itself'. [15] And

exclusion from the club of the rich may mean that there is

no way of ordering a rational experience at a more modest level in the same universe. For the rich who call the tune are continually changing it, too. The price of order and rationality for those who are neither rich nor in control, nor in a position to challenge control, is to withdraw.[16]

These are not caims that can be argued *a priori*. Their chief recommendation must be their power to explain aspects of human behaviour, such as our concern with order and with what is 'fitting', that might otherwise remain unexplained. What can be said, however, is that a concern with making sense of the kind to which Douglas appeals is to be expected in any being adapted for life in a cultural environment. As we have said, to be a language user is to have a concern to make sense and avoid nonsense, and there is no reason to suppose that this concern will be confined to language. What gives meaning to non-linguistic signs and symbols is not *so* very different from what gives words their meaning. Ultimately it comes down to our being sensitive to them, and thus disposed to react to them in certain ways, though in each case the sensitivity involved is one that is mediated by our reason—where the term 'reason' is here used in what Douglas calls 'the code-breaking, jigsaw puzzle solving' sense.[17] An active concern to create sense and avoid nonsense is a necessary part of the make-up of any being that has acquired the ability to distinguish sense from nonsense. How far we should see this concern as arising from an innate predisposition, and how far it is something generated by the individual's interaction with his or her cultural environment, is in a sense a secondary question, but it is worth emphasising that a concern to impose an intelligible order on the world is at the very least *continuous* with our nature as expressive, communicating beings. We must not be tempted to see it as something society imposes on us, like the contents of some Freudian superego.[18]

To return to the issue with which we started, the claim that society is natural to us undermines one kind of argument for the minimal state. It cannot be argued that the best society is that which places least constraint on the liberty of the individual on the grounds that it involves the least departure from our natural state. However, there is another, more Aristotelian, way of linking questions about human nature with questions about the good society. To say that we are social by nature is to say that only in society do we find the conditions necessary to the exercise and full development of our natural powers. It is possible that some societies provide better conditions than others in which to exercise those powers. The suggestion is not that we can identify a form of society that is uniquely natural, but rather that the merits of any given social order can be judged by the extent to which it enables individuals to develop their full potential as human beings.[19] The idea of human nature serves here to identify certain key powers, failure to develop which would constitute failure to become a fully developed human being.

Where this line of thought leads us depends, of course, on what we take these key human powers to be. A scientific understanding of human nature can take us only so far, for the choice is essentially political or moral. It is a question of what we value. Within the set of plausibly universal human powers, each culture chooses to highlight some and downplay others, offering its own list of key human virtues.[20] For example, if what we value most highly is the human capacity for a life of order and discipline, we may see here an argument for a fascist or even a monastic political ideal. J. S. Mill is best remembered for his insistence that there are many different forms of human excellence and that each of us has a different potential for self-development. But it is crucial to Mill's argument for liberty that any acceptable conception of self-development involves the cultivation of a capacity for making choices that are genuinely one's own. Only in this way do we exercise the key human faculties of 'perception, judgment and discriminative feeling'.[21] To follow custom merely because it is the custom is to make no choice. That, in the end, is why we must each be allowed the freedom to pursue our own conception of self-development in our own way, for Mill sees it as a condition of the development of these key human faculties that the individual be left as free as possible from the constraints of law and custom.

In affirming the importance of developing these particular faculties, Mill is, of course, affirming certain identifiably liberal values. For most of us, they will be values we share, but that does not mean we are forced to accept the political conclusions Mill draws. In part that is because we may want to strike a different balance between these and other competing values to which we are attached. But we also need to ask whether Mill has correctly identified the conditions conducive to the exercise and development of a capacity for making choices that are genuinely one's own. Is a situation of minimal constraint—the enterprise culture? the permissive society?—the best way of promoting the specifically *cognitive*, as distinct from economic, independence by which Mill sets such store? Or to put it in terms of Isaiah Berlin's famous distinction, we must ask whether Mill is correct in supposing that a situation of maximum 'negative' liberty is in fact, as he supposes, conducive to the development of the positive liberty which seems to be his ultimate concern.

These are large questions and I shall not attempt to pursue them here, but those who have read Mary Douglas on consumption patterns in a low-grid environment will know that she has done more than most to make us aware of the social dimension, and the social costs, of the pursuit of novelty and individuality. And more generally, her insistence on the social dimension of thought is a useful reminder to the philosopher not to exaggerate the extent to which cognitive independence is an achievable ideal for any of us.

NOTES

1 For a discussion of the way in which defenders of the free market seek to represent it as natural, see Professor Sugden's contribution to this volume.

2 Freud, of course, took himself to be operating within a biological framework, but it is arguable that he had not fully absorbed the implications of Darwin's theory, and he was obviously working without the benefit of modern palaeontological and ethological research. See John Bowlby, *Attachment and Loss, Vol. I*, Hogarth Press, London, 1969, and Frank Sulloway, *Freud, Biologist of the Mind*, Burnett Books, London, 1979.

3 Others who have seen communication as the central, defining feature of a social way of life include G. H. Mead, Claude Lévi-Strauss and Jürgen Habermas.

4 Sometimes only *one* of these two complementary dispositions will be found in a given individual, e.g. in the case of distress calls of young to which only adults respond. But I take it that we are interested in cases where communication can go in both directions.

5 David Hume, *A Treatise of Human Nature*, John Noon, London, 1739, Book II, Part I, Section XI.

6 See for example H. P. Grice, 'Meaning', *The Philosophical Review*, 1957, pp. 377–88, and Jonathan Bennett, *Linguistic Behaviour*, Cambridge, Cambridge University Press, 1976.

7 David Lewis, 'Language and Languages' in Gunderson (ed.), *Language, Mind and Knowledge*, (University of Minnesota Press, Minnesota, 1975), pp. 7–12. I have expressed other doubts concerning Lewis's account of language in 'Why do we believe what we are told?', *Ratio*, 1986, pp. 70–88.

8 To pursue the theme of increasing awareness, the utterer who varies his expressive activity in this way also manifests a degree of awareness of the goal of that activity, in that he shows himself capable of recognising when its goal has been achieved.

9 Mary Douglas, *The World of Goods*, Allen Lane, London, 1979, pp. 71 and 65. See also Chapter 2 of this volume.

10 See for example Mary Douglas, *How Institutions Think*, Routledge, London, 1987, and Chapter 3 above.

11 Douglas, *The World of Goods*, p. 65. See also Chapter 2 of this volume.

12 It might be objected that the view we express is often a view as to how the world *ought* to be, not simply how it is. But I take it that the kind of interpretation of the world with which Douglas is concerned always involves moral categories, and so always implies some conception of how things ought to be.

13 Though Douglas singles out David Hume for praise as the 'anthropologist's philosopher', the debt here is clearly to Kant.

14 Douglas, *The World of Goods*, p. 5. See also Chapter 2 of this volume and, for a discussion of our reaction to things and actions that threaten the intelligibility of our world, Mary Douglas, *Purity and Danger*, Routledge, London, 1966.

15 Douglas, *The World of Goods*, p. 198.

16 *Ibid.*, p. 93.

17 *Ibid.*, p. 4.

18 And nor, thinking of Freud, should we see a concern with order as particularly infantile.

19 Perhaps we should see this thought as already involving a political stand characteristic of a low-grid, low-group environment, in that it values the well-being of individuals rather than, say, the greatness of the nation or the triumph of the true religion.

20 Many cultures also recommend some virtues to the mass of citizens while reserving others to leaders, some to men and others to women, and so on. There is, of course, no evidence for the view that the potential for developing this or that power is confined to any identifiable class of individuals. That is another way in which factual questions about human nature can have a bearing on political debate.

21 J. S. Mill, *An Essay on Liberty*, London 1859; reprinted in Mary Warnock, ed. *Utilitarianism*, Fontana, London, 1962, Ch. 3: 'Of individuality as one of the elements of well being'.

10

Fear of fridges: some aspects of the politics of consumption

JOHN STREET

Suddenly it seems as if the key actor in democratic political life is not the citizen; it is the consumer. The democratic choice is the consumer's choice. The Conservative Party's 1987 election manifesto celebrated the ideas of consumer sovereignty as the theoretical grounding for its policies of privatisation and parental choice in education. Consumers and consumption are not, however, the exclusive preserve of the Conservatives. Indeed, the argument currently in favour within the Left is that the Labour Party lost the 1987 General Election precisely because it failed to lay claim to the politics of consumption. Equally, consumption has featured in explanations of the collapse of communism in Eastern Europe. Popular dissent was said to have been fuelled by the governments' failure to put goods in the shops.

It might be tempting to conclude, in the face of this new trend, that the Left's attempt to capture the consumer is another case of political opportunism, on a par with Harold Wilson's gift of the MBE to the Beatles. Such criticisms rest on the idea that there is something inherently unsocialist about consumption, that it embodies capitalism at its worst. The dignity of labour is not matched by the dignity of shopping.

Certainly, the Left has a traditional attachment to the *embourgeoisement* thesis—or the 'fear of fridges' theory of politics (Rentoul, 1988). According to this, the acquisition of goods has the effect of changing the attitudes and interests of individuals, causing them to adopt middle-class conceptions of their interests in preference to their real working-class interests. It affects voters and leaders alike—voters are 'bought off'; leaders 'sell out'. These political observations of the ill-effects of acquiring a bourgeois life-style, through the acquisition of bourgeois goods, are reinforced by a set of ethical claims about consumption. These derive from a puritan Christianity which inhabits British socialism. Worries about 'storing up treasures on earth' combine with anxieties about the rich and the eye of the needle, not to mention the commandment against covetousness. These concerns are given force by the thought that socialists, like Christians, should lead lives which exemplify their beliefs. Together they account for why the Labour Party celebrates Tony Benn's tea-drinking habits, and castigated Roy Jenkins for his claret-drinking ones; or why the General Secretary of the CPGB once offered this list of the iniquities of capitalism and the USA (the two being, it seems, synonymous): 'horror comics, Coca-Cola, juke-boxes, rock, tenpin bowling alleys, electric guitars, commercial TV . . .' (Boyd, 1973). These ethical doubts about consumption are given intellectual and institutional support through the legacy of Marx (for whom commodities, as 'congealed labour', stood as the alienated product of the worker's endeavour) and through the character of the socialist movement, organised around labour. Whatever its debt to Marx, the Labour movement (as its name confirms) shares the basic focus of his thinking. The Labour Party is a trade union party, and as such its interest is primarily with producers. This is all too apparent in its interpretation of Clause Four and in the very limited provision made for consumers in the original form of public ownership.

These various factors—whatever their intellectual or political coherence—have worked against the Left's development of a thorough account of the consumer within capitalism and her/his role in the move towards socialism. In constrast, the Conservative Party has been faced with none of the same ideological or institutional barriers to celebrating consumption, and has—it is claimed—captured the consumer and secured its political future, thereby demonstrating the importance of consumption and ensuring the death knell of socialism. My concern here is to unpick, with Mary Douglas's help, the assumptions that underlie such conclusions and to see what the politics of consumption involves. In doing this, I want to focus on the single issue of whether the Left's courtship of the consumer is in vain. Is there, in fact, a single-meaning message to be ascribed to consumption?

I shall begin by looking more closely at the Left's traditional opposition to capitalist consumption. There is a hypermarket-like range of these criticisms, each one threatening a more effective attack on the stubborn stains and ingrained dirt of consumerism. There is, for example, the grand, elitist tradition contained within the Frankfurt School of social theory which sees in mass consumption the mass oppression of people. There are two elements to this claim. The first is that mass oppression is revealed in the absence of any 'real' choice (all soap powders are essentially the same). The second element is the suggestion that the desire for something more, for a higher goal and a better choice, has itself been eliminated, and that citizens have become consumers who want nothing more than the false choices that they are presently offered. Recent versions of the Frankfurt School argument continue to appear. Stuart and Elisabeth Ewen write of 'the ideological lure of consumerism' which is tied to the 'decimation of customary bonds' and the creation of isolated and vulnerable individuals (1978, p. 48). The philosopher W. F. Haug offers one of the most unforgiving attacks on consumption. He focuses on the exchange relationship. On the one side there is the seller who values goods in terms of their exchange value; on the other side there is the consumer for whom an item's worth is measured by its use value. Commodity production, however, is only concerned with sales. Under these conditions, it is the *promise* of use value that seduces the purchaser, not the reality. This, says Haug, opens the way for goods to be sold only in terms of their illusory qualities: 'Appearance becomes just as important—and practically more so—than the commodity's being itself. Something that is simply useful but does not appear to be so, will not sell, while something that seems to be useful, will sell' (1986, p. 17). Hence the importance attached to brand names and to advertising generally.

Such thoughts find their way into the writings of one of the British Left's leading critics of consumerism, Jeremy Seabrook. In a series of articles and books, Seabrook has chronicled what he sees as the deadening effect of material goods. 'Simply because goods or services are marketed, and indeed achieve great sales,' he writes, 'does not necessarily mean that they *answer* a need' (1985, p. 14). What distinguishes Seabrook from the fatalism or determinism of the Frankfurt School is the thought that there is something going on beneath 'the driven and pervasive insistence on buying and selling'. He describes consumption as 'a means of crowding out all the precious things that cannot be had for money'; and he says that 'our "free" choices' may disguise 'formless and captive longings'. He recognises too that the desire for domestic consumption is in response to 'the growing coldness outside' (Blackwell and Seabrook, 1985, p. 183). But while Seabrook is prepared to acknowledge that consumption is more complex and ambiguous than the Left has recognised, he remains sceptical of its value. He clearly looks forward to a world which is warmer outside, where consumption is of little consequence and where what we buy satisfies real—if unspecified—needs. It is a world in which we can live 'without the right brand-name equipment and clothing' (pp. 174–5).

Another version of this critique of consumerism is advanced by Ursula Huws (1988) who echoes Seabrook's worries about the chill which mass consumption brings to human relations. While modern consumer goods create undoubted benefits, they also bring costs. The first of these is to be measured in terms of money. While washing machines, for example, relieve people of domestic drudgery, they increase the financial burden that falls upon individual workers, a burden that is exacerbated by the planned obsolescence of the technology. Furthermore, says Huws, the private provision of services inevitably erodes demand and support for public provision, and the loss of public services falls disproportionately on the poor who cannot afford the now necessary household items. The second form of hidden cost, argues Huws, is to be detected in the decline in collective or community identity. The world is privatised. A third effect of this trend is to increase domestic labour for those who can afford the consumer goods, even though such items promise to be 'labour saving'. As she observes of the truly rich, 'you don't catch them up ladders using the latest Black and Decker drill with sander attachment' (p. 6). Similarly, trends towards 'consumer choice' often conceal a shift in responsibility and effort. As the grocer's shop is replaced by supermarkets, we are forced to do more—to drive further, to walk the aisles, to keep the food fresh. Such tasks used to fall on the shopkeeper. For Huws, therefore, consumption acts to restrain and burden the people who have access to it, while also increasing the discrimination against the poor.

A variant on the costs of consumption argument is associated with the Green movement. Two main strands can be discerned. First, the Greens, like Huws, focus on the hidden costs, in particular on the notion that mass consumption is wasteful of precious resources (fast-food hamburgers don't taste the same once you know that they involve the artificial inflation of South American beef prices and the cutting back of much-needed rain forests). The second line of argument follows Fred Hirsch's *Social Limits to Growth* (1977) whereby the good itself is diminished or eliminated in the very process of its acquisition, either because of its positional character or because of the effect of 'commercialisation' upon it.

While these different attacks on consumption may only share a tenuous connection with each other, they are consistent in their view that consumption is politically suspect, either because of the effects it has on individuals or because of the interests it serves. There is a presumption that consumption is an integral part of the political and economic order which socialists oppose. It is noticeable that when Raymond Williams defines consumption in his *Keywords* he links its etymology to the rise of capitalist economic activity.

But while the Left has been dominated by those who decry consumption, theirs is not the only voice to be heard. There is a counter-argument which could begin by challenging Williams' etymology. The Latin root of consumption is, in fact, ambiguous: it can mean, negatively, 'to use up', or more positively, 'to sum up'. This second meaning provides the grounding for the Left's defence of consumption. Consuming becomes a site for participatory political activity. Rather than being a form of manipulation, consumption can be a source of political radicalism; it can function as a way by which citizens retain some hold on their society. Frank Mort and Nicholas Green write: 'Advertisers and marketers are not simply the "slaves of capital", driven by profit and the frantic search for markets. They are cultural entrepreneurs who construct a two-way dialogue between the market on the one hand and the lived experience of consuming on the other' (1988, p. 32). More radically still, in his *Rethinking Socialism*, Gavin Kitching (1983) has suggested that it is affluence and consumption that provides the conditions for democratic social change. It is in our role as consumers that we exercise our rights as citizens.

It is into these alternative arguments about the political importance of consumption that I want to introduce Mary Douglas and Baron Isherwood's *The World of Goods*. Although their book is directed primarily at economists, it seems that political science too can learn much from what they offer. Not only does *The World of Goods* confirm that consumption matters, it also shows us how we can add considerable subtlety to this key insight. After identifying briefly the elements of *The World of Goods* that are relevant here, I go on to examine the political importance of consumption, first by linking it to voting behaviour, and then by extending it into other aspects of the political process.

One of the key ideas in *The World of Goods* is that goods form part of an 'information system' (p. 10), and that the data so conveyed is 'about the hierarchy of values to which their chooser subscribes'. The transmission of these values depends on the way goods are understood, and this depends on the culture in which goods are the currency. 'Consumption,' write the authors, 'is the very arena in which culture is fought over and licked into shape' (p. 57). Goods are not just about survival and subsistence; they are the means by which we articulate our relations with each other. Consumption is the way we—literally—'make sense' of our world: 'Commodities are good for thinking' (p. 62). This argument for the positive value of consumption challenges the negative interpretation of the Frankfurt School for whom human beings are so often dupes of capitalism's tricks. For Douglas and Isherwood, the consumer is a wise and capable actor, managing a complex set of ideas and possibilities.

A second key idea in *The World of Goods*, which follows from the general question of how goods are to be understood, is the way they link or differentiate people. Consumption, it is suggested, is a way of belonging to a community. In contrast to those, like Seabrook, who emphasise the isolating effects of consumption, *The World of Goods* offers the idea that mass consumption can constitute a form of sharing. Such an idea is frequently expressed (but rarely analysed) in the study of popular culture where, for example, it is assumed that forms of dress are used to establish a sense of identity. This claim does not just refer to high fashion or bespoke clothes, i.e. clothes which are unique to the individual wearer. It is addressed to mass marketing and mass consumption. In *Adorned in Dreams*, Elizabeth Wilson argues that clothes and fashion are ways by which individuals replace loneliness with a group identity (1985, p. 12). But goods, too, serve to mark the differences between people. This is not just—or even—a matter of 'luxury' goods that betoken status, but rather of goods providing the means to live in a particular way: to marshall time. By this account, and in constrast to Huws' arguments about the burdens of consumption, poverty is experienced as a lack of control and a lack of 'free time'. Consumption is a way of obtaining control.

If goods are to be understood this way, then it is not difficult to see how they might form part of the way in which political ideas and interests are formulated. *The World of Goods* makes two central claims which link with the concerns of political scientists. First, there is the emphasis on the idea of choice which underpins consumption. It is informed choice. This exercise of consumer choice takes on political importance because it constitutes the means by which 'an intelligible universe' is constructed, and in doing this 'the individual uses consumption to say something about himself, his family, his location' (1979, p. 68). In her volume of collected essays, *In the Active Voice*, Mary Douglas reinforces this point in her description of a football fan: 'When he meets an alleged fellow consumer, a few sentences are enough to betray how much they really have in common and whether the joys of shared consumption will be released' (1982, p. 28). Such choices also establish differences and individuality: 'scratch underneath any disagreement on tastes and far-reaching metaphysical differences may be revealed' (1982, p. 73). In a democracy, consumer choices and the world they create are part of the material on which politicians work in attempting to win legitimacy for their views and actions (think of the rhetoric and meaning attached to home ownership). But *The World of Goods* does not just point to the link from citizen to representative or political party. It also raises the issue of the structure and culture within which those goods are used. The meaning and use of goods is dependent upon how items are perceived, who they belong to, and why. The selling of British Telecom (back to the people who already owned it) is an example of the way in which an act of consumption is created and then invested with a particular meaning. Equally, Labour failed to create the culture and conditions by which people felt they owned, and valued, those industries and services which were nationalised in 1945. These general thoughts fit with some specific developments in political science.

The study of voting behaviour is coming to recognise the importance of 'consumption' in explaining the political interests and identities of voters. Consumption, according to this thesis, is an independent variable, and it cannot be subsumed within traditional class accounts of voting behaviour. This theory is not just a reworking of the rational-individualist model of voting behaviour (Downs, 1957), in which the voter is understood to behave as if she or he were a consumer. The consumption model does not use consumption as a metaphor, but as a key variable.

The consumption theory of political behaviour marks a significant advance on earlier attempts to incorporate consumption into accounts of political behaviour. It sets itself against the *embourgeoisement*—or 'fear of fridges'—thesis of the late 1950s and early 1960s which suggested that acquisition of consumer goods led to a change in social status. The *embourgeoisement* thesis, in fact, was a claim about class rather than consumption. It contended that the acquisition of consumer goods altered one's sense of class location, and hence one's voting intentions. The thesis was decisively challenged by the empirical work done by Goldthorpe and Lockwood (1968/9). At a theoretical level, it failed because it offered no account of why consumption should alter social and political perceptions—a fridge is a fridge is a fridge, as Left critics commented.

The consumption theory of voting, by contrast, argues that political interests are significantly influenced by an individual's location in a particular consumption sector. A recent study of class in Britain pointed out that 'there is a clear association between housing tenure and voting intention' (Marshall *et al.*, 1988, p. 234). Dunleavy takes such evidence as indicating that consumption sectors (housing, transport, etc.) determine political alignment. Such sectors may cut across social class so that, for example, working class people who own their own home may place their political interests with middle-class home owners. But there is more at work. Within consumption sectors,

Dunleavy distinguishes between individualised and collective forms of consumption. For Dunleavy, it is the latter which has potential political importance because of the way values and meanings are attached to it. Individualised forms of consumption are explained by reference to household income, which in turn is determined by production relations. By contrast, collectivised consumption is highly politicised, and thereby forms the basis of political cleavages which cut across production interests (Dunleavy, 1979, pp. 418–20). In the collective mode, the key factor is not production, but consumption and its politics.

The political alignments which derive from collective consumption are established by the socially-defined interests which characterise each sector. Although particular consumption sectors under particular conditions will produce voters with particular interests, there is nothing fixed about this arrangement. The organisation of consumption is a political question. It is suggested, for example, that the inner-city working class adopted Labour 'as a means of controlling and ameliorating the operations of the local housing market' (Dunleavy, 1979, p. 433). The organisation and representation of collective consumption is, according to this approach, the way in which people come to acquire their political identity.

Thus, while some political scientists have been trying to write themselves (or rather their colleagues) out of a job by claiming that changes in voting behaviour are determined sociologically by changes in the UK's industrial and social structure, Dunleavy and others, (e.g. Heath *et al.*, 1985) have attempted to keep themselves in work by arguing that political factors are as important as sociological ones in explaining the current distribution of party support in Britain. Put simply, Labour's loss of support cannot just be explained by a decline in the size of the working class. Rather, it has to be accounted for in its failure to develop policies (or implement them when in power) which recognise the importance and meaning of consumption.

But while Dunleavy and others point to the importance of consumption, there are some gaps in their account (Harrop and Miller, 1987, p. 161). While they observe the effect of consumption on political behaviour, they do not explain it. How does experience of consumption become part of a set of political interests? Dunleavy's structuralist account of voting eliminates the process by which high-level political processes are translated into individual political responses. Political scientists need to go beyond the important observation that consumption affects political perceptions to ask how this process works. In doing this, they need to look more closely at the link between consumption and behaviour, and to consider the answers provided by the historian Patrick Wright (1985 and 1988). He argues that home ownership, for instance, is best understood as a means by which a person's public and private worlds are related. Furthermore, as that public world fragments, the private becomes a crucial source of order and control. Whatever the validity of this particular speculation, it does seem that there is a fruitful line of investigation to be pursued which links the idea of goods as means of communication, with the idea that political attitudes change with the organisation and experience of consumption.

Two recent studies of social history point to the wider political importance of consumption. Simon Schama's (1987) study of seventeenth-century Dutch culture not only adds further illustrations of the way goods demarcate ways of life, it also shows how the meaning of consumption was subject to competing public interpretations. Calvinist restraint fought with capitalist ambition to manage 'the embarrassment of riches'. The 'moral ambiguities of materialism' were played out in the more mundane mixture of spending (the pleasure) and domestic housework (the penance), giving form to the deeply ingrained folk-wisdom that 'if their cup ever ran over it would spill into a punishing flood' (Schama, 1987, p. 326). Rosalind Williams's (1982) study of the history of the consumer in nineteenth-century France starts from a similar premise: consumption brings pleasure, but also 'remorse and guilt, craving and envy ... as we sense that we have too much we want more' (p. 4). At one level, this ambivalence finds contemporary political expression in the Green movement, as the price of consumption is seen to be paid in the environment; at another, it is contained in the act of consumption itself where 'hard-headed accounting and dreamy-eyed fantasizing' are merged (Williams, 1982, p. 66). The two interact under the conditions of mass consumption:

> When a consumer decides to buy something, he does so because he has a mental image of how his life might be improved if he, and he alone, owned that object. At the

same time thousands and millions of other consumers may be forming the same mental image and arriving at the same decision. The collective reality which emerges is entirely different from the image that motivated the purchase. (Williams, 1982, p. 272)

The frustrations of the experience of consumption, of unmet desires, suggests that the cash nexus of consumption, where all are formally equal, implicitly threatens structures which seek to treat people unequally or serve them inadequately. Such thoughts seem to underpin recent left analysis of the idea of citizenship (Plant, 1988) and democracy (Kitching, 1983).

Emphasising these ambiguities in consumption focuses on both the experience of consuming and on its organisation. Williams, for example, distinguishes between democratic and elitist forms of consumption. 'Democratic consumers,' she writes, 'sought to make consumption more equal and participatory' and to raise it 'to the level of political and social statement' (1981, p. 110). Elitist consumption was about making an individual statement through consumption. But while these two forms of consumption differ, they share a common feature: they identify consumption as a creative process in which consumers make consumption a political activity.

To illustrate this line of thought, I have chosen an example which may be regarded as both peculiar and perverse. It is a pop song called 'Shopping for clothes'. In three minutes, this song—as delivered in the cool, wry tones of The Coasters—tells the story of a young black man who goes out to buy a suit. The smooth-talking salesman tempts him: 'that suit's pure herring bone'. Our hero falls for it: 'that's the suit I'd like to own'. He asks to sign on the dotted line, as he promises to get his payments in right on time. 'Wait a minute I gotta go back there do a little checkin' on you,' says the voice of authority. And then, curtly disrupting the young man's dreams, 'your credit didn't go through'. 'Pure, pure herring bone', reflects the young man; 'That's a suit you'll never own,' emphasises the salesman. And as the song fades, we hear the shopper plaintively remark, 'I've got a good job sweeping up every day.' Interlaced with this story, the hero displays a sophisticated knowledge of the cuts and styles of suits and of the kind of people who wear them.

In 'Shopping for clothes', the writers Leiber and Stoller eloquently capture the way an everyday consumer experience can become politically charged. However pretentious it may sound, clothes (and the purchasing of them) can be a source of passionate concern, engaging ideas of identity and self-respect. This concern has political, rather than purely personal, dimensions. Not only are there the barriers to consumption created by overtly political processes (access to wealth, practices of discrimination), but there are the statements which the act of consumption itself can make. In observing the dress of the black jazz star, the jazz critic Francis Newton (who doubles as the historian Eric Hobsbawm) wrote:

> he was an enthusiastic and flamboyant dresser, regarding his dress as a symbol of wealth and social status ... If he was a free spender it was for the same reason—casual earnings breed spending—and because his social standing in his world depended on him behaving like a king ... For the star was what every slum child and drudge might become: the king or queen of the poor. (1961, pp. 199–200)

What matters here is not so much whether such interpretations are accurate, but that clothes can form part of the way political goals and ideals are expressed.

There is, of course, no necessary political outcome from the adoption or refusal of certain items of clothing (consider the very different meanings to be attached to military clothes: soldier, terrorist, freedom fighter, follower of fashion). But what clothes do, like other goods, is to help forge identity, a sense of how we fit into the world and what sort of demands we can legitimately make on others. Consumption and citizenship become entwined. Such an idea, it seems, is apparent in *The World of Goods*, and in the work of writers like Judith Williamson and Simon Frith. Williamson and Frith see consumption as a mechanism by which a sense of self is fought for, if not established. Williamson speaks of the passion with which consumption is invested. 'We are consuming passions all the time,' she writes, 'at the shops, at the movies, in the streets, in the classroom' (Williamson, 1986, p. 11). Passion, the expression of our desires, is articulated through the way 'we invest the world with its significance' (Williamson, 1986, p. 14). The political importance of this is that these desires represent a key element in articulating what we want of life, what we identify as 'good'; and the political and economic arrangements both make possible and frustrate these desires. 'Cultural commodities,' writes Frith, 'may support the contemporary power of capital, but they may have their civilising moments, too' (Frith, 1978, p. 206). They are 'civilising' because, in buying these goods, we give some sustenance to our ideal sense of ourselves and our world. We are not simply manipulated, we explore our dreams. It is no coincidence that Rosalind Williams calls her history of consumption *Dream Worlds*, just as Elizabeth Wilson calls her study of women's fashion *Adorned in Dreams*.

The relationship between goods and consumers goes both ways. While consumers try to realise their dreams in consumption, those dreams are themselves a construction of commodity production. Just as we shape consumption, so it shapes us. It is not just that goods are useful *for* thinking, consuming *is* thinking. Furthermore, the thoughts which consumption engenders work both to separate and amalgamate us. It is not just that individuals as consumers and producers may have conflicting interests, nor that consumers will themselves be divided, but also that the process of consuming itself can link us into certain groups, while also establishing a sense of oneself as a discrete individual. So, at one level, being denied the access to goods is a form of disenfranchisement; at another level, we should expect even those with minimal resources to use their goods in politically small, but significant, ways. Teenage cults are classic examples of this: the way a designer label or style of dress (unlaced trainers) establishes membership of a group.

The implication of this is that advertising matters. It is one of the ways in which consumption acquires meaning. This, though, is not a manipulative process. Colin Campbell (1989) argues that it is wrong to see unmanipulated consumption as a 'rational calculation' which is devoid of 'emotion and imagination'. Like Douglas, Campbell doubts the premise upon which this case is made:

consumer behaviour is just as much a matter of emotion and feeling as it is of cognition, as the centrality of the issues of liking and disliking reveal. In fact, the dimension of affective attachment can be said to be more basic to consumption than any issue of rational calculation. There is, therefore, no good reason whatsoever for assuming that the emotional nature of many advertising 'messages' is indicative of the existence of 'manipulation' (or at least, no more than is true of all messages about the product). (Campbell, 1989, p. 48)

This returns us to the issue of the political Left and consumerism. If the meaning of a consumer good is partly a construct of those who market it, then it may be worth noting that, according to one advertising agency, consumer trends in the 1990s are towards 'affluent altruism' or *The Dawn of Us-ism*, as the advertisers' report called it (Rentoul, 1988). While it may be hard to take such evidence seriously, the ideas to be found in *The World of Goods* do suggest that students of politics would do well to study consumption. Much may turn on decisions about the organisation of, and opportunity for, consumption. More fundamentally, perhaps, the emphasis on consumption introduces into conventional politics and political science a set of words which, as Mort and Green point out (1998, p. 33), are not usually part of the vocabulary of formal politics: words like desire and pleasure and fun. While it is hard to imagine Labour riding to victory on the back of market trends towards the dawning Us-ism, it clearly needs to eliminate its 'fear of fridges'. At the same time, the Conservatives cannot assume that affluence and a consumer credit boom, irrespective of their economic implications, will ensure them a dominance in the political market. Consuming is, as Mary Douglas teaches us, a complex business. We clearly need to look cautiously at claims about 'false needs' and manipulation, to look closely at the organisation of the consumption, and to anticipate political challenges from the frustration experienced when the dreams are unfulfilled. We need to recognise, too, that the ability to raise your voice in protest will depend upon your inclusion in the political process; those without access to consumption processes may be rendered speechless. Carolyn Steedman (1986), in her book *Landscape for a Good Woman*, sums up the themes of this chapter better than I can:

My mother's longing shaped my childhood. From a Lancashire mill town and a working-class twenties childhood she came away wanting: fine clothes, glamour, money; to be what she wasn't. However that longing was produced in her distant childhood, what she actually wanted were real things, real entities, things she materially lacked, things that a culture and a social system witheld from her. The story she told was about this wanting, and it remained a resolutely social story. When the world didn't deliver the goods, she held the world to blame. In this way, the story she told was a form of political analysis, that allows a political interpretation to be made of her life. (p. 6)

ACKNOWLEDGEMENTS

My thanks to Sarah Beckwith, Marian Brandon, Shaun Hargreaves Heap, Angus Ross, Simon Frith and all the participants in the Mary Douglas Symposium for their help and comments.

REFERENCES

BLACKWELL, T. and SEABROOK, J. (1985) *A World Still to Win*, London: Faber & Faber.

BOYD, J. (1973) Trends in youth culture, *Marxism Today*, Vol. 13, No. 12, pp. 375–9.

CAMPBELL, C. (1989) *The Romantic Ethic and the Spirit of Modern Consumerism*, Oxford: Basil Blackwell.

DOUGLAS, M. and ISHERWOOD, B. (1979) *The World of Goods*, Harmondsworth: Penguin.

DOUGLAS, M. (1982) *In the Active Voice*, London : RKP.

DOWNS, A. (1957) *An Economic Theory of Democracy*, New York: Harper & Row.

DUNLEAVY, P. (1979) The urban basis of political alignment, *British Journal of Political Science*, Vol. 9, pp. 409–43.

EWEN, S. and E. (1978) Americanization and consumption, *Telos*, Fall, No. 37, pp. 42–51.

FRITH, S. (1978) *The Sociology of Rock*, London: Constable.

GOLDTHORPE, J. *et al.* (1968/9) *The Affluent Worker*, 3 vols., Cambridge: Cambridge University Press.

HARROP, M. and MILLER, W. L. (1987) *Elections and Voters*, London: Macmillan.

HAUG, W. F. (1986) *Critique of Commodity Aesthetics*, Oxford: Polity.

HEATH, A., JOWELL, J. and CURTICE, J. (1985) *How Britain Votes*, Oxford: Pergamon.

HIRSCH, F. (1977) *Social Limits to Growth*, London: RKP.

HUWS, U. (1988) 'Consumption', paper delivered to the Fabian Society conference on *Democratic Socialist Aims and Values*. (A revised version appeared as 'Consuming Passions', *New Statesman and Society*, 19 August, pp. 31–4.)

MARSHALL, G., *et al.* (1988) *Social Class in Modern Britain*, London: Hutchinson.

MORT, F. and GREEN, N. (1988) You've never had it so good— Again!, *Marxism Today*, May, pp. 30–3.

NEWTON. F. (1961) *The Jazz Scene*, Harmondsworth: Penguin.

RENTOUL, J. (1988) Who's afraid of the big bad fridge? *New Statesman*, 3 June, p. 14.

SCHAMA, S. (1987) *The Embarrassment of Riches*, London: Collins.

SEABROOK, J. (1985) *Landscape of Poverty*, Oxford: Blackwell.

STEEDMAN, C. (1986) *Landscape for a Good Woman*, London: Virago.

WILLIAMS, R. H. (1982) *Dream Worlds*, Berkeley and LA: University of California Press.

WILLIAMS, R. (1976) *Keywords*, London: Fontana.

WILLIAMSON, J. (1986) *Consuming Passions*, London: Marion Boyars.

WILSON, E. (1985) *Adorned in Dreams*, London: Virago.

WRIGHT, P. (1988) Brideshead and the tower blocks, *London Review of Books*, 2 June, pp. 3–7.

WRIGHT, P. (1985) *On Living in an Old Country*, London: Verso.

11

Naturalness and the spontaneous order of the market

ROBERT SUGDEN

Here is an economist, reviewing a book on market socialism: '[The author] gives the ... impression of not being sufficiently aware of the tremendous forces at work. His market socialist satellite would not find it at all easy to orbit capitalism without being drawn into its gravitational pull' (Collard, 1990). David Collard's satellite is a modern version of a common metaphor of economics, in which the workings of the market system are likened to natural forces. The tremendous forces of capitalism, it is suggested, are like the gravitational pull of a planet; in comparison, a market-socialist economy is like a man-made satellite, which will crash unless it is sent on exactly the right trajectory.

This chapter is an attempt to examine the analogy between natural forces and the workings of markets. The inspiration for the paper comes from Mary Douglas's *How Institutions Think* (1987). Drawing on a mass of anthropological evidence from primitive societies, Douglas argues that the institutions of any society are ultimately grounded in individual interest. An institution, she says, is a self-policing convention; it maintains itself primarily because it is in the interest of each individual to follow its rules. It is a mistake to suppose, as economists writing on modern societies often do, that individuals in primitive societies are motivated by their religious beliefs to follow customary rules. These people are not so different from us: 'The individual cost-benefit analysis applies inexorably and enlighteningly to the smallest micro-exchanges, with them as well as us' (p. 29).

An institution is more than a convention; it is a convention that, for the people who follow it, has *legitimacy*. Although an institution is only a social contrivance, its successful working depends on its not being thought of as such. Douglas interprets the religious and cosmological beliefs of primitive societies as devices that have grown up to legitimate the institutions of those societies. These beliefs typically take the form of analogies between the institutions of the society and the natural world. 'To acquire legitimacy,' she writes, 'every kind of institution needs a formula that founds its rightness in reason and in nature' (p. 45). I take this to mean that if a society is to survive and replicate itself, it must propagate a system of beliefs in which its own institutions are seen as extensions of the natural world.

Could this also be true for us as well as for them, for modern societies as well as for primitive ones? Do we need to be able to legitimate our institutions through analogies with the natural world? I shall be posing these questions in relation to the institution of the market, and in particular, to the distribution of income generated by a market economy. In a market economy the rewards that individuals receive are often uncorrelated with any kind of desert. The industrial revolution provides many tragic examples of this generalisation. Men built their lives around the expectation that the trades they learned as apprentices would provide them with a decent standard of living; they had no way of foreseeing that new technologies would make their skills worthless. Unforeseen and undeserved gains and losses are an essential part of a market economy. In a society whose economy is based on the market, these gains and losses must in some way be legitimated. If Douglas is right, we might expect the defenders of the market to make some kind of appeal to nature, to the *naturalness* of the market.

I shall be looking at the work of Friedrich Hayek, who has provided the most profound defence of the market system in our time. Hayek sees the market as *spontaneous order*. I shall examine Hayek's idea of spontaneity, and how it connects with the idea of naturalness. But first I shall look at two great eighteenth-century thinkers who developed the idea of spontaneous order, and whose work has greatly influenced Hayek— David Hume and Adam Smith.

THE NATURAL AND THE ARTIFICIAL IN HUME'S TREATISE

In his *Treatise of Human Nature* (1740/1978), Hume explains the origins of rules of justice in terms of spontaneous order: they are the product of a gradual process of social evolution. But Hume constantly stresses that justice is an 'artificial' and not a 'natural' virtue. For Hume, a natural virtue is one which is embedded in human nature—one which, to use modern language, is part of the genetic endowment of our species. Benevolence, for example, is a natural virtue. Our propensity to sympathise with one another's pleasures and pains is part of human nature. The force of this sympathy depends on the perceived degree of closeness between the two people; it is strengthened by physical closeness, by similarity of manners, character, custom and language, by blood relation and by long acquaintance (pp. 317–18). Thus 'there is no human, and indeed no sensible, creature, whose happiness or misery does not, in some measure, affect us, when brought near to us, and represented in lively colours' (p. 481); this property of our minds can even be manipulated by dramatists so that we feel sympathy for pleasures and pains that we know not to exist (p. 369). Such natural sympathy provides the motivation for spontaneous acts of generosity to people who are in distress (p. 579).

It is characteristic of a natural virtue that it produces behaviour that is psychologically rather than rationally consistent. Thus, to give a modern example, someone might give generously to the beggars she sees on holiday in India, and then on returning home, give nothing to a charity that is working to relieve Indian poverty in a systematic way. All things considered, the natural tendency to benevolence works for the general good; but it is too partial and too unsystematic to regulate the interactions of people in a large society. For that, we need a sense of justice.

To act justly is to follow rules. These rules, unlike the principles which determine our sympathetic feelings, are external to our minds. For example, justice requires one to repay a debt. The motive to repay a debt is not a feeling of benevolence towards the creditor. We are often under obligations of justice to people with whom we have little sympathy, and to whom we would feel no inclination to make a gift. Nor is the motive a feeling of 'public benevolence' towards mankind in general. There is, Hume asserts, 'no such passion in human minds, as the love of mankind, merely as such, independent of personal qualities, of services, or of relation to ourself' (pp. 479–81). We need to explain why people are motivated to follow particular rules of justice, and these rules are far too complicated, and differ too much in detail between cultures, to be natural.

Hume then offers an explanation of 'the origin of justice and property'. Man is a social animal, not naturally equipped to live in isolation. The original instincts to form social groups are sexual, maternal and paternal; these produce the family unit (p. 486). Hume seems to suggest that larger societies evolve from the family. It must be said that much of his discussion reads like a social contract theory. He points to the advantages that all human beings gain from social life (the ability to co-ordinate attack and defence, mutual aid, the division of labour). He then says that society is impossible without some rules of mutual restraint, and in particular, rules to secure the stability of property. These rules are not natural but must be created by man. This requires 'a convention enter'd into by all the members of the society to bestow stability on the possession of those external goods [i.e. goods which can easily be transferred from person to person], and leave everyone in the peaceable enjoyment of what he may acquire by his fortune and industry' (p. 489)

But though Hume, like social contract theorists, uses the language of agreement, he insists that this agreement is never made explicitly. There is, he says, only a 'general sense of common interest; which all the members of the society express to one another, and which induces them to regulate their conduct by certain rules'; the rule of property 'arises gradually, and acquires force by a slow progression, and by our repeated experience of the inconveniences of transgressing it'; the process is similar to that by which languages become established (p. 490). It seems clear that what Hume has in mind is a process of social evolution, in which the driving force is each individual's pursuit of his private interests. In this sense the rules of justice, though not natural, constitute a spontaneous order.

It is an essential part of Hume's argument that stability of possession works to the benefit of all; indeed, he seems to regard this as an adeqate explanation of the evolution of property. Hume sometimes uses the same kind of argument to explain the details of the rules of property, as when he says that the right of succession is natural because it is in 'the general interest of mankind ... that men's possessions shou'd pass to those, who are dearest to them, in order to render them more industrious and frugal' (p. 511). But at other times he draws on his theory of the workings of the human mind and argues that the details of property rules are grounded in the 'imagination' rather than in 'reason and public interest' (p. 506). Since property is a relation between a person and an object, it is natural for the mind to associate this relation with other relations between persons and objects, such as first possession; thus people are inclined to assign property rights to first possessors. Similarly, the rule of succession can be explained in terms of a conjunction of relations: the dead parent's property stands in a relation with the parent, and the parent stands in another relation with the surviving child; thus it is natural to associate the parent's property with the child (pp. 512–13).

Some commentators, such as Brian Barry (1989, pp. 346–7) and J. L. Mackie (1980, pp. 95–6), have seen Hume's discussion of the role of imagination as an unconvincing digression from his main argument about the *utility* of rules of property. But are we entitled to assume that the process of evolution will always produce those rules that are most efficient at promoting individuals' interests? We need an analysis of *how* property rules evolve out of self-interested behaviour. One possibility is that these rules were the product of conscious design, perhaps within the families which Hume sees as the original societies; then it is perhaps plausible to suppose that the rules would be chosen on grounds of utility. But then their utility would need to be understood in relation to societies very different from our own, just as our genetic endowment is adapted to a very different form of life than we now live.

Another possibility, however, is that rules of property were never consciously designed, but evolved as resolutions of conflicts between individuals or families. Thomas Schelling (1960) has shown how games of conflict are often resolved by the use of shared ideas of *prominence*; thus, for example, two opposing military commanders who each wish to advance as far as possible without coming into conflict with the other may recognise a river as the 'obvious' or 'natural' boundary between them. Schelling's concept of prominence has many similarities with Hume's ideas about the role of imagination in determining rules of property. I have argued elsewhere that the process of social evolution will tend to generate shared ideas of prominence, and that these ideas will be embodied in the rules of property that evolve (Sugden, 1986).

If we accept, as Hume clearly does, that the rules of property have emerged from an historical process, then we must expect these rules to reflect the contingencies of history. They cannot be explained as if they were consciously-designed and rationally-chosen solutions to the problems of the societies we now observe. Hume recognises this. For Hume, the broad features of property rules are universal, because they are a solution to universal human problems, or because they result from natural properties of the human mind. But the finer details are historical and cultural variables. Thus, for example, it is a universal feature of property rules that first possession counts for something; but how first possession is defined, and how much importance is given to first possession as against long occupation, are variables (pp. 501–13).

But this leads to a problem. If the rules of property we observe are the product of a chain of historical contingencies, how do they come to be morally binding on us? What gives them legitmacy? Suppose, for example, that I am the second son of a father who owned a great deal of land and has just died. Suppose there is a rule of primogeniture. I can see that this rule works against all my interests; my whole life would be better if it were the rule that all children inherited equally. Each of these rules can readily be explained in terms of the workings of the imagination; either might have evolved, but only one has. Why should I accept a rule which harms me, when it is no more than an historical accident?

The question can be posed in two different ways. One way is in terms of the morality of *individual* action in the context of a given society: does justice require me to abide by the established rules? Thus we might ask whether it would be just for the second son to compensate himself by stealing some of the first son's wealth, given that they live in a society in which primogeniture is the established rule. The second way is in terms of *political* action to change the established rules: are the rules just? Thus we might ask whether legislation to change the rule from primogeniture to equal division would be just.

When Hume explains 'why we annex the idea of virtue to justice', he is thinking in terms of the first of these questions. He argues that everyone benefits from the rules which secure the stability of possessions, and that 'disorder and confusion follow upon every breach of these rules'. In a large society, self-interest may tempt an individual to break the rules, but an impartial observer will recognise that such action is harmful to society as a whole. According to Hume, our ideas of virtue and vice correspond with the judgements we would make from the viewpoint of an impartial spectator. This provides a coherent account of why justice is a virtue, of why the rules of justice that happen to have evolved are regarded as morally binding on individuals. The further question, 'But are those rules just?', would perhaps not occur to someone writing in the middle of the eighteenth century. But in the twentieth century, it cannot be evaded.

ADAM SMITH AND THE SPONTANEOUS ORDER OF THE MARKET

The idea of spontaneous order is much more central to the work of Adam Smith. Smith begins *The Wealth of Nations* with a description of the division of labour in the economy of his time. This displays for our wonder the enormous complexity of the economic system. Even the coarse woollen coat of a common day-labourer is the product of the co-ordinated efforts of thousands of workers from all round the world: the shepherds, the wool-trade workers, the merchants and carriers, the ship-builders and sailors, the suppliers of tools for all these trades, and so on, and so on. Although we think of the labourer as poor, his standard of living is still something to be marvelled at—far better than that of 'many an African king, the absolute master of the lives and liberties of ten thousand naked savages' (1776/1976, pp. 22–4). How, we wonder, has all this been achieved? Then Smith gives us the answer.

> This division of labour, from which so many advantages are derived, is not originally the effect of any human wisdom, which foresees and intends that general opulence to which it gives occasion. It is the necessary, though very slow and gradual consequence of a certain propensity in human nature which has in view no such extensive utility; the propensity to truck, barter, and exchange one thing for another. (p. 25)

This theme pervades *The Wealth of Nations*. A market economy is driven by the independent efforts of individuals to increase their own wealth; the unintended consequence is that the wealth of the whole society increases. Smith sometimes uses the metaphor of the machine to present this conception of a self-regulating economic system. For example, he describes trade restrictions as 'a dead weight upon the action of one of the great springs which puts into motion a great part of the business of mankind'; they 'cramp' and 'clog' the workings of the system (pp. 592–3). At other times he uses the metaphor of the body. He argues that because Britain has monopolised the trade of its American colonies, its economy has become over-specialised so that 'it resembles one of those unwholesome bodies in which some of the vital parts are overgrown, and which, upon that account, are liable to many dangerous disorders scarce incident to those in which all parts are more properly proportioned'; if trade restrictions were gradually relaxed, the different branches of British industry could be restored to 'natural, healthful and proper proportion' (pp. 604–6). Arguing that the forces of individal enterprise are strong enough to overcome many legal restrictions, he remarks that the human body seems capable of maintaining a state of perfect health even under unwholesome regimens of diet and exercise:

> [T]he healthful state of the human body, it would seem, contains in itself some unknown principle of preservation, capable either of preventing or of correcting in many respects, the bad effects even of a very faulty regimen. ... [I]n the political body, the natural effort which every man is continually making to better his own condition is a principle of preservation capable of preventing and correcting, in many respects, the bad effects of a political economy, in some degree, both partial and oppressive. Such a political economy, though it no doubt retards more or less, is not always capable of stopping altogether the natural progress of a nation towards wealth and prosperity, and still less of making it go backwards. (p. 674)

Lying behind these metaphors is the idea that the unregulated economic system is a mechanism that is part of the natural world, and that the natural world is the design of a benevolent God. Smith's adherence to natural religion seems beyond doubt. This commitment is, I think, nicely revealed in a phrase in the *Theory of Moral Sentiments*, where Smith is mentioning some of the topics that people might discuss in an impersonal way.

Among these are 'the various appearances which the great machine of the universe is perpetually exhibiting, with the secret wheels and springs which produce them' (1759/1976), p. 19). Here again we have the idea of the universe as an intricate machine, working according to natural laws which in principle man is capable of understanding, but reflecting the design of a Being infinitely superior to man.

From this kind of natural religion, it seems a short step to the idea that it is wrong to interfere in the workings of the great machine of the universe. If Smith can say that the unregulated economic system is part of this machine, and that regulation by government is not, then he can perform the manoeuvre described by Douglas; he can found the rightness of a human institution in nature. The difficulty, however, is that *all* human action is part of the natural world. How can we say that the regulations which legislators impose on trade are dead weights on the machine and not more springs and wheels?

One of the ways in which Smith answers this question is familiar to all economists. He sets out to show that the unregulated market promotes human prosperity. Since we can presume that a benevolent God intends us to prosper, we are entitled to expect a machine designed by God to have this function. Human actions are unnatural to the extent that they prevent the machine from carrying out its intended function. Of course, this line of argument ultimately makes God and nature redundant. The fundamental criterion for appraising an institution is its contribution to human prosperity; the distinction between natural and unnatural seems to be doing no work, except as a rhetorical device. But it is still significant that Smith should be attracted by this device—that he should feel the need to establish the naturalness of the market.

Smith is on his strongest ground when he argues that an unregulated market is the most effective institution for increasing the *total* wealth of a society. In criticising the attempts of governments to intervene in the workings of the market, Smith argues that no single mind could possibly have the knowledge necessary to direct the resources of a nation to their most productive uses; each individual must be allowed to make the best use of his own knowledge and of the opportunities he can see.

But this kind of argument cannot be used in relation to

government action to influence the *distribution* of income. Have we any reason to expect the market to generate the distribution of income that a benevolent God would have chosen? Smith does not make the implausible claim that, in the natural order of things, the distribution of income corresponds with need or moral desert. Instead he claims that the rules of the market correspond with the principles of *natural justice* and *natural liberty*.

The idea of natural justice is a recurring theme in *The Wealth of Nations*. Smith's term for the market system is 'the system of natural liberty' (e.g. p. 687). In the system of natural liberty: 'Every man, as long as he does not violate the laws of justice, is left perfectly free to pursue his own interest in his own way, and to bring his industry and capital into competition with those of any other man, or order of men' (p. 687). Similarly, in a society in which 'things were left to follow their natural course, where there was perfect liberty', every man would be 'perfectly free both to chuse what occupation he thought proper, and to change it as often he thought proper' (p. 116). This is a matter of right:

> The property which every man has in his own labour, as it is the original foundation of all other property, so it is the most sacred and inviolable. The patrimony of a poor man lies in the strength and dexterity of his hands; and to hinder him from employing this strength and dexterity in what manner he thinks proper without injury to his neighbour is a plain violation of this most sacred property. It is a manifest encroachment upon the just liberty both of the workman and of those who might be disposed to employ him. (p. 138)

Each person, then, has a natural right to use his labour and his possessions in any way that he sees fit, subject only to the property rights of others. Force, theft and fraud are unjust. So too are laws which give monopoly rights to particular traders, or enforce apprenticeship systems, or restrict the free movement of labour between areas. Notice that laws of this kind do not work unambiguously against human prosperity, but tend to make some people better-off at the expense of others. Smith's attack on such laws depends crucially on his conception of natural rights.

But what makes these rights natural? Smith provides no

answer to this question in *The Wealth of Nations*. We must go back to his discussion of justice in *The Theory of Moral Sentiments* (pp. 78–91). Here Smith argues against Hume's claim that justice is an artificial virtue. Recall that for Hume, the rules of justice are human conventions, and our approval of justice results from our recognition of the general utility of these rules. Smith disagrees, arguing that our resentment at acts of injustice, and our desire to retaliate for them, are original principles of human nature. It is true that this sense of justice is useful to us, since society would be impossible without it; but this is another case of secret wheels and springs. By acting on our natural passions we are led to promote an end which we have never intended. Smith uses his favourite metaphors of the human body and the machine. Our blood does not circulate with the intention of preserving our lives, but that is its function. The wheels of the watch do not turn with the intention of telling the time, but that is their function:

> But though, in accounting for the operations of bodies, we never fail to distinguish in this manner the efficient from the final cause, in accounting for those of the mind we are very apt to confound these two different things with one another. When by natural principles we are led to advance those ends, which a refined and enlightened reason would recommend to us, we are very apt to impute to that reason, as to their efficient cause, the sentiments and actions by which we advance those ends, and to imagine that to be the wisdom of man, which in reality is the wisdom of God. (1759/1976, p. 87)

Smith argues that we discover general moral rules by a process of induction. Thus the first person to see an act of murder would naturally condemn it, without any sense that murder was a category of unjust acts; but as we accumulate experience of the kinds of acts that inspire our abhorrence and resentment, we learn that our natural responses have a pattern, which we call a moral rule (pp. 159–60).

Smith is pointing to a genuine weakness in Hume's theory of justice. At the psychological level, Hume's claim that our resentment at injustice rests on some kind of utilitarian calculation does not ring true; resentment seems to be a more primitive response than this. But at the same time, it is hard to deny the truth of Hume's conclusion that the rules of justice, at least in matters of detail, are matters of convention which vary across ages and cultures. These rules are not instincts. It may be that, as Smith claims, there is an instinct to retaliate against attack, but what counts as an attack must in some degree be a matter of convention.

Smith never really addresses Hume's argument about the conventional nature of justice. He seems to take it as self-evident that we have a natural inclination to resent any violation of those particular principles which define the system of natural liberty. Thus, for example, Smith says:

> In the race for wealth, and honours, and preferments, [each man] may run as hard as he can, and strain every nerve and every muscle, in order to outstrip all his competitors. But if he should jostle, or throw down any of them, the indulgence of the spectators is entirely at an end. It is a violation of fair play, which they cannot admit of. ... They readily, therefore, sympathize with the natural resentment of the injured, and the offender becomes the object of their hatred and indignation. (1759/1976), p. 83)

But the metaphor of the race tells against Smith's argument. The rule against jostling in a running race is certainly not natural; it is human convention. (In a game of rugby, the action of bringing down an opponent may be applauded by a neutral spectator.) The resentment of the runner who is jostled may be natural enough, but it occurs only in the context of a man-made rule of fair play. Smith's principles of natural liberty may, it seems, be no more than human conventions.

HAYEK'S CONCEPTION OF SPONTANEOUS ORDER

The work of Friedrich Hayek, particularly his *Constitution of Liberty* (1960) and the three volumes of *Law, Legislation and Liberty* (1973, 1976, 1979), represents an attempt to re-state the insights of Hume, Smith and other classical liberals for twentieth-century readers. Like Smith, Hayek sees the market as a spontaneous order, and argues that (subject to some important exceptions) governments ought to interfere with its workings as little as possible.

Hayek's conception of the market system is somewhat different from Smith's. Where Smith uses the metaphors of the machine and the human body (and Smith thinks of the human body as a kind of machine), Hayek speaks of growth, spontaneity and evolution. Casting around for a suitable label for his political position, he says he wants a name for 'the party of life' the party that favours free growth and spontaneous evolution' (1960, p. 408). Phrases such as 'spontaneous change', 'undesigned change', 'freely grown institutions' and 'the growth of the undesigned' recur throughout the *Constitution of Liberty*. For Hayek, the market is a process, like biological evolution, rather than an intricate machine, like a watch; although we can understand the general principles which drive the process, we cannot predict its outcomes. This difference may in part reflect different understandings of the natural world; Hayek knows much more than Smith could possibly know about biological evolution.

Smith sees the division of labour as the main mechanism by which the market increases human prosperity. Hayek emphasises the division of knowledge. No single mind, Hayek argues, can comprehend more than a tiny fraction of the body of human knowledge. The market puts all this knowledge to use, by allowing each person to act on what he knows; it can thus achieve feats of co-ordination that are beyond the powers of any planner:

> Knowledge exists only as the knowledge of individuals. It is not much better than a metaphor to speak of the knowledge of society as a whole. The sum of the knowledge of all the individuals exists nowhere as an integrated whole. The great problem is how we can all profit from this knowledge, which exists only dispersed as the separate, partial, and sometimes conflicting beliefs of all men. (1960, pp. 24–5)

The market provides the solution to this great problem. So far, this is not dissimilar to Smith's (1776/1976, p. 687) argument that no human wisdom or knowledge could ever be sufficient for the duty of superintending the industry of private people. But Hayek goes beyond Smith in stressing the *discovery* of knowledge. Hayek sees the market as an outstandingly effective procedure for discovering useful knowledge.

The market's success as a discovery process is the result of two properties. First, a market economy has a very large number of centres of planning; each individual, or at least each family, is an agent which makes its own plans in the light of its own knowledge, beliefs and objectives. As a result, many experiments are made; although many fail, some succeed and can be imitated by others:

> Liberty is essential to leave room for the unforeseeable and unpredictable; we want it because we have learned to expect from it the opportunity of realizing many of our aims. It is because every individual knows so little and, in particular, because we rarely know which of us knows best that we trust the independent and competitive efforts of many to induce the emergence of what we shall want when we see it. (1960, p. 29)

But it is not enough to have experiments; these need to be directed towards the discovery of what is useful. This is where the second property of the market comes in. In a market, each person is rewarded according to the value of his contribution to other people's plans, as valued by those people. Thus a person is rewarded for discovering new ways of assisting other people in the pursuit of their aims—for discovering what is useful to others. This reward attract yet others to imitate the first person. Within the basic framework set by the rules of the market, there is thus a continuous process of change, as new practices (new ways of making things, new ways of organising firms, new markets for existing goods, new kinds of goods, and so on) are discovered and imitated.

This is the process of spontaneous change and free growth. It is 'spontaneous' and 'free' in the sense that its outcomes are not the result of conscious design, and cannot be foreseen. However, our understanding of the general rules of the process allows us to predict that it will lead to the growth of practices that benefit us, even though we cannot predict what those practices will be.

Hayek sometimes makes the much more general claim that, in *any* society, rules of conduct that are beneficial to the members of that society will tend to evolve, since the groups which practise the most beneficial rules will tend to be most 'successful' and so 'displace' the others (e.g. 1973, pp. 17–9). On this view, the mere existence and survival of a rule of conduct is evidence of the benefits of that rule. Thus we might seek to justify the market, not by showing that it tends to promote the spontaneous growth of beneficial practices, but by showing that its rules are themselves the result of spontaneous growth in some more fundamental process. But this way of defending the market is, I think, much less convincing. Hayek does not provide any real analysis of how, in general, successful groups displace less successful ones, while his conception of the market as a discovery process is a profound contribution to economic theory. It would be ironic if the former analysis made the latter redundant.

Further, as many readers of Hayek have pointed out, it is not clear that there is any consistent historical tendency for market societies to displace other kinds of society. In North America and Western Europe the general trend from the middle of the nineteenth century has been towards greater intervention in markets by governments. Hayek is well aware of this trend, and tries to persuade us that it should be reversed—presumably through the political process. Using the term 'liberalism' for his own position, and contrasting this with conservatism, Hayek says:

> Liberalism is not averse to evolution and change; and where spontaneous change has been smothered by govern-ment control, it wants a great deal of change of policy. So far as much of current governmental action is concerned, there is in the present world very little reason for the liberal to wish to preserve things as they are. It would seem to the liberal, indeed, that what is most urgently needed in most parts of the world is a thorough sweeping-away of the obstacles to free growth. (1960, p. 399)

All this seems to imply that we must think of the set of rules which establish the market as a social contrivance, to be justified by its utility and not by its spontaneity. Spontaneity is a property of the *consequences* of following these rules; the utility of the rules derives from the generally good properties we can expect these consequences to have. Thus Hayek is in much the same position as Smith: recall that Smith has to show that the market promotes human prosperity in order to support his claim that it, and not the actions of the governments that restrict it, is part of God's design for the universe.

This leaves Hayek with the problem of giving legitimacy to the distributional consequences of the market. The most consis-tent line for him to take, I think, is to argue that, although these consequences are sometimes unfair and distressing, they are the necessary price we have to pay for the many advantages we get from the market. And Hayek often does argue this. He is clear-sighted in recognising that the rewards given by the market are often unrelated to merit or desert; a large part is played by luck. Nevertheless, he says, it is an essential part of the market system that rewards are based on the *actual* contribution that a person makes to the aims of others; this is what provides the incentive to try to discover what is useful to others, and to imitate those who do discover this:

> [T]o hold out a sufficient incentive for those movements which are required to maintain a market order, it will often be necessary that the return of people's efforts do *not* correspond to recognizable merit. ... The long and the short of it is that men can be allowed to decide what work to do only if the remuneration they can expect to get for it corresponds to the value their services have to those of their fellows who receive them; and that *these values which their services will have to their fellows will often have no relation to their individual merits or needs.* (1976, p. 72)

What, then, are we to say to those who, through no fault of their own, come out as losers? One (rather Humean) answer is that the rules of the market, considered as a whole, work to *everyone's* benefit; each of us must accept occasional losses as the price of these more general benefits. This claim can be made more plausible by conceiving of benefit in terms of long-run expectations; in this sense we may all benefit from the market *ex ante,* even though some of us turn out to be losers *ex post.* Thus:

> [I]t should be obvious that we will achieve the best results if we abide by a rule which, if consistently applied, is likely to increase everyone's chances. Though the share of each will be unpredictable, because it will depend only in part on his skill and opportunities to learn facts, and in part on accident, this is the condition which alone will make it the interest of all so to conduct themselves as to make as large as possible the aggregate product of which they will get an unpredictable share. (1976, p. 122)

In a similar vein, Hayek (1960, pp. 90–1) argues for allowing private inheritance, even though this will generate substantial and unmerited inequalities; his main argument is that the possibility of leaving one's wealth to one's children has a useful incentive effect.

From Hayek's point of view, the problem with arguments of this kind is that they open the way to trade-offs. We might grant that a totally planned economy would eventually make everyone worse off than they would have been in a market society—at least if that market society had, as Hayek advocates, some minimal safety-net of income support. (If this proposition now seems trite, we should remember that many people in the 1930s would have thought it absurd. Our present understanding of the problems of planning owes an enormous amount to Hayek's early work.) But there are degrees of intervention. Is it so clear that Hayek's almost unconstrained market would benefit *everyone* more than, say a German-style social market or a Swedish-style welfare state? Or that the disincentive effects of a tax on inheritances outweigh the benefits of a more equal distribution of wealth?

To justify the distribution of income generated by the market, Smith had to rely on arguments about natural rights as well as on arguments about general utility. Hayek seems to need some comparable device to complete his defence of the market. This, I think, is to be found in his argument that the concept of social justice is meaningless. He tries to show that the person who loses from the workings of the market has no basis for making any kind of claim on the rest of society.

This line of argument appears in *The Constitution of Liberty* when Hayek asks whether, in a market economy, one person's 'witholding a benefit' from another can be counted as coercive:

> The use of such power by another may indeed alter the social landscape to which I have adapted my plans and make it necessary for me to reconsider all my decisions, perhaps to change my whole scheme of life and to worry about many things I had taken for granted. But, though the alternatives before me may be distressingly few and uncertain, and my new plans of a makeshift character, yet it is not some other will that guides my action. I may have to act under great pressure, but I cannot be said to act under coercion. Even if the threat of starvation to me and perhaps to my family impels me to accept a distasteful job at a very low wage, even if I am 'at the mercy' of the only man willing to employ me, I am not coerced by him or by anybody else. So long as the act that has placed me in my predicament is not aimed at making me do or not do specific things, so long as the intent of the act that harms me is not to make me serve another person's ends, its effect

on my freedom is not different from that of any natural
calamity—a fire or a flood that destroys my house or an
accident that harms my health. (Hayek, p. 137)

Notice the analogy between the impersonal forces of the
market and the natural forces of fire and flood. There is a sense
in which the person who has been harmed has been harmed as a
result of the actions of other people. (The craftsman whose
livelihood is destroyed by a change in fashion has been harmed
by the consumers who choose to stop buying the goods he is
skilled at producing.) But these others have not intended to
harm him, or to make him serve their ends; they have simply
pursued their own ends. Thus, Hayek says, the first person has
not been coerced; his freedom has not been invaded, any more
that it would have been invaded if he had been harmed by a
natural accident.

Can this person claim to be the victim of any injustice? Again
Hayek says 'No'. In a passage in *Law, Legislation and Liberty*, he
recognises that we all often feel that life is unjust: 'the deserving
suffer and the unworthy prosper'. And when effort is rewarded,
we feel a sense of satisfaction or fitness. But:

[W]e experience the same feelings also with respect to
differences in human fates for which clearly no human
agency is responsible and which it would therefore clearly
be absurd to call injustice. Yet we do cry out against the
injustice when a succession of calamities befalls one family
while another family steadily prospers, when a meritorious
effort is frustrated by some unforeseeable accident, and
particularly if of many people whose endeavours seem
equally great, some succeed brilliantly while others utterly
fail. ... And we will protest against such a fate although we
do not know anyone who is to blame for it, or any way
in which such disappointments can be prevented. (1976,
pp. 68–9)

Here again we have the analogy between losses inflicted by the
market and natural calamities. In neither case is there any
genuine injustice, because no one has acted unjustly: 'there is no
individual and no co-operating group of individuals against
which the sufferer would have a just complaint' (p. 69).

Clearly it is true that, *within the rules of the market*, there is no
ground for complaint. But does this mean that the concept of
social justice is 'strictly empty and meaningless' (1976, p. 68)? It

does, but only if we have already accepted those rules as morally binding. (This is precisely what Smith does when he invokes natural justice.) But if instead we say that these rules are only social contrivances, to be justified by their general utility, then it seems that one might complain that the rules themselves are unjust—that the society, through its political process, ought to change the rules. Hayek seems to be urging us to forget that the rules of the market are, in Hume's sense, artifical. We are being asked to treat them as though they were natural laws—just as Smith does.

There are even faint echoes of Smith's natural religion in Hayek's professions of faith in the value of progress. For Hayek, 'progress' summarises the kind of changes we can expect if we follow the rules of the market order—'progress in the sense of the cumulative growth of knowledge and power over nature'. Hayek admits, with typical honesty, that progress may not make us any happier:

> Though progress consists in part in achieving things we have been striving for, this does not mean that we shall like all its results or that all will be gainers. And since our wishes and aims are also subject to change in the course of the process, it is questionable whether the statement has any meaning that the new state of affairs that progress creates is a better one. (1960, p. 41)

In the course of progress, much may be lost. Hayek mentions the peasants of the remote mountainous areas of Europe, whose cherished ways of life are being destroyed by economic developments. He is sympathetic, but can counsel only a Stoic acceptance of the inevitable: every human being, after all, 'is being led by the growth of civilization into a path that is not his own choosing' (1960, p. 50). Hayek is still ready to urge us to have 'courage and confidence', to be prepared 'to let change run its course even if we cannot predict where it will lead' (p. 400). And he can dedicate *The Constitution of Liberty* 'to the unknown civilization that is growing in America'. It is almost as if some great plan, beyond human understanding, is unfolding.

In Hayek's writing we get glimpses of a distinctive conception of virtue. This, we might say, is a conception of virtue that could underpin a market order; it is virtue for an enterprise culture. Progress depends on the willingness of individuals to act on their own beliefs even (and perhaps especially) when others' beliefs are different. This requires courage and self-reliance. Some people's plans will succeed, while others will fail; success and failure cannot be foreseen. The failures are as necessary a part of progress as the successes, and those who fail may be as meritorious as those who succeed. In success, then, we should show humility, recognising 'how uncertain is the connection between [market] value and merit' (1960, pp. 98–9). In failure, we should show self-command, accepting the cards that fate has dealt us. We should see the insignificance of our own successes and failures when set against the whole scheme of progress—a scheme which we believe to be in some way the proper destiny of mankind.

This is a humanist form of Smith's natural religion, with the same Stoical undercurrents. It is in many ways an inspiring vision. That it can inspire us is, I think, a testimony to the truth of Mary Douglas's insight, that we all feel a need to conceive of our institutions as part of the natural order. But however important the belief in the naturalness of our institutions may be in securing their stability, whatever psychological needs of ours it may satisfy, we must still ask whether it is true. And in the end, I have to side with Hume.

REFERENCES

BARRY, Brian (1989) *Theories of Justice*, Hemel Hempstead: Harvester-Wheatsheaf.

COLLARD, David (1990), Review of *Market, State and Community* by David Miller, *Times Higher Education Supplement*, 23 March, p. 20

DOUGLAS, Mary (1987) *How Institutions Think*, London: Routledge & Kegan Paul.

HAYEK, Friedrich (1960) *The Constitution of Liberty*, London: Routledge & Kegan Paul.

HAYEK, Friedrich (1973, 1976, 1979) *Law, Legislation and Liberty*, Chicago: University of Chicago Press. Vol. 1: 1973; Vol. 2: 1976; Vol. 3: 1979.

HUME, David (1740/1978) *A Treatise of Human Nature*, edited by L. A. Selby-Bigge, Oxford: Clarendon Press.

MACKIE, J. L. (1980) *Hume's Moral Theory*, London: Routledge & Kegan Paul.

SCHELLING, Thomas (1960) *The Strategy of Conflict*, Cambridge, Mass.: Harvard University Press.

SMITH, Adam (1759/1976) *The Theory of Moral Sentiments*, edited by D. D. Raphael and A. L. Macfie, Oxford: Clarendon Press.

SMITH, Adam (1776/1978) *The Wealth of Nations*, edited by R. H. Campbell, A. S. Skinner and W. B. Todd, Oxford: Clarendon Press.

SUDGEN, Robert (1986) *The Economics of Rights, Co-operation and Welfare*, Oxford: Basil Blackwell.

12

The dynamics of cultural theory and their implications for the enterprise culture

MICHAEL THOMPSON

'There is no such thing as society,' Mrs Thatcher asserted, 'there are only individuals and families.' Unfortunately, the fact that opinions of this particular individual and mother are immediately pounced on by the media, while those of a million others go unrecorded, only serves to confirm that there is at least one more level above the two she allows: the government of which she was the Prime Minister. But, with that omission remedied, I am happy to operate with Mrs Thatcher's definition. Her three levels readily map on to the three that will provide the main foci of this paper: the social being, the household, and the regime. Though she (and many a beleaguered academic) may feel that sociology (not to mention social*ism*) has now been done away with, these three levels provide all the justification I need for the sort of social science I wish to practise.

Mrs Thatcher's individuals are free-standing agents, each equipped with his or her distinctive set of preferences, and each transacting on an equal footing with whosoever it pleases him or her to transact with. Her individuals, in other words, are what markets are, reputedly, made of. Most economists, too, would go along with this, insisting for good measure that certain agglomerations of individuals (firms, for instance) can also be treated as 'economic individuals'. But of course there are always *some* restrictions on what the individual can drag into the market-place. For instance, we tend to disapprove of those individuals who are prepared, as the saying goes, to sell their grandmothers, and this is where Mrs Thatcher's second level—the family—comes in.

The relationships that define and stabilise the family are sacrosanct in some way. They, and the transactions they sustain, are largely insulated from the market-place. Social sanctions, ranging from public disapproval to imprisonment, are meted out to those who do not respect this insulation. Families, of course, are quite capable of generating and expressing public disapproval, but something more is needed to hand out prison sentences. Something more is also needed to keep the market functioning: some sanction-wielding institution that, standing firmly and authoritatively outside of the market, can enforce the law of contract without which that market could not function. From all of this we can see that Mrs Thatcher's parsimonious definition takes us a long way. Indeed, in giving us *markets* and *hierarchies*—clearly separate yet clearly interdependent—it takes us about as far as social science has got. I wish to go further.[1]

Markets and hierarchies, I concede, allow us to understand an awful lot about our lives together, but not everything. In the midst of Mrs Thatcher's Britain there is something—'the work-starved/work-greedy bifurcation', as it is called—that, according to the markets-and-hierarchies account of things, should not (indeed, cannot) be there. It is, in Imre Lakatos' delightful terminology, a 'monster'—something that, according to prevailing theories, cannot exist.[2] This same monster is also to be found in the United States, where it goes under a number of names, the most familiar of which is 'the underclass': a whole tier of people (of all ages) who are simply not needed by the rest. And anthropologists of Melanesia, if consulted, will admit that this monster is an old friend of theirs. Throughout the highlands of New Guinea, it manifests itself in a self-perpetuating distinction between 'big men' (as they are called in pidgin—the *lingua franca* of the region) and 'rubbish men'.

In any inner-city area in Britain, those who know will tell you that you do not go to the Job Centre (the renamed Labour Exchange) if you are looking for work. You go to see your uncle at his vegetable stall in the local street-market, or your mate's cousin in the building trade, or your mum's friend's husband who has a crash repair workshop round the corner. Work comes through networks, often in such quantities that it cannot all be done by the recipient, even though he or she may be prepared to work all the hours God sends. But you do not refuse such work; to do that would be to risk closing down the network by which you live and, more importantly, would jepoardise your standing in your local community. No, you pass the work you cannot take on yourself to others. Those others then stand in the same sort of relationship to you as you stand to those from whom you obtained your work in the first place. These networks can proliferate rapidly and quite informally, often becoming reciprocal as recipients pass work back to their initial benefactors, and sometimes turning round on themselves to create circular flows that, in a manner of speaking, keep it all in the family. Such networks, of their very nature, are work-greedy. Only if you are work-starved, because you have no networks to draw on, do you go to the Job Centre.

What makes this divide so monstrous is that, since it is all on one side (the markets side) of the markets-and-hierarchies distinction, it cannot be accounted for by that distinction. Worse still, it cuts right across something (the labour market) that, according to the markets-and-hierarchies account of things, has to be a seamless whole. If the markets-and-hierarchies frame is unable to account for this increasingly visible monster, that must be because it does not contain the requisite variety. A single dimension of sociality (market incentives *v.* social sanctions is the economist's favourite) clearly is not enough. So let us try two. That, in essence, is what cultural theory does. If two dimensions give us more explanatory grip than one, then that decides it. But why stop there? Why not go on to three, four, five, or even n dimensions? And, if you do that, what was so special about those first two? Would not any two have done just as well?

My reply is that I use these two dimensions because they are the only dimensions there are. Or, to be more precise (since you can dream up any number of dimensions), my reply is that any set of dimensions can be reduced to just these two *without any loss of explanatory power.* This, of course, is a statement of the *impossibility theorem* that sits at the heart of cultural theory, and the exercise I embark on below provides me with an opportunity to be persuasive about it. I aim to show, first, that cultural theory's two dimensions make good the variety that the single dimension lacks and, second, that these two dimensions between them capture everything that can be captured. I begin with the monster and its discovery by social science (as opposed to the street-smart who, of course, has always known all about it).

A TROUBLESOME DIVIDE

The work-starved/work-greedy bifurcation is one of the most interesting, and most surprising, results of the work of two of Britain's leading sociologists, Jan and Ray Pahl.[3] It is interesting because it gives us some valuable, and perhaps alarming, pointers to the sort of future we are moving towards (not to mention the present we are already in). It is surprising because, as an instance of *structural imbalance*, it seriously contradicts the basic assumptions—margin-adjusting and general equilibrium —that underpin the neoclassical economics on the basis of which most policies are justified, and on which most theories and analyses of the household (and of 'post-industrial' society generally) are based.

What I mean by 'structural imbalance' is that, left to their own devices, the work-starved and the work-greedy portions of the population do not gradually erode the differences between them, thereby moving from initial disequilibrium to eventual equilibrium through myriad small and continuous adjustments at the margin. There is no margin; there is a gulf. What is more, the persistence of this imbalance is maintained by the interaction—the dynamic connectedness—of the two parts. Though the work-greedy do not set out with the deliberate aim of depriving the work-starved of opportunities, they nevertheless end up doing just that. And it is this dynamic connectedness that makes the imbalance structural. The Matthew Principle, of which this bifurcation is one example, tells us that disequilibrium, not equilibrium, is what makes our social systems function. They are disequilibrium systems: the more the more, the less the less; to those that have shall be given, from those that have not shall be taken away, even that which they have.

If social systems are equilibrium systems, which is what neoclassical economics (and Parsonian social theory) insists, then the work-starved/work-greedy divide is a temporary upset that will soon sort itself out.[4] If it does not disappear of its own accord, this must be because something is preventing the labour market from functioning properly. The sensible policy, then, is to leave well alone and, if need be, to get in there and remove the institutional obstacles to the proper functioning of the system. But if social systems are disequilibrium systems, these policies will be totally ineffective; persistent divides then tell us, not that something is preventing the system from working, but that it is working perfectly! This is what makes the Pahls' monster so alarming, for we can now see how it is that many institutions, academics and policy advisers have a vested interest in seeing it discredited.

One popular discrediting ploy is to point out counter-examples[5]—households among which there is no sign of this bifurcation (those of members of the armed forces, for instance, or of senior civil servants). It is at this point that cultural theory can come to the rescue by showing that these counter-examples, far from discrediting the bifurcation hypothesis, actually reinforce it. This particular bifurcation, it insists, is inherent to individualised social contexts—to markets; it is one of the essential features that stabilise them and enable them to function. Cultural theory shows us that markets function, not because they are made up of autonomous agents free from the impediment of social sanctions (the neoclassical view), but because they are made up of distinctive *social beings* who, in acting in a particular way and in generating a particular set of social sanctions, are able to stabilise and promote their preferred way of life. Some—the energetic, the skilful, the adventurous, the lucky—are able to operate through the impressive personal networks that this mode of operation inevitably gives rise to. Others—those less energetic, less skilful, less adventurous, less lucky—find themselves always out at the peripheries of other people's networks and never at the centres of their own. This bifurcation—network centrality versus network peripherality— is, therefore, the normal state of affairs when group relationships are absent or little developed.

Cultural theory then goes on to show that a quite different bifurcation is found in those reaches of social life where group relationships predominate and individualism is muted. Here it is the various dynamics of group formation—boundary creation, internal differentation, incorporation, exclusion, and so on— that continually act to separate the hierarchists and the egalitarians. The dynamic interconnectedness of these two ways of life derives from the either/or nature of the choice between instituting status differences as an organising principle or instituting complete equality. Status differences enable bounded groups to enter into ranked relationships with one another, thereby creating complex hierarchical structures; complete equality makes relationships between groups impossible, each group generating its own intense internal warmth, and in the process, insulating itself from all the others (and from the markets and the hierarchies) (Figure 12.1).

Now we have the full picture, of which the work-greedy/ work-starved bifurcation is one half. But the relative strengths of the four basic ways of organising—markets, margins, hierarchies, and egalitarian bounded groups—are not fixed. They can and do fluctuate for all sorts of reasons. In Britain, at present, it is hierarchy that is under attack. New technologies

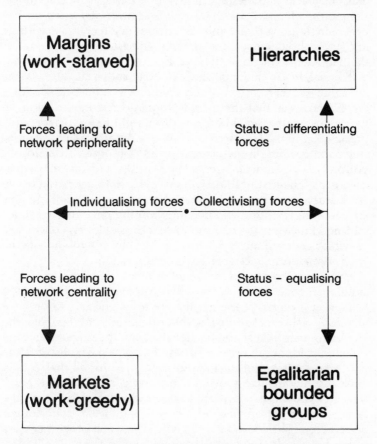

Figure 12.1 The complete disequilibrium system (the Douglesian axes, *grid* and *group*, intersect at the centre point of the figure).

(desk-top publishing, for instance) are undermining it; 'knowledge-intensive' forms of organisation (which are the forms best suited to the development and exploitation of technologies based on information-harnessing rather than on energy-harnessing) are everywhere succeeding the hierarchical structures that characterise the sunset industries that for so long have dominated the economy. On the political right, Thatcher-ites are anxious to sweep away the clutter of institutional structures based on the careful balancing of privilege and obligation (the gentleman, for instance), which they see as the major obstacle to the establishment of an 'enterprise culture'; on the radical left, environmental activists, feminists, and a host of other single-issue public-interest groups see hierarchy, with its institutionalised inequalities and its endless compromising, as the betrayal of the collectivist ideal.

If hierarchy is under attack—if that, above all else, is the nature of our current transition to the post-industrial world—we can now see that there are two quite separate directions in which it is being dismantled: one (from right to left on the grid/group diagram) away from collectivised patterns of relation-ships and towards individualised ones; the other (from top to bottom) away from differentiated statuses and towards equa-lised ones. The first of these will give us an intensification of the work-starved/work-greedy bifurcation; the second will give us an increasingly critical and uncompromising rejection of econo-mic individualism, and a withdrawal into egalitarian collectives, in which everything that is despised by devotees of the enterprise culture is celebrated and vice versa.

These two trends (which have already emerged in earlier cultural theory work at the level of policy debates over technology, poverty, energy, the environment and so on)[6] are identical to those identified, within households, by Jan Pahl: the increasing marginalisation of the wife, and 'the gradual seepage of feminist ideology into everyday discourse'.[7] The first fits the wife who finds herself losing out in the free-for-all that cuts in once the hierarchical principles that used to guarantee her a certain share of the household's resources, in return for the conscientious performance of her wifely duties, can no longer be enforced. The second fits the wife who, with other members of her household, joins together with similarly situated house-holds in rejecting both the 'sexist assumptions' that helped stabilise the hierarchical household and the 'grasping material-ism' that is now taking its place.

Quite apart from its effortless bridging of the gap between the household and the whole political system—the regime—that contains it, this two-dimensional scheme has enabled us to understand how it is that we can have both of these trends at the same time and in the same polity. If there was only one dimension of sociality, these two trends would be irreconcilable: the increased enslavement of women could never coexist with their increasing liberation. Once we go into two dimensions, however, we can immediately see how it is that we are now getting more of both (and less of the hierarchical option). A scheme that can be made to speak to all this deserves a closer look.

AN OUTLINE OF THE DYNAMIC THEORY

Cultural theory's focus is on those values and convictions that are intimately tied to consistent patterns of behaviour: to ways of acting. The two dimensions of sociality, and the four rationalities that they give us access to, can be expanded into an impressively long list (see the Appendix to this chapter) of predictions about the beliefs, the ways of organising, the decision heuristics, and the moral justifications that go with each of the four ways of acting that these four sets of heuristics give rise to. The result is nothing less than four distinct *ways of life*: four internally consistent bundles of values, behaviours, learning styles, and justificatory bases, each of which seriously contradicts the other three. These four ways of life are not just *there*, nor are their adherents locked into them for all time. They are, rather, the recurrent regularities that are somehow thrown up by an unending flux of people and things: transitive transactions and shared meanings. It is this relationship between the eternal four-fold patterns and the flux that gives rise to them that a *dynamic* cultural theory must get to grips with.

There are three questions a dynamic cultural theory must answer:

1 How are the four ways of life stabilised?

2 How do individuals sometimes find themselves 'tipped' from one of these ways of life into another?

3 How is it that, as this tipping proceeds, one way of life does not eventually win out over all the others?

The first question is answered by the *cultural hypothesise*.
Actions based on each particular set of convictions as to how
the world is and how people are promotes just one possible
way of organising relationships and, as it is doing this, it
demotes the other possible ways.

The second question takes us into the *theory of surprise*. The
world, at times and in places, can be any of the four ways it is
asserted to be. If it happens that it is the way you are insisting it
is, then you will probably find that things work to your
advantage more often for you than for those who are insisting
that it is some other possible way. As more and more of those
people are surprised into your way of life so their actions, in
aggregate, alter the world itself until eventually it becomes more
conducive to one of the other ways of life. (This, incidentally,
raises the whole question of whether our world is currently in the
state that is most conducive to an 'enterprise culture'. There are
many who argue that the post-industrial world we are entering
rewards carefully co-ordinated teams and actually punishes one-
man bands.) I have, with Paul Tayler, developed a computer
simulation of this 'surprise hypothesis', which gives us a
surprisingly orderly, but never-ending, cyclical alternation of
states of the world and ways of life: a disequilibrium system that
continually reasserts the four-fold pattern that drives it. This
simulation—we call it 'The Surprise Game'[8]—shows us that
change (the movement of individuals from one way of life to
another) is not some additional complication that the basic
cultural theory framework has somehow to cope with; it is
essential to that framework's very existence. Those who cry,
'Wait a minute, let's get the static framework straight before we
try setting the whole thing in motion,' have missed the point.
Since change is essential to the very existence of all these four-
fold patterns, what they are saying is equivalent to insisting that
we learn to balance ourselve on a stationary bicycle before we
try to turn the pedals. But just as riding a bicycle is a *dynamic*
activity, so change and surprise are the essential ingredients of
cultural theory.

This mechanism that, from time to time, tips an individual out
of one way of life and into another can be given a quite precise
description. It cuts in whenever successive events (that is,
surprises) intervene in such a way as to prevent the preferred
pattern of relationships delivering enough towards the expec-

tations it has generated in its consitituent individuals. This, of course, is the theory of rational expectations, seriously complicated by the fact that there are as many rationalities as there are ways of life that can be lived.

The third question—the non-extinction of the four ways of life—can be rephrased as a question about their emergence: how do these four patterns of relationships together gain some sort of advantage over all those millions of other combinations that are logically possible? The answer is that they, and only they, happen to form themselves into a *hypercycle*. Each way of life, it turns out, does something for the next that it cannot do for itself. The hierarchists, for instance, enforce the law of contract for the individualists, the inegalitarian excesses of the individualists and hierarchists give the egalitarians something to criticise, and the fatalists give the hierarchists someone to sit on top of and the individualists someone to take work from. For all their contradictions and contentions, each way of life ultimately needs the others. Their 'game', in other words, is positive-sum, whilst that of all the other possible combinations is not. Since each way of life is acting as the 'catalyst' for the formation of the others, the disappearance of one would result in the disappearance of them all. That is why none of them can ever go into permanent extinction.

Now, having established that change is an essential feature of cultural theory, let us take a look at the various transitions individuals can make. There are twelve of these in all (Figure 12.2). Of course, just because you can draw these twelve transitions on a piece of paper, it does not follow that you can make them in real life. Some of them may be socially impossible. So a sensible first step will be for us to run through all twelve and see whether we can spin a plausible story around each of them. Better still, can we see that plausible stories have already been spun around some of them and not around others?

1 From fatalist to individualist is the familiar 'rags to riches' story. More gradually, it is 'pulling yourself up by your own bootstraps'.

2 The reverse, from individualist to fatalist, is the 'downward spiral of poverty' or, in terms of New Guinea anthropology, from 'big man' to 'rubbish man'. Transitions 1 and 2 together, when spread over a sizeable span of family history, is 'clogs to clogs in three generations'.

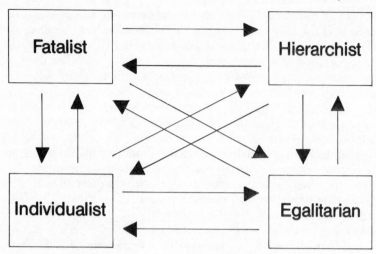

Figure 12.2 The twelve micro-changes (expressed in terms of the four social beings who constitute each of the four ways of organising that are set out in Figure 12.1)

3 From egalitarian to hierarchist is Max Weber's 'routinisation of charisma'. In more secular terms, it is the path taken by the troublesome outsider who finds himself co-opted by the establishment.

4 The reverse, from hierarchist to egalitarian, is the path taken by the schismatic: the loyalist who becomes the heretic. In more secular terms, it is the whistle-blower.

5 From fatalist to hierarchist is Marx's 'dictatorship of the proletariat'. His description, of course, assumes this to be a macro-change (one that is taken by everyone) but it is also the path taken by, say, the Ronan Point Tenants' Association as its initially atomised members come together to resist those—the local authority, etc.—who they think are (and may indeed be) oppressing them. It corresponds to much of what is nowadays called 'empowerment'.

6 The reverse, from hierarchist to fatalist, is the most extreme form of a 'fall from grace'. It corresponds to 'defrocking', being 'drummed out of the regiment', 'discharged with ignominy', 'disbarred', 'struck off'.

7 From individualist to egalitarian is 'Saul on the road to Damascus'. One minute he is a 'Big Man' in a growth

industry—Christian persecution; the next minute he is the charismatic leader of an egalitarian and persecuted sect. Captains of industry who lose their achieved positions (through retirement or take-over) sometimes take this path, becoming prominent figures in activist groups (like the Soil Association or the Findhorn Community).

8 From egalitarian to individualist fits the person who, having been rudely expelled from his tight little group, 'lands on his feet'. Many small-scale entrepreneurs—in new energy technologies, in wholefood retailing, and in high-tech waste treatment, for instance—have followed this route. Where they then go, if they prosper and become large-scale entrepreneurs, take us on to the first of the diagonals.

9 From individualist to hierarchist is Max Weber's 'bureaucratisation'. At first, the ex-activist's business bowls along on casual but efficient first-name terms. Face-to-face and few in number, he and his employees just get on with it, sweeping up, serving, driving the van, or whatever, in an agreeably higgledy-piggledly confusion of people and jobs to be done. As the firm grows, however, so the roles and the people who perform them crystallise out into job descriptions, separate departments, salary grades and so on.

10 From hierarchist to individualist is the 'gamekeeper-turned poacher': the civil servant, for instance, who, having spent many years devising and implementing some regulatory framework, leaves his secure niche and sets up as a consultant. In recent years many tax inspectors have taken this route.

11 The other diagonal, from egalitarian to fatalist, fits the person who is rudely expelled from the activist group and does not land on his feet. Resourceless, unprepared, and suddenly quite alone, he has no choice but to go straight into ineffectuality.

12 The reverse, from fatalist to egalitarian, is the path taken by the isolated individual who, by chance, happens to display the characteristics that the members of some tightly-knit group are looking for. Squatting co-operatives in London, for instance, are always on the lookout for real, working-class, homeless families who are willing to join them and have their consciousnesses raised in the process.

Since a plausible story can be (or already has been) spun around each of these twelve transitions, we must conclude that they are all socially possible. We must also conclude that any *macro-change* (that is, any significant changes in the shape of the whole) will be the aggregation, in differing proportions and relations, of some or all of these twelve *micro-changes*.

FROM MICRO TO MACRO

If we take the simplest indicator of macro-change—a shift in numerical dominance from one quadrant to another—we can isolate four sets of micro-changes, each of which will produce one of the four possible dominances

1 Movements into fatalism from all three of the other quadrants:

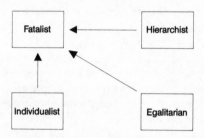

This is the process that social scientists call 'marginalisation'. Our diagram shows that, though there is but a single outcome, there are three distinct processes by which that outcome can be reached.

2 Movements into hierarchy from all three of the other quadrants:

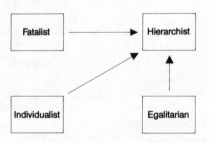

This outcome usually goes by the label 'bureaucratisation', and we can see that the process the sociologist Weber[9] and the economist Williamson[10] have isolated is but one (the individualist to hierarchist transition) of the three distinct processes that give this particular outcome. The dictatorship of the proletariat (the fatalist to hierarchist transition) and the routinisation of charisma (the egalitarian to hierarchist transition) are brought about by processes quite different from the increasing division of labour and the spiralling transaction costs that accompany the individualist to hierarchist transition.

3 Movements into egalitarianism from all three of the other quadrants:

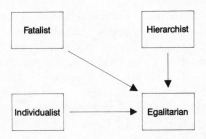

This is the outcome usually called 'radicalisation' and, again, we can see that this singular outcome is reached by three quite distinct processes. The label 'radicalisation', however, is not just indiscriminate in that it fails to distinguish between these separate processes; it also fails to cope with 'radical conservatism', which, as our last possibility shows, goes with a completely different three-fold set of transitions.

4 Movements into individualism from all three of the other quadrants:

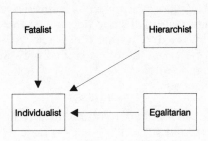

This is the explicit goal of Thatcherism, of radical conservatism, it goes by the clear if unlovely name, 'privatisation'. (The fact that it has no sociological name lends support to the thesis that sociology, as a social activity, is biased against economic individualism.)[11] Again, we can see that there are three quite different paths by which this outcome can be reached. An attack on hierarchy, by itself, may well tip some hierarchists into individualism, but the diagram shows that it may just as easily (perhaps more easily) tip others into fatalism and still others into egalitarianism. This, as we have seen from the work of the Pahls and others, is what is currently happening in those countries—Britain and the United States—where radical conservatism is being tried.

Finally, to summarise this brief excursion through the micro-changes and the macro-changes that the 'surprise game' (and the four eternal bases it is played between) give rise to, I can say that it has opened up a can of very nasty social, economic, and political worms. Can I now sort these worms out? Can I draw upon the increased discriminating power that these twelve varieties of micro-changes have given me to reorganise the mess I have created among the conventional distinctions of social science? This is indeed a tall order, and one that is best take on one step at a time. Here I have restricted myself to just the fourth macro-change: to radical conservatism and what its pursuit is doing, first, to the household and, second, to the wider whole of which the household is so vital a part. My argument, which I have set out in terms of the transitions that are at present taking place within the households, is that, since there are always three routes into (and out of) each of the four quadrants, policies that are aimed at creating an 'enterprise culture' (by radically shifting social transactions away from hierarchies and into markets) will also be creating (or, rather, strengthening) a 'culture of poverty' (fatalism) and a 'culture of criticism' (egalitarianism). This is not to say that such policies should not be pursued, only that those who believe that those policies will bring about a world peopled only with individualists will be disappointed.

CONCLUSION

What I have been describing, with the help of just three out of the twelve micro-changes, is a macro-change—the decline of hierarchy—that is, in some ways, the opposite of the one Weber was trying to get a conceptual hold on. But the one is not simply the reverse of the other. There are three routes into hierarchy and there are three routes out of it, and it is highly improbable that the weights of traffic on these routes will remain the same through all the upheavals that lead to their directions of travel being completely reversed. This is not something that worried Weber (or, indeed, any of the other masters of social thought) because they (in the absence of a theory of culture) were not able to distinguish between the available routes, but it takes us right into the last great mystery of the social sciences: the relationship between micro and macro.

The conceptual separation of micro and macro (the individual and society, for instance, or politics and the political arena) has become the 'central dogma' of the social sciences. To understand the micro, the macro is held constant: the macro becomes the conditioning environment of the micro, never something that is within the 'organism' itself. And to understand the macro, some 'reasonable' assumptions about the micro have to be made so that it can then be aggregated: for example, Keynes' celebrated 'fundamental psychological law' which states that 'men are disposed, as a rule and on the average, to increase their consumption as their income increases but not by as much as the increase in their income'.[12] With the micro thus reduced to a single principle, rather than treated as the repository of all the contending principles that are socially possible, macroeconomics can then take on its splendid separate existence. But there is a price to be paid for all this: the fundamental irreconcilability of micro and macro. Hence the central dogma.

In cultural theory, however, micro and macro are not separate, or even separable. Each, rather, *constitutes* the other. They are mutually reducible cosms ('As above,' as the Albigensian heresy has it, 'so below'). The central dogma, confronted with a flock of starlings, has to insist that the flock (the macro-level) is one thing and the individual birds (the micro-level) is something else. But the individual starlings do not fly around *inside* the flock. They *are* the flock and flock *is* them. Sorting out that conventional nonsense, it seems to me, is the most glittering of all the prizes that we are now within the grasp of a fully dynamic cultural theory.

NOTES

1 Much of the argument in this chapter is derived from two more
  extensive treatments of cultural theory: Michiel Schwarz and
  Michael Thompson, *Divided We Stand: Redefining Politics, Technology and Social Choice*, Hemel Hempstead, Harvester–Wheatsheaf, 1990 and Michael Thompson, Richard Ellis and Aaron
  Wildarsky, *Cultural Theory*, Boulder, CO and Oxford, West View,
  1990.

2 Imre Lakatos, *Proofs and Refutations: The Logic of Mathematical
  Discovery* Cambridge, Cambridge University Press, 1976.

3 R. E. Pahl, 'The social and political implications of household
  work strategies', *The Quarterly Journal of Social Affairs*, I, 1, 1985,
  pp. 9–18; 'Does jobless mean workless?', *Annals of The American
  Academy*, 493, September 1987, pp. 36–46.

4 Of course, the neoclassicist will point out that such divides are to
  be expected if some people have skills that are increasingly in
  demand (computer programming, for instance) while others can
  only do work for which there is less and less call (labouring, for
  instance). But this is not what lies behind the Pahls' divide. There
  is nothing to distinguish the two sides in terms of skills, and the
  re-skilling of the work-starved (the sensible solution to the only
  sort of divide admissible by the neoclassicists) would be of little
  avail.

5 Mrs Thatcher, for instance, has sought to discredit the idea of a
  north/south divide by pointing to places like Harrogate and
  Kendal that compare quite well with Winchester and Milton
  Keynes.

6 The many and various applications are listed in a bibliography of
  cultural theory in Michael Thompson *et al.*, *Cultural Theory*.

7 Jan Pahl, personal communication.

8 M. Thompson and P. Tayler, *The Surprise Game: An Exploration of
  Constrained Relativism*, Warwick Papers in Management, No. 1,
  Institute for Management Research and Development, Univer-
  sity of Warwick, Coventry, CV4 7AL, UK, 1986.

9 Max Weber, *The Protestant Ethic and The Spirit of Capitalism*, New
  York, Free Press, 1958.

10 Oliver Williamson, *Markets and Hierarchies*, New York, Free
   Press, 1975.

11 D. Marsland, *The Seeds of Bankruptcy*, London, Claridge, 1988.

12 J. M. Keynes, *The General Theory of Employment, Interest and
   Money*, London, Macmillan, 1936.

APPENDIX TO CHAPTER 12:
THE FOUR WAYS OF LIFE

	Hierarchical	*Egalitarian*	*Individualistic*	*Fatalistic*
Preferred way of organising	Nested bounded group	Egalitarian bounded group	Ego-focused network	Margins of organised patterns
Certainty (myth of nature)	Nature perverse/ tolerant	Nature ephemeral	Nature benign	Nature capricious
Rationality	Procedural	Critical	Substantive	Fatalistic
View of resources	Scarce	Depleting	Abundant	Lottery
Scope of knowledge	Almost complete and organised	Imperfect but holistic	Sufficient and timely	Irrelevant
Learning style	Anticipation	Trial without error	Trial and error	Luck
Social context	Positive group/ positive grid	Positive group/ negative grid	Negative group/ negative grid	Negative group/ positive grid
Desired systems properties	Controllability (through inherent orderliness)	Sustainability (through inherent fragility)	Exploitability (through inherent fluidity)	Copeability (through inherent chaos)
Ideal scale	Large	Small	Appropriate	—
Engineering aesthetic	High-tech virtuosity	Frugal and environment-benign	Appropriate (as cheap and cheerful as possible)	—
Ideal of fairness	Equality before the law	Equality of result	Equality of opportunity	Not on this earth
Cultural bias	Ritualism and sacrifice	Fundamentalism/ millenarianism	Pragmatic materialism	Inconsistent eclecticism
Preferred economic theory	Bureaucratisation through increasing transaction costs (O. Williamson)	Buddhist and Thermo-dynamic economics (E. F. Schumaker and N. Georgescu-Rogen)	Neo-Austrian: competition without equilibrium (F. Hayek, A. Alchian)	Marginalisation through structural imbalace (Neo-Marxist)
Energy future	Middle of the road (technical fix)	Low growth (radical change now)	Business as usual	What you don't know ...

	Hierarchical	Egalitarian	Individualistic	Fatalistic
Perception of time	Balanced distinction between short term and long term	Long term dominates short term	Short term dominates long term	Involuntary myopia
Preferred form of governance	Leviathan	Jeffersonian	Laissez-faire	It doesn't matter who you vote for ...
Salient Risks	Loss of control (i.e. of public trust)	Catastrophic, irreversible and inequitable developments	Threats to the functioning of he market	—
Model of consent	Hypothetical consent	Direct consent	Implicit consent	No consent
Method for applying model of consent	Natural (or other ideal) standards	Expressed preferences	Revealed preferences	—
Risk handling style	Rejection and absorption	Rejection and deflection	Acceptance and deflection	Acceptance and absorption
Latent Strategy	Secure internal structure of authority	Survival of the collectivity	Preservation of the individual's freedom to contract	Survival of individual
Commitment to institutions	Correct procedures and discriminated statuses are supported for own sake. *Loyalty.*	Collective moral fervour and affirmation of shared opposition to outside world. *Voice.*	Only if profitable to the Individual. If not, then *exit.*	—
Relationship between needs and resources	Can manage resources but not needs	Can manage needs but not resources	Can manage needs and resources	Cannot manage needs or resources
Need-and-resource management strategy	Manage resources up (collectively) to meet socially fixed needs	Manage needs down (collectively) meet naturally fixed resources	Manage needs and resources up (individualistically) as high as possible	Devise short term responses to cope with erratic mismatches of needs and resources
Matching of man and environment	Control	Harmony	Exploitation	Happenstance
Nature of pollution	Human defilement of social order through nature	Social transgression of natural order	Matter in wrong place at wrong time	Fecalmonism

	Hierarchical	Egalitarian	Individualistic	Fatalistic
Pollution solution	Change nature to conform to society	Change society to conform to nature	Market incentives (transferable rights to pollute, etc.)	—
Information rejection style	Paradigm protection	Expulsion	Networking	Risk absorption
Anomaly handling style	Monster-adjustment	Monster-barring	Monster-accepting	—
Audit criteria	Legality of expenditures	Equalisation of differences	The bottom line: profit, cost-effectiveness, popularity	—
Search and change behaviour	High on search; low in (internal) change	High on search; high on (external) change	'Satisficing'; enough search for enough change	No search; fatalistic acceptance of change
Leadership	Pro-leadership	Anti-leadership but will accept charismatic leadership under certain contitions	Leadership – minimisation (through self-organisation)	Leadership – enduring
Blame-pinning	The victim	The system	The non-productive individual (or external distortions of the market)	'It's the poor that gets the blame'
Tragedy	Technique triumphs over purpose	Crabs in a barrel	Tragedy of the commons	(Inescapable ignorance)
Triumph	Sacrifice of parts to whole (noblesse oblige etc.,)	Brotherhood of man	The hidden hand	Dignity
Consumption Style	Traditionalist: strong links to past and others	Naturalist: rejection of artificiality and excess	Cosmopolitan: neophiliac and wide-ranging	Isolated: traditionalist but with weak connections to past and to others
Impact on production system	High product differentiation/ low product innovation	Low product differentiation/ low (or negative) product innovation	High product differentiation/ high product innovation	Low product differentiation/high product innovation
Advertising and and history (claims in present versus evidence of the past)	Advertising has to fit itself to a gradually accommodating history	Apocalyptic history rejects almost all advertising	Advertising an essential input to a rapidly accommodating history	Advertising re-writes a vestigial history

	Hierarchical	Egalitarian	Individualistic	Fatalistic
Style of cheating	*Wolves*: cheat in hierarchical and exclusive teams, unequal redistribution of proceeds	*Vultures*: cooperative, but difficulties in equalising proceeds often leads to scism	*Hawks*: competitive back stabbing/shifting allegiances	*Donkeys*: sabotage and cheat, when possible, to excess (no group or network controls)
Evolutionarily stable stable strategy (and its power implication)	Collectivist manipulation (power-wielding and power-deflecting)	Collectivist survival (power-deflecting)	Individualist manipulative (power-wielding and power-deflecting)	Individualist survival (power-absorbing)
Idea of nature (deduced from social and cultural constraints)	*Isomorphic*: nature holds up a mirror to society	*Accountable*: society must fit itself to rigid natural frame	*Cornucopian*: (skill-controlled) 'If you can do it it's natural'	*Cornucopian*: (lottery – 'When your number comes up'

13

Close encounters of the third sector kind

ALBERT WEALE

INTRODUCTION

The purpose of this chapter is to bring together two sets of concerns. The first relates to the cognitive dimensions of social life and in particular to the research programme instituted by Mary Douglas into how institutions think (e.g. Douglas, 1978, 1986 and Douglas and Wildavsky, 1982). The claim that institutions think and that different types of institutions think in their own distinctive ways is one that should be taken seriously by the social sciences. Traditional economic or rational choice approaches taken for granted the generation of belief systems and assume that members of a society share a common understanding of the social world in which they live. As an anthropologist, Mary Douglas constantly reminds us that these assumptions cannot be taken for granted. There is no more reason to expect homogeneity of belief and interpretation than there is to accept homogeneity of preference. We need to understand the social context in which individuals seek to interpret the world, thereby appreciating how institutions provide a framework within which interpretation emerges.

The second concern is to be found in the work of James Douglas, and in particular in his book *Why Charity?* (Douglas, J., 1983). At a time when the political debate rages between individualism and collectivism, it is useful to be reminded that no society need face a harsh and uncompromising choice between reliance on the state and reliance upon individual initiative. There is in all liberal democracies a third sector that is neither state nor market, but something distinct. Douglas has shown how much of this third sector activity can be understood as a response both to the market failure and to its analogue in the political realm, 'majority rule' failure. Because there are certain sort of preferences to which neither the economic nor the politcal market are sensitive, a third sector will emerge that will seek to satisfy these preferences. The world of the third sector, then, is one that seeks to cater for minority or intensely-held preferences.

It is not my intention to question the understanding of the third sector offered in *Why Charity?* Instead I wish to supplement it by considering the role of the third sector in relation to the cognitive dimensions of public policy. In other words I shall be seeking to shift the focus from a preference-based understanding of third sector activity to a cognitive and belief-based understanding. One way of putting the relevent issues into perspective is to say that I shall be concerned with how policy-making institutions may think differently once a contribution is made from the third sector. In order to bring this focus into sharper relief I shall be taking as examples one particular type of third sector institution, namely the foundation. Alan Ware (1989, pp. 8–12) has shown how difficult it is in general to identify a set of institutions that fall neatly between profit and state, but he does identify the chief characteristics of the modern foundation: 'it derives most of is income from endowments; it makes grants to agencies for projects or administers projects directly; it is controlled by a self-perpetuating board of trustees; and it is run by a professional staff which operates independently from the original benefactor' (Ware 1989, p. 135). Among social scientist examples of such trusts are household names: the Ford Foundation, the Rowntree Trust, the Thyssen Foundation and the King Edward's Hospital Fund for London.

In seeking to make the links between the question of how institutions think and what the role of third sector bodies might be within the policy-making processes of liberal democracies, I shall draw upon an idea that has gained much currency recently in the literature on policy analysis, namely the idea of 'social learning'. Treating policy-making institutions as instruments of social learning provides, I shall argue, a constructive way of thinking about the cognitive dimesions of public policy. However, before discussing these basic notions, it will be sensible to give some illustrations of the way in which foundations have contributed to the policy-making process in recent years.

EXAMPLES OF FOUNDATION ACTIVITY

One of the most interesting contributions in recent years from a foundation to the development of public policy in the UK was the decision of the Wellcome Foundation to finance a survey of sexual practices as part of the research background for the development of AIDS policy. The story behind the decision is simply told. In 1988 the Economic and Social Research Council launched a £1·5m. research programme into AIDS related issues. The programme comprised a linked series of projects and there was a high degree of co-ordination and co-operation among the individual research teams. As part of the programme the researchers decided that it was necessary to have a survey of sexual practices among the general population in order to establish baseline data for comparisons with particular groups. There was no question about the intellectual merits of such a survey—the only available data being from the Kinsey surveys—but there did arise an issue of how the costs were to be borne. The ESRC sought to interest the Department of Health and Social Security (as it then was) which was in principle willing to collaborate, but which needed approval from higher up the system. Mrs Thatcher, as Prime Minister, had always taken an interest in science policy and the proposal for Department of Health and Social Security involvement landed on her desk, where it stayed for ten months. In the end the Prime Minister refused to allow the involvement of a government department in the funding of such a survey on the (insubstantial) grounds that it would be resented by the population as an intrusion into domestic privacy, and those responsible for the research programme found themselves denied an intellectually essential research project. Enter stage right the Wellcome Foundation in December 1989, who within a matter of weeks were able to supply the funds necessary to carry out the survey.

The second example is less dramatic but it provides an idea of the contribution that foundations can make it to the quality of public debate. In 1986 the King's Fund established a health policy institute, the King's Fund Institute, in order to improve public debate about the health service. The role of the Institute is not so much to conduct original research itself but to synthesise existing work and draw out its policy implications.

Given the political controversy over health service spending, one of its main roles since its inception has been to provide a dispassionate analysis of public spending on health care, not only in general terms but also in relation to specific measures like the cost improvement programmes. This role has become particularly important during the 1980s given the growing concern about the abuse by the government of official statistics for the purposes of propaganda. Remarkably for so contentious a field, the King's Fund Institute rapidly established a reputation both for its independence and for its authority.

I take these two examples because in their different ways they illustrate the contribution that third sector institutions can make to the development of public policy. In both cases the contribution arises essentially from the financial independence from government that foundations enjoy, thus enabling them to take on public policy research. This means that they can follow the logic of argument and reasearch relevant to the formulation of public policy and it also provides them with a neutrality in the policy process which may be essential if policies are to be put on a sound intellectual footing. Financial independence from the machinery of government is important, because there is likely to be more credibility in the professional communities affected by public policy if the processes of research affecting policy formation are seen to be independent of a department of state that is being harrassed by the Treasury for cost-cutting measures.

Yet is such independence really necessary? Is there an essential place for third sector institutions or is it simply a matter of happenstance and the peculiarities of UK policy-making institutions? To say that independence is necessary may be to say that there is a characteristic way in which third sector institutions think that makes a distinctive contribution to the policy-making process. To see why there might be a need for such a distinctive contribution, it is useful to place the discussion in the context of social learning theories of public policy.

SOCIAL LEARNING THEORIES OF POLICY

Social learning theories of policy and politics lay stress upon the role that understanding, and in particular the understanding that policy-makers have of complex social systems, has in the process of policy-making. According to such theories, we miss an essential feature of the policy-making process unless we see it as a struggle to acquire and utilise knowledge for the purposes of public action. Such theories have been implicit in many approaches to policy analysis for some time. For example, Herbert Simon's (1957, 1983) insistence that organisational decisions-makers need to be understood in terms of 'bounded rationality' provides an obvious source one we see that policy-making, whatever else it is, takes the form of an organisational process within public bureaucracies. Graham Allison (1971) took this insight and applied it creatively to the study of decision-making about the Cuban missile crisis using it as the second of his conceptual lenses in the form of the organisational process model of decision making. Heclo takes the idea a stage further by seeking to characterise the whole of politics in terms of problem-solving in the face of uncertainty: 'Politics funds its sources not only in power but also in uncertainty—men collectively wondering what to do. Finding feasible courses of action includes, but is more than, locating which way the vectors of political pressure are pushing, (Heclo, 1974, p. 305). Like many creative notions, the idea of social learning was obviously 'in the air' at the time Heclo was writing. Steinbruner (1974), for example, sought to draw explicit analogies between policy-making and cognitive processes at the level of individual psychology. Steinbruner appeals to what he calls the 'known principles of cognitive operations' (1974, p. 91) to explain the behaviour of decision-makers in the face of uncertainty. For example, if we ask why decision-makers do not simply yield to passivity in the face of tremendous uncertainty and complexity, the answer, according to Steinbruner, is that there are powerful cognitive processes of simplification, value separation, inferential memory and consistency that come into play and which reduce complex bodies of information to something that can be managed by human decision-makers. In a more recent work Majone (1989) draws upon the ideas of policy argument and persuasion to show how policy developments can be understood by analogy with theory change in the sciences, in which rival hypotheses are tested and refined by competing partisans.

The conceptualisation of policy-making as a system of social learning would be little more than an interesting metaphor if the forms of comparison remained at a very general level. We need to appreciate not simply *that* policy-making has a cognitive dimension, but *how* the cognitive dimension produces the characteristic forms of policy development. Sabatier (e.g. 1987) has suggested that policy-making be characterised in terms of 'advocacy coalitions', groups of actors within a policy community who share a common belief system. Competing belief systems serve both to clarify the terms of the policy debate and unite otherwise diverse groups of political actors around a common policy stance whose advocates seek to institutionalise their own particular belief system within the prevailing principles of public policy. The cutting edge of this view is to be found in Sabatier's claim (1987, pp. 663–4) that it is belief systems that define interests, not interests that define belief systems.

Within the framework of an advocacy coalitions approach, politics and policy-making involve competition over the plausibility of different belief systems, and various strategies will be employed by different advocacy coalitions in order to secure some intellectual, and hence political, advantage. If social learning, rather than a ritual exchange of sophisticated insults, is to take place, then certain conditions of public debate will have to be satisfied. Among these conditions Sabatier (1987, pp. 679–80) suggests one of the most intriguing. He argues that one of the most important conditions for informed analytical debate is a relatively apolitical forum in which experts from competing coalitions are forced to confront each other. The forum must be prestigious enough to force professionals from competing coalitions to participate and it should be dominated by professional norms, to reduce the dangers of intellectual sharp practise. By bringing differences of belief and judgement into the open in a forum of peer review, the conditions for learning are created within which relatively weak or implausible beliefs are eliminated by a process of intellectual winnowing.

It seems to me that this model of politics as a process of social learning is well suited to certain types of policy issues, typically those like environmental or health policy, in which there is a considerable body of technical expertise involved and in which the relationships between expert appraisal and political judgement are manifold and complex. (It does not worry me that it is less suited to issues, like prayers in schools or immigration policy, in which the decision-making process is usually more visceral.) Where policy-making necessarily calls for some understanding of complex cause-and-effect relationships and their implications, then the notion of collective or social learning surely has some bite. We can say in some meaningful sense that we develop a better understanding over time of how to control pollution or deliver health services and that if anyone aspires to contribute to policy development, he or she must show a certain competence in the basics in order to be plausible (compare Simon, 1983, pp. 103–4). Social learning produces genuine understanding even when it also serves to underline how little we really have knowledge of how to solve particular problems.

It also seems to me that the notion of social learning provides an interesting context for Mary Douglas's views about how institutions think. The essence of the Douglas approach draws heavily on the fundamental assumptions of the anthropological approach to society; before people can have preferences they must first have meanings, and these meanings come from beliefs sustained and transmitted by social institutions. Douglas's contribution is to note that certain types of institution typically sustain and transmit certain types of belief system. If we put this insight together with social learning theories of public policy, we have the makings of an interesting brew. In particular, how and for whom policy learning takes place will depend upon the type of institutions involved, and perhaps, as I shall argue, the role of the third sector can become crucial.

GRID, GROUP AND SOCIAL LEARNING

For Douglas different types of social institution will involve different types of thinking. Using the familiar two-fold grid–group classification, institutions can fall into various categories. Three in particular are of interest in the present context: egalitarian and voluntary associations (high group and low grid); institutions typical of a competitive market order (low group and low grid); and hierarchical, compartmentalised organisations, like public bureaucracies and corporations (high group and high grid). For Douglas organisations and associations that fall into these groups will typically display certain characteristic styles of thought. Thus, egalitarian, voluntary groups, whom Douglas sometimes labels sects, will be typically risk-averse, distrust impersonal knowledge and in the extreme will tend towards an apocalyptic view of the world. Hierarchies, by contrast, will see the world as a stable order to be managed for the achievement of certain purposes. Competitive market institutions are exemplified by the small firm with its own way of thinking—sceptical of regulation, impatient of order and risk-loving rather then risk-averse. This classification is not meant to be rigid, and institutions or organisations may be classified in some ways for some purposes and in different ways for other purposes. Looked at in the context of the market, the small firm may seem to be freewheeling, but looked at from the point of view of internal organisation even quite small firms can seem hierarchical. But the classification does serve to pick out salient features of the styles of thought associated with different types of institutions.

Douglas is surely right to seek to impose some sort of pattern on the variety of intellectual and cognitive styles that different organisations use, and she is also surely right to point out how these differences can prevent or obstruct communication. Thus, during the 1970s there grew up in a number of liberal democracies a series of social movements, typically focused on environmental concerns, who were sceptical of the claims made by goverment or business of the safety of modern production processes, including pesticides, factory farming, supersonic transport and nuclear power. Not all of the critical fell strictly into the category that Douglas labels 'sects', but there clearly have emerged strong currents of thought within the culture of liberal democracies sceptical of the postitivistic assumptions of institutionalised science and hostile to the bureaucratic cast of mind. As Douglas and Wildavsky (1982) point out in their study of cultures of risk, cultural attitudes have become so polarised in some cases that it is difficult to see how any constructive dialogue can be carried on.

And here is the rub. Many of the most pressing problems in public policy, particularly in the fields of health and the environment, involve policy communities whose membership is made up of sects, hierarchies and entrepreneurs. At one time key members of the health and environmental policy communities would have been made up of public bureaucrats, key members of the government and legislature, and a few select interest groups. Now the universe of membership has expanded in all liberal democracies to include the courts and legal institutions, public interest groups, environmental activists, patient groups, specialist reporters in the media, alternative technology firms, international agencies, professional institutes, universities and other institutions in higher education, independent policy institutes and what the Home University Library series used to refer to as the generally educated reader. So whereas at one stage styles of policy-making appropriate to hierarchies would have been sufficient to secure consent, now more attention must be paid to involving a wider range of perspectives and points of view.

An example will illustrate the change in the nature of policy-making and the concomitant change in the composition of the policy community. In 1989 the Ministry of Agriculture, Fisheries and Food proposed to renew a set of licenses under which certain firms could dump liquid waste in the North Sea. There was well established procedure under the Paris Commission by which such renewals could be handled. However, during the renewal process Greenpeace drew public attention to what was happening and pressure mounted for the licenses not to be renewed. In the middle of the campaign at least one major company discovered that it had a perfectly feasible land-based disposal route for its waste and withdrew its application for renewal. A new entrant to a previously closed policy community had gained a significant victory.

Examples like this impose considerable inefficiencies upon the operation of the economic system. They raise transaction costs, and lower the returns on investment, as well as increasing search and policy-choice costs. Such costs are not marginal or incidental to the successful operation of an economic system; they are central and considerable. They figure prominently among Liebenstein's (1966) 'X-inefficiencies' and they have to be reckoned with. Moreover, as in the case of North Sea waste disposal, increased transaction costs may well be associated with technical inefficiencies in the choice of available technologies. If a firm can quickly come up with an alternative to its previously selected waste disposal strategy, that suggests that the original choice was less well grounded than it need have been, and that all the factors bearing on the choice were not fully scanned by key decision-makers in the first place.

In this example, as in others, considerable inefficiencies therefore arise in the implementation of environmental policy through a failure to take into account the changing composition of the policy community. And yet if the policy community has been enlarged to include not simply an increasing number of actors but also a wider range of actors, then Mary Douglas's analysis suggests a dilemma. For as the range of actors increases, so it comes to include different types of organisation on the grid–group analysis, and these different types of organisation are characterised by different styles of thinking. Moreover, those adopting these divergent styles of thinking will run the danger of talking past one another because they are drawing upon competing paradigms and presuppositions.

If anybody is able to provide a communicative mechanism for the members of an increasingly diversified policy community, then the third sector is the most likely candidate. Neither business nor government can play this role. Businesss is clearly too partisan and government is too often perceived, and sometimes rightly perceived, as being in hock to business. (For a persuasive academic account of this indebtedness, see Lindblom, 1977). Sectarian groups have little incentive to create institutions promoting communication with what many of their members will see as the functional equivalent of the Antichrist. And by definition freewheeling, entreprenurial institutions will not possess the organisational infrastructure to set the appropriate institution-building in motion. Of course, social nature does not abhor a vacuum, and there is no reason to believe that, just because some institutional device is needed, some functional mechanism will come into play to provide it. Yet there are grounds for supposing that foundations can play a role in promoting a constructive exchange of views in the health and environmental policy-making communities.

One reason why foundations may have a special role is that they have themselves been instrumental in changing the character of certain policy communities. For example, the Ford Foundation in the US provided crucial support to fledgling environmental organisations. During the 1970s its total grants to the Environmental Defense Fund and the Natural Resources Defense Council totalled $21 million, and its support therefore enabled such public interest legal organisations to get off the ground (Bosso, 1987, pp. 147–8). similarly, in the UK the Rowntree Trust was important in changing the character of the policy community concerned with social security policy through its long-standing support for the Child Poverty Action

Group. A record of support for public interest groups and social movements, especially during periods when it was unfashionable or politically suspect to do so, seems to be an essential condition for a foundation to establish its 'street credibility' with sectarian organisations. The larger foundations can usually do this without compromising unnecessarily their relations with the world of hierarchy since their trustees are normally drawn from the ranks of the good and the great.

However, the funding strategies of foundations are in some sense preliminary to the task of effective social learning. Having the respect of diverse parties may be a necessary condition for creating social learning, but it is unlikely to be sufficient. What is needed in addition is some sense of the way in which the research and intellectual agenda of politics needs to be shaped and a familiarity with techniques to improve the understanding of policy problems. Here, it seems to me that foundations are likely to have several advantages over conventional public policy-making institutions. Their main advantage is that they are not bound by a system of formal political accountability in which the government is answerable for its actions. This means that they have the freedom to explore politically unfashionable issues or currently unpopular points of view. This is particularly important when seeking to draw out the implications of novel and unconventional viewpoints. Many problems in the health or environmental field are long-term, and attention devoted to them in the policy cycle waxes and wanes over time. The ability of foundations to select problems that are not part of a currently fashionable focus of attention, which stems from their independence of the standard mechanisms of political accountability, is crucial to the persistent investigation of these long-term problems.

A further advantage of foundations is that they can provide an example of Sabatier's apolitical forms in which professionals and experts can address issues that divide members of the policy community. The King's Fund consensus conferences provide an example of this process at work. Consensus conferences were developed in the 1970s by the US National Institutes of Health. They provide a forum in which there can be an informed discussion of the advantages and disadvantages associated with various types of clinical activity. The activity chosen is one where there is controversy, both about clinical technical matters and about the welfare of patients. For example, an early King's Fund conference was concerned with the treatment of breast cancer in women, an issue in which there is controversy about both the need for and the psychological and social consequences of mastectomy. The nature of the conference is what makes it distinctive. Instead of there being simply a succession of papers relevant to the topic, a panel, usually comprising a dozen people, is asked to draw up a statement summarising their consensus of opinion of the questions involved and indicating where any unresolved issues remain. The purpose of the conference therefore is to obtain, so far as it is possible, a consensus 'state-of-the-art' statement on the principal questions associated with a particular type of clinical activity. The King's Fund has been running conferences, the topics of which have covered: the treatment of breast cancer in women; the treatment of stroke; ischaemic heart disease; the need for asylum in society; and the practice of genetic and pre-natal screening. In such a forum those with expertise or experience can put forward competing views within a framework that is intended both to identify points of disagreement and to come to a disinterested judgement as to where the balance of argument lies over particular questions. An interesting feature of the King's Fund consensus conferences, as distinct from those organised by the US National Institutes of Health, is the attempt to move beyond the purely professional issues of clinical practice to questions of ethics and the patient's perspective.

Many of the issues involved in health and environmental policy require technical expertise. The extent to which the technical component of public policy disenfranchises the layperson is, I believe, much overdone. Within a post-industrial society (even one like the UK where public policy seems Neanderthal in respect of higher and further education) the skills of technical policy appraisal are widespread in the population. Data analysis, model building and report writing are no longer the privilege of a cultivated few, and plenty of experts will confess that they have been floored at public meetings by the skill of those opposed to their development plans. But even with these widespread skills, there comes a point where technical knowledge has to give way to personal knowledge. It is here that the expansion of the policy communities in health and environmental affairs are of importance. These are policy areas in which technical expertise may be necessary for the development of sound policies, but in which they can never be sufficient. The effects of clinical procedures upon a patient's sense of personal well-being or family relationships and so on are inseparable from the appraisal of the effectiveness of those procedures. A similar point applies in the environmental field. As Majone (1989) points out, it is in societies like the Soviet Union, where professional engineering judgement has been most isolated from public anxieties, that there has been a failure to build adequate safety precautions into the design of nuclear reactors.

The ability to draw together technical questions with issues of general public concern seems to me to be the decisive comparative advantage that third sector insititutions have over government or official bodies, and the nature of the advantage can be expressed in terms drawn from Mary Douglas by saying that these institutions can be characterised as mixed in terms of their grid–group features. Trustees and officers of foundations normally have the social background and skills to move easily in the hierarchical world of public and corporate bureaucracies, but their funding policies typically put them in contact with voluntary and egalitarian organisations. Moreover, since foundations, at least in the UK, are relatively flat hierarchies, those responsible for forming foundation policy are not too far away from the street-level agents responsible for implementing it. The organisational flexibility of foundations also means that they should be able to make contact with the more maverick, and therefore more creative, entrepreneurs who occupy a low grid-low group niche of the competitive market.

So far as I am aware there is no parallel in the field of environmental policy to the consensus conference process in the field of health, despite the fact that both policy fields share the charcteristic that the questions they raise are often technically complex *and* emotionally charged. The process of planning inquiries, even when inspectors are seriously looking to separate the intellectual wheat from the propaganda chaff, does not serve the same function. A planning inquiry is the focal point of intense political controversy, and the participants to the process have too great an incentive to secure a particular decision to allow their minds to be changed by the arguments that are advanced. The political and adversarial nature of the proceedings makes it difficult for an exchange of views to take place with a modification of positions occurring, as was well illustrated in the inquiry over the building of the Sizewell B nuclear power station (O'Riordan, *et al.*, 1988). Moreover, even when public bodies have tried to initiate impartial debate about the nature of the public interest in relation to environmental policy, they have found it difficult to gain credibility among members of the policy community. For example, where the work of the Health and Safety Executive on the tolerability of risk from nuclear power stations has not met public indifference, it has met pressure group hositility (Health and Safety Executive, 1988). So there is a clear need for the lines of communication to be opened up.

IMPLICATIONS

My argument so far is that institutions of the third sector have a decisive role to play in certain areas of public policy once we see that the cognitive dimension of policy requires processes of social learning within changing policy communities. Since the policy communities that are involved in health and environmental policy now comprise groups that are mixed on Mary Douglas's grid–group dimension, there is a need for relatively neutral agents to become involved. I now want to end by speculating about what might be the more general implications of this argument.

The first of these is that it is a mistake to pose a sharp alternative of the form 'either government or charity'. Those on the new right of the political spectrum who are advocating the rolling back of the state have sometimes accompanied their rhetoric with claims about the ability of the charitable sector to substitute in the delivery of services. Empirical evidence suggests that this is too sanguine a view, however. Voluntary activity is simply too variable in quantity and quality to plug increasing gaps in a diminishing welfare state safety net (Ware, 1989, pp. 141–3). To say that there are certain tasks in the field of public policy that the third sector is best able to perform is not to claim that it makes sense for the third sector to substitute for wide areas of legitimate public action. Indeed, it may be argued that to have identified a specialist niche for third sector activity is to reinforce the urgency of public action across more general and less specialist programmes of service delivery and income maintenance.

Secondly, to have identified a niche is not to have made an empirical generalisation. To say that there are some things that foundations can do especially well is not to say that these are things they do in practice. It may still be true, as Ben Whitaker (1974) once argued, that the potential role of foundations as experimenting pioneers or iconoclastic critics is an opportunity largely missed. The point to stress is that the changing character of the policy communities in health and the environment creates a need that foundations are as well equipped as anyone to fulfil.

I offer my analysis to complement the work of James Douglas. As he insists, majoritarian preference with the competitive political market of modern liberal democracies will ignore minority interests and preferences. In addition, however, the dominant institutions of policy-making with such democracies will be biased towards certain styles of thought and certain patterns of perception. The inefficiencies that this is now imposing on the operation of the policy process in health and environmental matters is such that close encounters with and through the third sector are no longer optional, but essential if policy is to be made coherently at all.

REFERENCES

ALLISON, Graham, T. (1971) *Essence of Decision*, Boston: Little, Brown & Company.

BOSSO, Christopher J. (1987) *Pesticides and Politics: The Life Cycle of an Issue*, Pittsburgh: University of Pittsburgh Press.

DOUGLAS, James (1983) *Why Charity? The Case for a Third Sector*, Beverly Hills: Sage.

DOUGLAS, Mary (1978) *Cultural Bias*, London: Royal Anthropological Institute of Great Britain and Ireland, Occasional Paper No. 35.

DOUGLAS, Mary and WILDAVSKY, Aaron (1982) *Risk and Culture*, Berkeley, Calif., : University of California Press.

DOUGLAS, Mary (1986) *How Institutions Think*, London: Routledge & Kegan Paul.

HEALTH AND SAFETY EXECUTIVE (1988) *The Tolerability of Risk from Nuclear Power Stations*, London: HMSO.

HECLO, Hugh (1974) *Modern Social Politics in Britain and Sweden*, New Haven and London: Yale University Press.

KAUFMAN, F-X *et al.*, *Guidance, Control and Performance Evaluation in the Public Sector*, Berlin: Walter de Gruyter.

LIEBENSTEN, Harvey (1966) Allovative efficiency versus X-efficiency', *American Economic Review* 56, pp. 392–415.

LINDBLOM, Charles E. (1977) *Politics and Markets*, New York: Basic Books.

MAJONE, Giandomenico (1989) *Evidence, Argument and Persuasion in the Policy Process*, New Haven: Yale University Press.

O'RIORDAN, Timothy *et al.*, (1988) *Sizewell B: An Anatomy of the Inquiry*, Basingstoke: Macmillan.

SABATIER, Paul A. (1987) Knowledge, policy-oriented learning and policy change, *Knowledge: Creation, Diffusion, Utilization*, 8: 4, pp. 649–92.

SIMON, Herbert A. (1957) *Models of Man*, New York: Wiley.

SIMON, Herbert A. (1983) *Reason in Human Affairs*, Oxford: Basil Blackwell.

STEINBRUNER, J. (1974) *The Cybernetic Theory of Decision*, Princeton: Princeton University Press.

WARE, Alan (1989) *Between Profit and State*, Cambridge: Polity Press.

WHITAKER, Ben (1974) *The Foundations*, London: Eyre Methuen.

Index

actions
  intentions and belief, 50–1
  rules constraints, 72–3
advertising, 6, 149, 157–8
advocacy coalitions, and policy-
    making, 208
agreement
  and communication, 4–5, 129,
    134–5, 136–7
  institutions, 33, 164
Allison, Graham, 207
Aoki, M., 96–7, 99

bargaining games, 87–8
Barry, Brian, 165
behaviour, rational, self-regarding
    motives, 64–5
belief
  actions and intentions, 50–1
  cultural theory, 189
  epistemology, 70–9
  expression, and contexts, 133,
    134–5
  and extraneous information, 1–2,
    9, 91–2, 203
  grid and group insights, 10–13
  individualism problems, 14
  necessary to enterprise culture
    progress, 179–80
  and policy-making, 207–8
  rationality of, 88
  shared, and communication, 6,
    131–3
  system, naturalness, 6, 161
benefits
  and voluntary organisations, 36
  see also market system, gains and
    losses
Berlin, Isaiah, 143
bias, sociological typologies, 34, 35
bifurcation see work-starved/work-
    greedy bifurcation
blaming procedures, institutions, 33,
    38, 58–9

body/mind link, 45–9
bureaucratisation, 193, 195
Burke, Edmund, 63, 66–7, 74–5

Campbell, Colin, 157–8
categories see culture, categories
change, cultural, 1, 2
  dynamic theory, 190–7
charities, private see third sector
    bodies
Child Poverty Action Group,
    212–13
choice
  analysis, 19
  contributing factors, 19–20, 25,
    137, 143
  individuals and institutions, 33
  political importance, 151
  shift of responsibility and effort,
    148
  spurious, 147
Christianity, 77
  and self, 42
  and wealth, 65–6, 146
citizenship
  in enterprise culture, 1, 16–17,
    63–79, 122, 149, 155–56
  good, undermined by enterprise
    and initiative, 66
claims system
  conflict, 6, 57–8
  and cultural situation of self, 6,
    51–3, 55, 57–8
  downgrading and exclusion, 55–6
class, goods markers, 27
clothes, as expression of identity,
    150–1, 155–7
Club Theory, 37
coercion, 111–12, 113, 118, 177–8
cognitive systems (societies), 70–2
Collard, David, 161
collective consumption, and political
    identity, 153